Technology Enhanced Learning and Cognition

Benjamins Current Topics

Special issues of established journals tend to circulate within the orbit of the subscribers of those journals. For the Benjamins Current Topics series a number of special issues have been selected containing salient topics of research with the aim to widen the readership and to give this interesting material an additional lease of life in book format.

Volume 27

Technology Enhanced Learning and Cognition
Edited by Itiel E. Dror

These materials were previously published in *Pragmatics & Cognition* 16:2 (2008) and 17:1 (2009)

Technology Enhanced Learning and Cognition

Edited by

Itiel E. Dror
University College London

John Benjamins Publishing Company
Amsterdam / Philadelphia

∞™ The paper used in this publication meets the minimum requirements of American National Standard for Information Sciences – Permanence of Paper for Printed Library Materials, ANSI Z39.48-1984.

Library of Congress Cataloging-in-Publication Data

Technology enhanced learning and cognition / edited by Itiel E. Dror.

p. cm. (Benjamins Current Topics, ISSN 1874-0081 ; v. 27)

Includes bibliographical references and index.

1. Educational technology. 2. Learning, Psychology of. 3. Education--Effect of technological innovations on. I. Dror, Itiel E.

LB1028.3.T39682 2011

371.33--dc22 2010046578

ISBN 978 90 272 2257 2 (Hb ; alk. paper)

ISBN 978 90 272 8745 8 (Eb)

John Benjamins Publishing Co. · P.O. Box 36224 · 1020 ME Amsterdam · The Netherlands

John Benjamins North America · P.O. Box 27519 · Philadelphia PA 19118-0519 · USA

Table of contents

About the authors

Katherine Aguero graduated from the University of Pennsylvania with a B.A. in Psychology. She completed her degree of Master of Science in Education at Bank Street College of Education while teaching in Brooklyn through the Teach for America program. She is currently teaching at Promise Academy II, a charter school that is part of Harlem Children's Zone.

Timothy Burke is Lead Developer for the UCLA Human Perception Laboratory and Vice President of Insight Learning Technology, Inc. He is a graduate of UCLA where he received a Bachelors of Science in Cognitive Science with a Specialization in Computing and a minor in mathematics.

Itiel Dror received his PhD from Harvard University in human performance, cognition and learning. He specialises in applying theoretical and academic research about how humans learn to increase efficiency in real world domains. In addition to dozens of scientific articles that he has published about his research in learning and technology, Dror has used this work to design and evaluate a variety of learning applications in governmental agencies (such as the US Air Force and the UK Identity and Passport Services), as well as in commercial companies (such as IBM, Orange, and PricewaterhouseCoopers). Dror is editing a five year series on Technology and Cognition for *Pragmatics & Cognition*, and has received numerous research grants for his work on merging technology, learning, and cognition. For more information, please see: www.cci-hq.com

Robert Goldstone is a Chancellor's Professor of Psychological and Brain Sciences, and Director of the Cognitive Science Program, at Indiana University. He won the 1996 Chase Memorial Award for Outstanding Young Researcher in Cognitive Science, the 2000 APA Distinguished Scientific Award for Early Career Contribution to Psychology in the area of Cognition and Human Learning, and a 2004 Troland research award from the National Academy of Sciences. He served as editor of *Cognitive Science* from 2001 to 2005.

Philip J. Kellman, PhD, is Professor and Chair of the Cognitive Area in the Department of Psychology at the University of California, Los Angeles, and Director of the UCLA Human Perception Laboratory. He is also the founder and President of Insight Learning Technology, Inc. and the author of patents in learning and display technology. His research spans basic and applied areas in visual perception, cognition, and learning.

Janet Kolodner addresses issues in learning, memory, and problem solving in computers and people. She pioneered the computer method called case-based reasoning. She has used its cognitive model to design formal and informal science curriculum for middle school. Learning by Design™ is a design-based learning approach and an inquiry-oriented project-based approach to science learning. In Kitchen Science Investigators, 5th and 6th graders learn science in the context of cooking. In Hovering Around, they learn to explain in the context of designing hovercraft. She is founding Editor in Chief of *Journal of the Learning Sciences* and a founder and first Executive Officer of the International Society for the Learning Sciences.

Christine Massey, PhD, is the Director of Research and Education at the Institute for Research in Cognitive Science at the University of Pennsylvania. Her research interests connect basic research in developmental cognitive science with mathematics and science learning in educational settings.

Shailey Minocha is Senior Lecturer of Human-Computer Interaction in the Department of Computing of the Open University, UK. Shailey's research focuses on the effective design of electronic environments, with two related strands: (a) Customer Relationship Management and service quality of e-business environments, and (b) information design and pedagogical effectiveness of e-learning environments. The core thrust of her research has been on investigating user behaviour with computer systems, users' requirements from technologies, and the nature of the user-system interactions, which influence the design and usability of electronic environments. She has a PhD in Digital Signal Processing from the Indian Institute of Technology in Delhi, India, a Post-Doctorate in Adaptive User Interfaces from the Technical University, Braunschweig, Germany, and an MBA from the Open University in the UK.

Inge Molenaar is a doctoral student at the University of Amsterdam, Department of Educational Sciences. Her research deals with scaffolding of self regulated learning in innovative learning arrangements. She is also the initiator and CEO of the e-learning application Ontdeknet, which has been devoloping since 2001. She received different national an international awards for the development of Ontdeknet and was involved as project manager for Ontdeknet in the EC- sponsored project Atgentive.

Claudia Roda is a Professor of Computer Science at the American University of Paris. She received her PhD from the University of London. Claudia's current research focuses on theoretical models for attention computing. She has organized academic meetings, edited collections, and published her work on attention computing and multi-agent systems in several international conferences and journals. Her latest book "Human Attention in Digital Environments" will appear in 2011.

Brian Reiser is a Professor of the Learning Sciences in the School of Education and Social Policy at Northwestern University. His research concerns the design and study of investigation environments and inquiry support tools for science. The goal of this work is to develop a model of "reflective inquiry" and the pedagogical principles for its support. He has led a number of large scale projects in this area, and is currently leading the NSF funded project: *A Learning Progression for Scientific Modeling.*

Dave Roberts Dave Roberts has recently retired from a long career at IBM. During his time with IBM Dave was a leader in the establishment of 'user experience' as a part of every product's life cycle. He led the team which produced many of the standards used in user interfaces. He also developed model-based methods for system design and the integration of the disciplines involved. Dave is currently a Visiting Senior Research Fellow in the Faculty of Mathematics, Computing and Technology at the Open University, UK. He also teaches interactive system design to undergraduate and graduate courses at the University of Birmingham. Dave's main interests lie in the improvement of design methods, particularly better integration between human factors and other disciplines.

Zipora Roth is the director of curriculum development at PENNlincs, the pre-college education group at the Institute for Research in Cognitive Science at the University of Pennsylvania. For nearly four decades she has been invested in mathematics and science learning at the elementary and middle-school levels, both as a classroom teacher and as a curriculum developer. In recent years she has focused on linking current research on learning with educational practice, creating technology-based instructional tools to support mathematics learning.

Amanda Saw is a graduate student in cognitive psychology at the Claremont Graduate School. She is interested in learning and evaluating educational technologies. She helps to maintain and develop the Web Interface for Statistics Education website which features interactive tutorials and other statistics education resources.

Ji Son Ji Y. Son is a Professor of Developmental Psychology at California State University, Los Angeles. Her research focuses on the development of abstract and higher-order understanding. Currently, she is investigating the role of perception and embodied experiences in traditionally cognitive domains. The results of these studies are used to fuel a research-teaching loop that produces incremental improvements to pedagogy in science and mathematics.

Iris Tabak Iris Tabak is a Senior Lecturer in the Department of Education at Ben Gurion University of the Negev, Israel, an Associate Editor of The Journal of the Learning Sciences, and a past President of the International Society of the Learning Sciences. She holds a PhD in Learning Sciences from Northwestern University and a B.S.E in Computer Engineering from the University of Michigan. Her interests include scientific inquiry, medical education, learning technologies, discourse processes, scaffolding, identity formation, and design-based research.

Swaroop Vattam is a PhD student driven by fundamental questions about cognition and learning. His research interest lies at the intersection of artificial intelligence (AI) and human-centered computing. His current research deals with issues related to interactive learning environments, human–computer interaction and the use of AI technology to enable communicative interactions between humans and computers.

Joseph A. Wise is the director of The Center for Effective Learning at New Roads School. Formerly, he was a science teacher at Crossroads Upper School for Arts and Sciences for fourteen years, and served as the Science Department Chair from 1988–1996. While at Crossroads, Mr. Wise was founder and director of the W. M. Keck Math Science Institute from 1996–2001.

Joel Zucker is Director of Research for the UCLA Human Perception Laboratory and Chief Information Officer for Insight Learning Technology, Inc. He has over 20 years experience in the technology industry as an IT professional, programmer, and Head of Engineering for Lava2140, LLC. He is a graduate of UCLA and holds a Bachelors of Science in Cognitive Science.

Brain friendly technology: What is it? And why do we need it?:

Itiel E. Dror
Institute of Cognitive Neuroscience, University College London

Technology is so widespread and used that it is an integral part of people's lives and learning. However, too often technology is driving the development and its usage, and in many ways it is detached and even isolated from the human user. The human user, who the technology is supposed to serve, is subservient to the technology, rather than the other way around. The technology needs to be 'brain friendly' so it fits and complements the cognitive processes of the human user. This is critical if technology is going to be used, and if it is going to be efficient and effective. If technology is not brain friendly, it may not be used, or its use may be detrimental; or at least cumbersome on the human who should be benefiting from it.

More and more people are talking about 'brain friendly' technology and 'brain friendly' learning (e.g., Yu-Ju, Yao-Ting, & Kuo-En, 2008; Sykes, 2005; Berninger & Winn, 2006), but what does it mean? How do we make technology or learning 'brain friendly'? To answer these questions one must know a great deal about the human brain and cognitive architecture and consider its application to technology (see Kosslyn, 2006, 2008; Dror, 2011-a). However, even without deep understanding, one can take rather simple principles of how the brain works, and apply them successfully in developing technology. For example, cognitive load is a key issue and principle that should guide and constrain technology, and I will illustrate the idea of brain friendly technology and its practical implication using the notion of cognitive load (for details, see Dror, in press). Of course, there are many other important considerations in brain friendly technology, such as mental representations, attention, top-down processing, task switching, depth of processing, and a whole range of cognitive issues that constitute brain friendly technology. I use cognitive load to illustrate what is brain friendly technology and why we need it.

Let's start off with a simply and widespread example of how technology is far from brain friendly; an example that illustrates well how technology is detached from the most basic notions of cognitive load and the human user. Consider, for example, passwords: We all use passwords to gain access to everything from buying online books and plane tickets, to downloading articles, banking online, logging onto e-mail accounts, Facebook, and accessing a variety of databases and other services. An important principle in password security is not to use the same single password for a variety of accounts, as if one account is breached, then all the accounts are breached (this is especially important when some accounts are of low level security, while others are of a more sensitive nature). Furthermore, we are told to never write down our passwords. Therefore, it seems that technology security experts require and expect us human users to memorize dozens of different passwords. Furthermore, they design the technology to force us to have passwords with minimal length, use uppercase letters, as well as numbers, and other constraints; and many times – even low level security systems – require that you change your password every 6 months (and they do not enable you to choose a similar password to the one you already had, or a password you used in the past). You do not have to be a cognitive neuroscientist to know that these technological requirements are absurd, unrealistic, and do not fit the constraints of human cognition; that they are not brain friendly (or even brain realistic in this example).

Sometimes I wonder from what planet these technological experts come from, when they expect and require ordinary people to carry out cognitive operations that do not fit the most basic notions of human cognition and brain. Let me assure you that most people either write down their passwords, or use the same password for multiple accounts – both are clear violations of security, but are necessary because the 'brain blind' technologies are doomed to fail as they do not consider and fit the human brains of the users.

I hope that now it is becoming intuitively clear that: (1) Brain friendly technology is needed; if the technology does not fit the human brain, then it is just not going to work (either effectively or at all), and (2) That technologies that are not brain friendly, that are developed and deployed without considering the users' cognition, do in fact exist and are even widespread. The issues of passwords was only a simple and clear illustration of the problem, and brain friendly technology is much more complex as we delve into different constraints of the brain and consider how to best build technology that works with the brain, rather than 'against' it.

Following the notion of cognitive load, that the brain has limited resources and uses selective attention, we can further develop the practical implication of how we translate these to technology in general, and e-learning in particular. Technology enhanced learning (TEL), should be built to maximize the learning for the learners. That means that the learning needs to drive the technology and that it needs to make life easy for the learner to focus on the actual learning, so they acquire the information, remember it, and use it. How can technology be made brain friendly? For example, consider navigation. Many e-learning modules make navigation complex and cognitively demanding, thus taxing brain resources for navigation through the learning module rather than focusing on the learning content. A specific example for this would be that sometimes the ‘next’ button is on the bottom left of the screen, sometimes it is on the top right of the screen, and sometimes there is no ‘next’ button at all as the next screen automatically appears. TEL requires flexibility to use different navigation tools as appropriate, but one should strive to minimize the cognitive load on the learner so they can focus on the learning and not on figuring out the navigation. This can be achieved by cognitive consistency that sets up top-down expectations where the ‘next’ button appears on the screen.

By setting up expectations, via consistency, the technology is guiding and helping the brain figure things out, and hence reducing cognitive load. Of course, we want to engage the brain and make learning interesting and interactive (e.g., Cairncross & Mannion, 2007). Boring e-learning technology is not good; but we want the cognitive attention and engagement to focus on the learning materials (as will be illustrated below). Another issue that relates to consistency and lack of clarity for the brain is the use of sound. Many TEL have some auditory components, but it is far from clear when text is read out aloud and when it is just displayed as text.

The use of auditory components in e-learning is many times also confusing and taxing on the brain because it is hard to follow what is being read. The lack of correspondence between two sensory streams (the visual text and the auditory sounds) is confusing and requires the brain to spend resources figuring it out. A simple and practical solution is to be clear when auditory sounds are going to be used, and when used, to have the technology itself (rather than the user) match and unify the two (e.g., by using ‘karaoke’ that bold the text that is being read, as it is read).

Moving up to more complex ways of making e-learning more brain friendly is by having the technology do a lot of the work for the brain, and thus releasing cognitive resources. Take for example training people to code information into a database using certain rules and syntax. As you provide the learning examples, some information is more important than others (the syntax, for example, of when a ‘;’ or a ‘,’ should be used, etc.). This information should be highlighted and emphasised during learning, by making it bold, a different color or size. This helps the brain pick up and focus on the important information. If you do not do that, then the brain will figure it out, but that will require it to spend some of its limited cognitive resources; why not help the brain learn by directing it to the important information?

This can be applied to almost any learning; if you are training how to use computers, then you can emphasize and exaggerate the important keys, menus, and functions; if you are training to understand and compare different machines or procedures, then you can over emphasize the distinct components; if you are training on new regulations, software, or machines, then you can emphasize where the new is different from the old (rather than just give all the information about the new in the same manner and letting the learners figure it out).

Using technology in such a brain friendly way helps the cognitive system learn. Research into aircraft identification has shown that if you want to train people to identify different aircraft, then you can use such brain friendly TEL. It will not only enable quicker learning, but the learners will remember it better and are more likely to use it. In aircraft identification, for example, one highlights and exaggerates the unique and distinct components of each aircraft, and thus helps and guides the learners' cognitive system to pick up the information it needs. This takes the load off the brain of the learners, and makes the learning technology much more brain friendly. The article: "Helping the Cognitive System Learn: Exaggerating Distinctiveness and Uniqueness" (Dror, Stevenage, & Ashworth, 2008), details how to construct such technology, and provides experimental data comparing between learning using such brain friendly exaggerations and learning which does not use exaggerated examples.

Technology can also be brain friendly in terms of how it engages the users, making sure cognitive resources and attention are properly used and focused. This can be achieved by using technology to make proper interactions, involvement, participation, and engagement of the learners (e.g., Cairncross & Mannion, 2007; Shephard, 2003; Laurillard, 2002). However, a word of caution: Too much 'fun' and interactions, such as often occurs in gaming, although well intended to engage the learners, sometimes results in decreased learning. The detriment in such cases is that the entertainment component is not used properly to embed the learning, and it takes over the cognitive system while the learning is sidelined. One must remember that technology offers great opportunities to create interactive learning, but that should be with the goal of increasing learning, through brain friendly technology. In other words, interaction is not the goal, it is a tool, a means, to help maximize the goal of learning, enhanced performance, and outcomes. It is not the technological or the visual fidelity that is important, as much as the 'cognitive fidelity' in terms of how it all fits and works with the human cognitive system of the learners.'

An innovative use of technology that makes it cognitively engaging, and thus brain friendly, is interactive videos. Such technology takes the commonly used standard video which is passive (see Laurillard, 2002; Shephard, 2003), and makes it interactive. Hence, rather than learners watching a video to discuss later, the video is interactive. The interactions entail 'hot spots' that the viewer has to click on, answering multiple choice questions, competing with other learners, and so forth. The paper: "Making Training More Cognitively Effective: Making Videos Interactive" (Cherrett, Wills, Price, Maynard, & Dror, 2009; see also Dror, 2011-b) provide concrete and practical examples of how to create such interactive videos. The use of technology in a brain friendly way provides further opportunities to increase learning, both in terms of performance and outcomes.

A new paper: "A Novel Approach to Minimize Error in the Medical Domain: Cognitive Neuroscientific Insights Into Training" (Dror, 2011-b), illustrated how brain friendly technology can revolutionize how training is conceptualized and used. It demonstrates that when you let the cognitive architecture and brain guide how you think about training and technology, rather than letting technology drive and guide training, then new ways of training can emerge. The article suggests a different approach to train in the medical domain, an approach that is especially effective in minimizing error – a critical problem in medicine. Rather than training medical staff to 'be careful', to 'pay attention', to 'remember', to 'follow procedures', etc., all with the goal of reducing the occurrence of error, this new approach suggests that training focuses on *error recovery* rather than error reduction.

The suggested error recovery training will not only result in knowledge of what to do when an error occurs, but it will help reduce errors occurring in the first place. The brain and cognitive system will learn more effectively how to reduce error by training that focuses on error recovery: it will guide their attention more effectively to the vulnerabilities, make them remember better how errors occur, make errors more salient, and so forth (for details, see Dror, 2011-b). The point is that thinking about the cognitive system of the learner, making the technology brain friendly, brings about novel ways and approaches to use technology and produce effective learning.

This paper starts off with a discussion and examples of cognitive load issues, but it has also shown that brain friendly technology and learning is much wider in scope. Another way of using TEL that is brain friendly is making sure that the most effective mental representations are formed. For example, when presenting images during learning, you would want to present them in the most similar way that the brain would represent them, and in a representation that is most effective for the task that needs to be performed. Rather than letting (and burdening) the learners' brain in forming these mental representations (by processing and transforming the images used in learning to mental representations used by the brain), it is much more effective to provide the brain with representations that are most appropriate and that conform to its internal representations. For example, if you are training to identify certain patterns in images, in what orientation should you present the learning examples? Which learning examples are best to present? And in what order? From a brain perspective, there are clear and scientific answers to these questions, and learning that is brain friendly will take this knowledge to guide design and development of training and e-learning (e.g., see specific example in the paper: "Object Identification as a Function of Discriminability and Learning

Presentations: The Effect of Stimulus Similarity and Canonical Frame Alignment on Aircraft Identification", Ashworth & Dror, 2000).

These were only illustrative examples of what brain friendly technology is, and why we need it. The complexity of the brain gives a huge scope of how we can further make technology brain friendly. Clearly, taking traditional training and transcribing it to technological medium is not what e-learning should be all about. The potential for TEL is huge, but if all it entails is putting lectures on podcasts, making a PowerPoint to a flash e-learning module, and putting paper text on the web, then we have not really used the technology to fulfil its potential. If we take advantage of what technology offers, and use it in a brain friendly way, learning can (and will) be transformed.

Sometimes making learning brain friendly is intuitive and self-evident, but other times it is not. For example, much attention and effort is placed on visual fidelity and realism. However, training can often be more effective when it intentionally distort certain elements in a way that enhances the learning outcomes, such as artificially exaggerate and make salient the critical learning knowledge (Dror et al., 2008). This entails distorting the realism, but e-learning is often promoted as providing 'realistic and real life experience' (similarly, animation, video, and gaming often emphasizes visual fidelity). However, from a brain-cognitive perspective, such things may not be needed for effective training. Sometimes, the visually distorted, less realism and visual fidelity, provide better and more enhanced learning (for details, see Dror, in press). Therefore, understanding and being guided by the cognitive system can give counter-intuitive insights how to make learning brain friendly.

References

Ashworth, A.R.S., & Dror, I. E. (2000). Object identification as a function of discriminability and learning presentations: The effect of stimulus similarity and canonical frame alignment on aircraft identification. *Journal of Experimental Psychology: Applied, 6 (2)*, 148-157.

Berninger, V.W. & Winn, W.D. (2006). Implications of advancements in brain research and technology for writing development, writing instruction, and educational evolution. In C. A. MacArthur, S. Graham, S, & J. Fitzgerald, J. (Eds.). *Handbook of Writing Research.* NY: The Guilford Press. (pp. 96-114).

Cairncross, S. & Mannion, M. (2007). Interactive multimedia and learning: realizing the benefits. *Innovations in Education and Teaching International. 38,* 156-164.

Cherrett, T., Wills, G., Price, J., Maynard,S ., & Dror, I.E. (2009). Making training more cognitively effective: making videos interactive. *British Journal of Educational Technology, 40 (6),* 1124-1134.

Dror, I. E. (in press). A cognitive perspective on technology enhanced learning in medical training: Great opportunities, pitfalls and challenges. *Medical Teacher.*

Dror, I. E. (Ed.) (2011-a). *Technology Enhanced Learning and Cognition.* Amsterdam: John Benjamins Publishing.

Dror, I. E. (2011-b). A novel approach to minimize error in the medical domain: Cognitive neuroscientific insights into training. *Medical Teacher, 33 (1).*

Dror, I. E., Stevenage, S. V., & Ashworth, A. (2008). Helping the cognitive system learn: Exaggerating distinctiveness and uniqueness. *Applied Cognitive Psychology, 22 (4),* 573-584.

Kosslyn, S.M. (2006). *Graph Design for the Eye and Mind.* Oxford University Press.

Kosslyn, S.M. (2008) *Clear and to The Point: 8 Psychological Principles for Compelling PowerPoint Presentations.* Oxford University Press.

Laurillard, D. (2002). *Rethinking University Teaching: A conversational framework for the effective use of learning technologies.* London: Routledge

Shephard, K. (2003). Questioning, promoting and evaluating the use of streaming video to support student learning. *British Journal of Educational Technology, 34 (3),* 295-308

Sykes, J.A. (2005). *Brain Friendly School Libraries.* Westport, CT: Greenwood Publishing Group.

Yu-Ju, L., Yao-Ting, S., Kuo-En, C. (2008). A mobile-device-supported brain-friendly reading system. *Wireless, Mobile, and Ubiquitous Technology in Education, 5,* 170-172.

Fostering general transfer with specific simulations

Ji Y. Son and Robert L. Goldstone
California State University, Los Angeles / Indiana University

Science education faces the difficult task of helping students understand and appropriately generalize scientific principles across a variety of superficialy dissimilar specific phenomena. Can cognitive technologies be adapted to benefit both learning specific domains and generalizable transfer? This issue is examined by teaching students complex adaptive systems with computer-based simulations. With a particular emphasis on fostering understanding that transfers to dissimilar phenomena, the studies reported here examine the influence of different descriptions and perceptual instantiations of the scientific principle of competitive specialization. Experiment 1 examines the role of intuitive descriptions relative to concrete ones, finding that intuitive descriptions leads to enhanced domain-specific learning *but* also deters transfer. Experiment 2 successfully alleviated these difficulties by combining intuitive descriptions with idealized graphical elements. Experiment 3 demonstrates that idealized graphics are more effective than concrete graphics even when unintuitive descriptions are applied to them. When graphics are concrete, learning and transfer largely depend on the particular description. However, when graphics are idealized, a wider variety of descriptions results in levels of learning and transfer similar to the best combination involving concrete graphics. Although computer-based simulations can be effective for learning that transfers, designing effective simulations requires an understanding of concreteness and idealization in both the graphical interface and its description.

Keywords: abstraction, analogy, complex systems, concreteness, generalization, grounded learning, learning, science education, simulation, transfer

1. Introduction

A central purpose of science is to produce models that provide unifying explanations of diverse phenomena and to generalize these models appropriately.

Following the axiom of preaching what we practice, a corresponding goal of scientific education should be to teach students to appreciate and use these overarching models, not just particular instances. Models in physics seek to explain all types of masses under a variety of circumstances, not just a particular cube on an incline plane. Chemistry seeks to explain many types of reactions across different environmental conditions, not just the result of exposing magnesium oxide to water. Biological models that provide explanations that apply across organisms and psychological explanations that cut across particular situations move these fields forward. Because scientific models typically capture deep principles that govern concretely dissimilar phenomena, they are largely sparse descriptions of structure. But novices in a domain are often more likely to attend to rich concrete information than relational structure (Chi, Feltovich, and Glaser 1981; Rattermann and Gentner 1998; Markman and Gentner 1993), so although fostering an understanding of deep structure is the very purpose of science, this is also what makes science education challenging. How can sparse relational structure be highlighted in the midst of the rich salient details of the particular phenomena? Indeed this has been a source of much dissatisfaction with students' (and teachers') conceptions of science (Duschl 1990; Lederman 1992).

In the research presented here, the focus is on two, sometimes divergent, goals of scientific education: (1) the understanding of general models and (2) transferring that general structure across specific phenomena. Technological innovations such as computer simulations play an increasingly important role in science education by helping students build working models. However, to develop effective simulations we need to know how students understand and interact with simulations. Our research is an attempt to maximize the pedagogical impact of simulations to foster both learning of particular phenomena but also to promote appropriate transfer. To such an end, we will provide a review of complex systems, an example of a scientific approach that necessitates an understanding of general models. Then we will review previous research that shows the impact of simulations in learning. Finally, we will present theoretical and empirical motivations for strategically choosing a level of concreteness in simulations (perceptually and contextually) that effectively fosters transfer.

2. Complex systems for science education

Complex adaptive systems (CAS) provide a particularly striking example of a situation where there is common structure shared among dissimilar concrete phenomena. CAS models phenomena use the simple interactions of individual units (or agents) to explain complex behavior at the macroscopic level. The key idea of these models is that even without a leader or centralized process, sophisticated high-level organization can emerge from low-level interactions (Bar-Yam 1997; Resnick 1994; Resnick and Wilensky 1993). Many real-world phenomena, from biology to social sciences, can be modeled with the formalisms of CAS. These principles often provide useful unifying descriptions across traditional scientific boundaries (Casti 1994; Flake 1998). For example, the growth of human lungs (Garcia-Ruiz et al. 1993), snowflakes (Bentley and Humphreys 1962), and cities (Batty 2005) can all be modeled by Diffusion Limited Aggregation, where individual units enter a system randomly and if a moving unit touches another one, they become attached. The same pattern of fractally connected branches emerges across all these systems. Although lungs, snowflakes, and cities seem to belong in different domains of inquiry due to salient differences among these phenomena, the structural regularities highlighted by this CAS construal (Ball 1999) are highly useful for prediction and quantification. A CAS perspective can provide a unifying explanation for the development of spots on mammalian skin as well as the distribution of religious communities over a country (Turing 1952); oscillations in chemical reactions as well as predator-prey populations (Ball 1999); the specialization of ants over food resources as well as neurons over perceptual stimuli (O'Reilly 2001).

There are also some specifically pedagogical reasons to bring CAS principles to the science classroom. First, since transfer of structural principles unifying superficially dissimilar domains is particularly problematic for students, CAS theories provide many examples of models that do just that. This has the potential to overcome students' resistance to science classes that they frequently view as overly particularistic. CAS principles are mechanistic descriptions of phenomena and offer compelling accounts of the similarity between otherwise dissimilar phenomena. Also, since CAS models are of authentic scientific interest, this can foster productive cross-fertilization across fields. The bridging is not only across phenomena, but also within phenomena since CAS principles offer bridging causal explanations among microscopic elements in a system and observed macroscopic emergent behavior. Building these links across and within scientific domains demonstrates different levels of description and offers students new ways of parsing phenomena. Finally, these systems provide situations where analogical reasoning and transfer naturally emerge as cognitively crucial ingredients. This last reason is of particular importance to educators and students who hope that their efforts and study will transfer between the classroom and the real world as well as between domains (Anderson, Greeno, Reder, and Simon 2000).

However, the very characteristics that make CAS principles good as science and potentially good for research in science education also make them particularly difficult to understand. First, because CAS modeling requires multiple levels of understanding, emergent and local interactions (Wilensky and Resnick 1999), students often only learn one-level of analysis and typically it is the overall structure that is most difficult to grasp. Second, past research has shown many failures of the spontaneous transfer of principles between superficially dissimilar contexts (e.g., Gick and Holyoak 1980; Reed, Ernst, and Banerji 1974). Third, relatively little research has been done to inform the design of CAS curricula, hands-on experiences, exercises, and laboratories to promote deep understanding of complex systems. Educational technology that is optimized for maximizing performance on a system will often not be the technology that is optimal for transferring knowledge and skills from one domain to another. For example, for training people to drive a car, developing a driving simulation that is as realistic as possible is sensible. However, it does not follow that realism and incorporating details faithful to a domain are beneficial if we are principally interested in transfer understandings to new domains with different details.

We propose to use recent developments in technology to address educational challenges. Technological advances have given rise to new tools for studying complex systems. Because effective real-life observation of whole system, such as an entire population of neurons or a predator-prey ecosystem, is often difficult, too complex, or too cumbersome, computer-based simulations provide a powerful new tool for scientific inquiry (Casti 1997) as well as education. Simulations offer promise in meeting the challenges of learning complex systems. We will discuss the broad advantages of using simulated environments to (1) effectively allow interactive control coupled with (2) perceptually grounding of higher order principles.

2.1 Advantages of simulations

Dynamic simulations instantiate scientific principles with simplified perceptual models, representing only the main elements and their interactions. These computer simulations have been called "artificial worlds", providing a functional laboratory for testing hypotheses (Casti 1997). Traditional laboratories are ideally controlled environments and computer simulations similarly constrain the potential influences on the environment via the availability of parameters. Students can explore these models by changing key parameters and examining the subsequent effects on the system (Miller, Lehman, and Koedinger 1999; Resnick 1994; Schank and Farrel 1988).

Such an interaction between a student and a simulation is particularly powerful because actions in this environment are coupled with ordered consequences. Often this coupling is designed to show students immediate visual consequences that correspond to changes in particular parameters (e.g., Jackson, Stratford, Krajcik, and Soloway 1996; Resnick 1994; Wilensky 1999). The organization of what gets learned is often directly connected to actions in the world (Scribner 1985), and so there has been an increasing interest in understanding cognition as the product of interactions with the environment. Embodied accounts of learning suggest that such coupling between activity and the environment is what leads to flexible and useful knowledge (Winn 1995; Smith and Gasser 2005). Even simple learning mechanisms can be flexibly 'intelligent' when they are sensitive to these couplings (Brooks 1991). Giving students feedback in these simulated environments gives them information about the system in a less direct, but potentially more effective, way than traditional textbook exposition. Particularly because CAS principles are often instantiated at the agent-level, it is difficult for students to connect changes at the micro-level to patterns at the global-level (Penner 2001). Simulations couple their micro-level changes to global consequences.

More specifically to scientific inquiry, simulations also provide economical opportunities for practicing skills. Because the environment is conducive to predictive problem-solving, students can test their theories and examine the consequences (White 1993; White and Fredericksen 1998). Resetting a computer simulation is easy to do, allowing students to start over and try out several tests in succession, something that might be costly or difficult in the real world or even a real laboratory. Additionally, as much as science is interested in predicting reality, the real world is unpredictable. Simulations are highly regular worlds that are created as perfect instantiations of scientific models. This allows a students' experimentation to be highly predictable, if they have a good understanding of the model. In the real world, a predictive failure is possible because either one's model is wrong or one does not understand the implications of one's model. By allowing students to explore simulations governed by exact and simple rules, the former possibility is eliminated and students can concentrate on understanding why a set of rules gives rise to the behavior describable at several levels.

Dede and colleagues (1997) have used simulated environments in ScienceSpace to help students realize when they do not have adequate models of the physical universe by allowing them to remove friction or gravity from the simulation. These impossible and extreme ways of controlling simulations are particularly needed to illustrate CAS principles. Emergent explanations are often overlooked for centralized ones (Resnick and Wilensky 1998; Jacobson 2001) and students are likely to seek a centralized authority or plan (i.e., one of the agents being a special leader), so being able to truly make every agent behave identically is important. This control allows students to see that the emergent structures they see are not caused by seeded differences among the elements, but come about because of their interactions. Also, because these interactive systems are made up of independent agents, they can seem perceptually noisy. Simulated environments allow students to have control over "the noise" in regular ways.

These visual interactive simulations are perfect models and, perhaps equally importantly, are also tools for constructing mental models. Although mental models have been implicated in effective scientific understanding (Gentner and Stevens 1983), actually being able to model simultaneous agents and interactions poses high demands on working memory and other cognitive processes (Narayanan and Hegarty 1998). CAS principles may be particularly difficult to instantiate mentally because the behavior of the components may be very different from the global patterns that arise. Students are surprised when they find that a traffic system composed of cars moving forward creates traffic jams that move backwards along the highway (Wilensky 1997; Wilensky and Resnick 1999). They only realize that this is a consequence of the system by observing it in the simulation.

These are a few of the potential benefits to complex systems education that visual simulations might provide. Undoubtedly this potential has been recognized given the recent proliferation of simulations used in educational settings. A noteworthy example is the StarLogo/NetLogo environment developed by Resnick and Wilensky (Resnick 1994; Resnick and Wilensky 1998; Wilensky 1999, 2001). StarLogo/NetLogo provides a platform for creating virtual environments made up of fixed patches and moving agents that can interact with patches and each other. Students can control various parameters to change the nature of those interactions. Simulations such as NetLogo systems often foster intuitions for complex systems such as slime-mold aggregation and predator-prey oscillations better than abstract equations and noninteractive animations (Resnick and Wilensky 1998; Wilensky and Resnick 1999).

However, not all simulations are created equal and there have been relatively few attempts to test the effectiveness of particular design choices (for notable exceptions, see Jackson, Stratford, Krajcik, and Soloway 1996; Klahr and Carver 1988; Miller et al. 1999). Although simulations on the whole might offer potential advantages over more traditional tools, systematic differences between simulations might also influence their actual effectiveness, particularly for transfer. Simulations should not be seen as panaceas to science education, just as concrete manipulatives or other learning tools should not be seen as generic solutions to the aims of education (see Uttal, Scudder, and DeLoache 1997 for a defense of this claim). Cognitive studies of learning and transfer offer valuable direction for designing simulations that are optimal teaching tools for the aims of science education: Unifying structural construals and generalizable skills.

3. Fostering transfer

Complex systems principles are cognitively influential because they lead to situations being construed in new and productive ways. The student or scientist armed with a model of Diffusion Limited Aggregation sees striking similarities between lungs and snowflakes that are missed by most others. Complex systems concepts are thus inductively productive; however, they are highly perspective-dependent. When corrosion on tin organ pipes speeds up the spread of further corrosion, it is exactly an autocatalytic process, with the rich mathematically governed behaviors that characterize all autocatalytic processes. However, the organ pipes not only instantiate an autocatalytic process, but also a resonating chamber and a harmonic series generator. An effective science education arms students with new perspectives to apply to the world.

The problem with these scientific construals is that they reflect a particular perspective out of a number of reasonable descriptions. Because of human processing limitations, differing construals compete against each other. However, appropriate generalization and transfer may require understanding multiple construals at once. At one level, participants do need to understand specific phenomena and how they instantiate certain principles. However, they also need to understand that these individual phenomena are in equivalence classes organized according to abstract principles. The specific and the general, the individual and the aggregate, the superficial and structural construals — all compete against each other, and every learning situation is wrought with these possible perspectives.

In the domain of science education, there is a wide variety of what could be considered critical transfer, from broadly generalizable skills, such as the ability to ask testable questions, to more specific instances of transfer, such as recognizing the link between a particular equation and a linguistic description of phenomena (for more detailed analysis of the types of transfer, see Barnett and Ceci 2002). Choosing the right perspective to apply to a situation may be important in many types of transfer but because we are limited in our ability to explore these in a series of short experiments, our empirical investigations will be restricted to transfer as solving problems similarly across deeply related phenomena, despite superficial differences. Thus, our aim is to design simulations that help students recognize structural similarities between two dissimilar contexts. Teaching or exposing students to a perspective that emphasizes deep structure may be critical for this type of transfer.

What can we do to emphasize structural information? One answer comes from evidence that deep processing can be facilitated with concrete representations (Barsalou 1999; Cheng 2002; Goldstone 1994a, 1994b; Goldstone and Barsalou 1999). When concrete details support relational reasoning, learners benefit from this redundancy (Gentner and Toupin 1986; Gentner and Rattermann 1991; DeLoache et al. 1991). There are many ongoing attempts to make simulations more similar to their real world referents (DiFonzo, Hantula, and Bordia 1998; Grady 1998; Heim 2000).

As vivid and interesting as these representations may be, it remains to be seen whether concreteness leads to better learning. Particularly if we are interested in learning that transfers, a detailed and concrete construal may not be desirable. For instance, in the case of math manipulatives, detailed interesting objects may distract children from actual principles of mathematics (Uttal, Liu, and DeLoache 1999). These details are particularly critical when they detract from relational construals (Goldstone, Medin, and Gentner 1993).

Even in situations where the details are not irrelevant but in fact relevant to structure, there is evidence to show that idealizations are better for generalization. Bassok and Holyoak (1989) examined transfer from algebra-to-physics versus physics-to-algebra. Even though physics is a fairly abstract domain, doing physics problems did not transfer to algebra as much as algebra to physics. Algebra captures the pure structural commonality shared by the two situations and this isolation of critical information may promote transfer. A particularly striking instance of relevant concreteness' detrimental effect on transfer comes from Kaminski, Sloutsky, and Heckler (2005, 2006). They taught students a version of modular arithmetic either through arbitrary abstract symbols or meaningful concrete representations of cups (see Figure 1). They taught students a system of relations structured according to addition modulo 3, a math system where there are only three numbers. Under modulo 3, 1+1 = 2, 2+2 = 1, and 1+2 = 0. When students were taught this system with arbitrary symbols in place of numbers, learning was more difficult than learning with cups iconically filled 1/3 or 2/3 of the way. However, transfer to another modulo 3 system was better for the arbitrary condition than the iconic condition. They attributed this advantage of simple symbols to be by virtue of their similarity to other abstractly related systems. Another aspect of the transfer disadvantage of relevant concreteness is that these vivid details are conflated with relational structure. These findings demonstrate how even concreteness

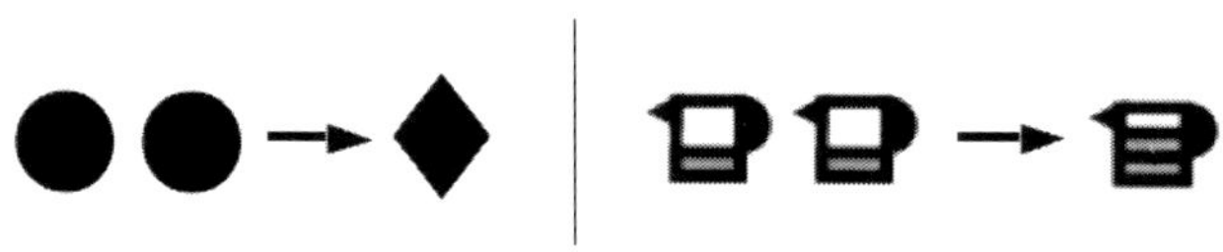

Figure 1. Training stimuli used in Kaminski, Sloutsky, and Heckler (2005, 2006) to teach students modular arithmetic. Although the modular arithmetic system is naturally instantiated by the cups scenario, instruction using the cups led students to generalize their knowledge less effectively than training with the more simplified geometric shapes.

perfectly correlated with abstract structure can result in an overly concrete construal, because learners do not have to rely on abstract structure to comprehend the situation.

Because the benefits of concrete understanding and abstract transfer seem to map well to the concrete/idealized perceptual dimension, we want to examine their role in designing effective simulations. There are two ways of understanding concreteness that may be important to simulation design. One is in terms of situational concreteness with a high degree of similarity between the model and the real world situation that it represents (model-to-modeled-world relation). A second way of being concrete is to be perceptually-based. This way of being "concrete" is closer to Barsalou's Perceptual Symbols Theory (1999) which proposes a central role of perceptual processes in comprehending even abstract concepts such as logical relations. Simulations may include aspects of both situational and perceptual concreteness but we believe that these are separable. Presenting a general Diffusion Limited Aggregation system using the domain of water spreading into viscous oil, but with simple blue patches representing water and black patches representing oil, would count as situationally concrete but perceptually idealized. Presenting the same system in terms of two unidentified fluids but with slickly rendered, three dimensionally shaded graphics, would count as situationally idealized but perceptually rich.

Based on evidence that suggests that perceptual processes may ground conceptual ones (see Goldstone and Barsalou 1994 for a review), all of this research here on simulation design has been based on perceptual simulations. The magnitudes of situational and perceptual concreteness were adjusted to examine the resulting effects on learning and transfer. Our research group has conducted several studies aimed at informing the design of effective interactive simulations. The aim is to foster a flexible understanding of structural principles, the kind that transfers across dissimilar phenomena. To do this, these studies use simulations of two dissimilar phenomena, both governed by the CAS principle of "Competitive Specialization," to examine the effects of concreteness/idealization on transferable learning. First, here is a review of competitive specialization and an introduction to the simulations. Then we will summarize experiments that examined several aspects of the simulations' design.

4. Case study: Competitive specialization

One advantage of teaching complex systems to study transfer is that these principles are of authentic scientific interest and the phenomena described by these systems are the result of real applications of these principles. We have focused here on one of the principles taught in our undergraduate CAS course at our university, "competitive specialization." This principle describes situations where units start off homogenous and undifferentiated but by uniformly obeying simple rules, become specialized and individualized. A well-worked out example of Competitive Specialization is the development of neurons in the primary visual cortex that start off homogenous and become specialized to respond to visually presented lines with specific spatial orientations (von der Malsburg 1973). Another example regards the optimal allocation of agents that specialize to different spatial regions of territory. In such situations, specialization is required for optimal covering of all regions, so that every region has a reasonably close agent. For example, if oil drills are to optimally cover a territory or waitstaff are to optimally cover a party, they will each need to cover different regions. Inefficient covering means that there are some regions redundantly covered by multiple oil drills or waitstaff, while some regions are not covered at all. The same structure can be seen in neuron specialization if the range of visual stimuli is construed as a space where distance represents similarity: Efficient covering is achieved when each stimulus region has a neuron or neural assembly responsible for it.

A centralized solution might involve some sort of algorithm, plan, or leader to instruct these individual agents (e.g., oil drills, waitstaff, or neurons) to distribute over a territory (e.g., Texas, a party, or a range of stimuli). However, competitive specialization offers a *de*centralized solution to achieving optimal covering, by executing three simple steps repeatedly. In order to get agents to specialize over a territory: (1) randomly select one region from the entire territory to be covered, (2) determine the agent closest to the selected region, (3) adapt the closest agent towards the region with a relatively fast rate while adapting all other agents toward that region with a slower rate. These steps iterated repeatedly will result in agents specializing towards regions they are already close to. Agents that are not close to selected regions move slowly towards them so that they are free to cover other regions that may be selected later. The two critical parameters of competitive specialization are the adaptation rate of the closest agent and the rate of the other agents. Although there are other parameters that can be changed such as the number of agents or regions of space, the rates of adaptation are critical to achieving optimal specialization. Combinations of these critical parameters will be demonstrated in the next section.

Laboratory and classroom investigations have shown that simulations can foster transferable learning between instances of competitive specialization (Goldstone and Sakamoto 2003; Goldstone and Son 2005; Goldstone, Landy, and Son 2008). In these experiments, students are directed in a period of focused exploration with a relatively literal spatial instance of agents covering a territory. Then, students are probed with another simulation that instantiates the principles of competitive specialization in a metaphorical space — in particular, a similarity space. Their understanding of each simulation is measured with multiple-choice quiz questions in all experiments. Some of the studies also examine how quickly students apply learned solutions as well as the quality of written out observations. An example simulation of agents covering a literal space (ants covering food patches) and another with agents covering metaphorical space (neuron sensors covering similarity space) will be shown in further detail. All simulations have been developed in NetLogo (Wilensky 1999).

4.1 Specialization in literal space

These simulations of competitive specialization involved agents spreading evenly over territory drawn by users. One example involves ants foraging food resources. At each time step, the ants-system iterates the rules described generally above and specifically here: A piece of food is randomly selected, the closest ant moves towards it with one rate while all other ants move toward it with a different rate. When a piece of food was selected, it was highlighted (yellow dot on the green patches, see Figure 2). Learners were told that there were no hidden complexities and these

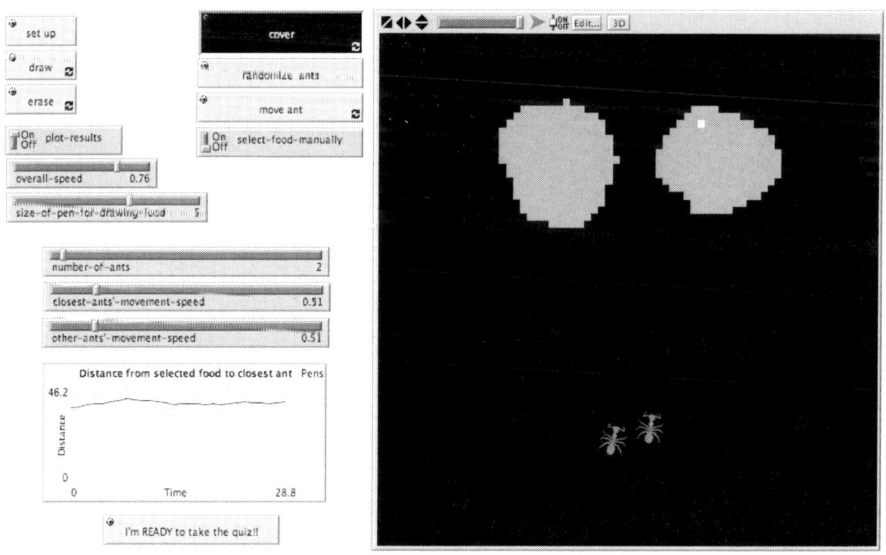

Figure 2. Screenshot of Ants and Food simulation created with NetLogo. Randomly selected food pieces (one is shown by the small yellow square) are sampled from the green regions drawn by the user. The ants move toward the sampled food with parametrically controllable speeds.

rules governed the behavior of the ants (by pressing the 'cover' command). To explore the simulation, students could draw food, add ants to the system, move ants, and randomize the ants' positions. They were also encouraged to explore various parameters (described as controlling factors) of the system, the critical ones being the 'closest-ant-movement-speed' and 'other-ants-movement-speed' that could be adjusted on sliders (see Figure 2). We will call these parameters the 'closest rate' and the 'not closest rate.'

To guide their explorations of the parameters, a worksheet with several steps asked students to think about and perform a number of actions to the simulation (this worksheet and corresponding simulation can be downloaded at http://www.calstatela.edu/centers/learnlab/simulations). (1) Students were asked to consider how to achieve an efficient covering solution such that the pieces of food each have an ant nearby. (2) Students were asked to manually place ants far away from the food in nonoptimal configurations and note that the graph (in the bottom left

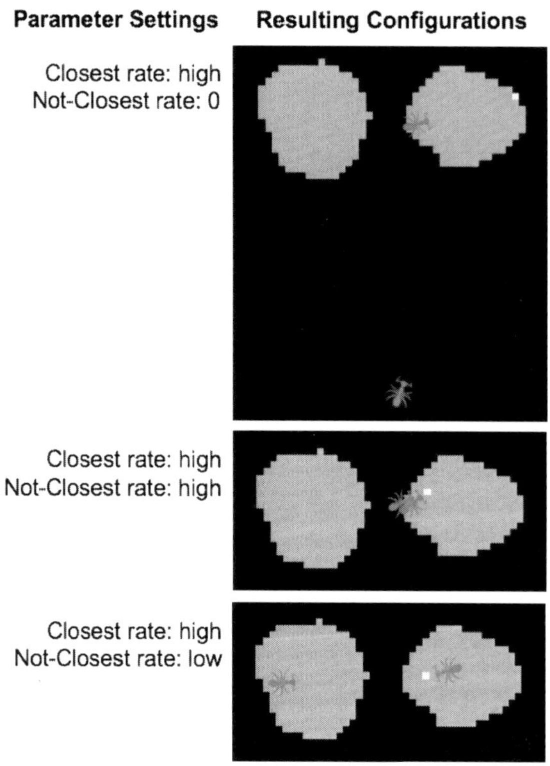

Figure 3. Resulting configurations from various parameter settings of the Ants and Food simulation. Only when the ant closest to randomly selected pieces of food moves quickly and the other ants move slowly does the optimal covering pattern (lowest panel) emerge.

corner of Figure 2) depicting the average distance between selected food to the closest ant was high. Then students were asked to manually place the ants in optimal configurations (i.e., one on each region) and note that the graphed distance was low. (3) Students were asked to randomize the position of the ants and have the ants automatically achieve this optimal configuration by finding parameter values (instead of the manual 'move ant' command) to achieve low average distance.

Starting with the initial configuration of two ants and two food patches shown in Figure 2, the results of different parameter settings are shown in Figure 3. If only the closest ant moves, and the not-closest ant does not move at all, then the ant slightly closer to the food will move closer to all of the food regions because the food regions are all relatively close together. In subsequent iterations, this ant will continue to be the closest ant no matter what piece of food is selected. The other ant will never get the opportunity to be the closest ant and will never move at all. On the other hand, if both closest and not-closest rates are equally high, all ants will move closer to the food. However, because all ants will be moving equally quickly toward selected food regardless of their initial positions, their movements and positions become identical after several iterations. These are both sub-optimal parameter settings because either one ant or a group of ants are trying to cover the entire food space instead of specializing for different regions. In these cases, either one or all ants will eventually hover around the center of mass of the available food. The solution for competitive specialization is instantiated by having the closest ant move quickly while the other ants only move very slowly. Even if one ant starts off covering most of the available food, soon the other ants will come close enough to cover peripheral patches. Eventually, each ant will occupy a local center of mass (the entire space is divided by the number of available ants).

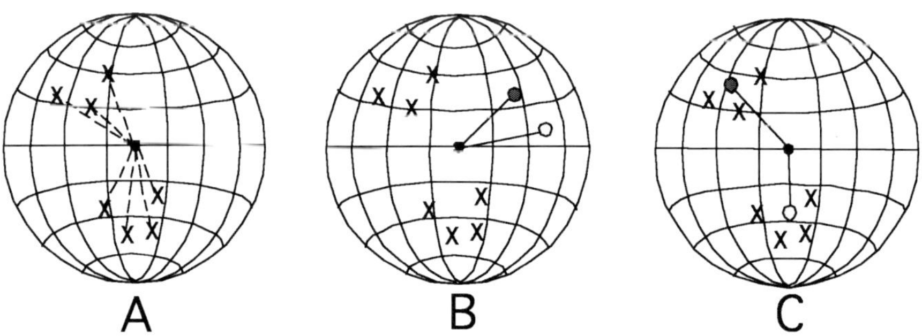

Figure 4. Rumelhart and Zipser's (1985) geometric construal of competitive learning shows (A) input patterns, represented by x's, as vector endpoints in a multidimensional space, (B) initially random pattern sensors are circles, and (C) the result when a sensor that "wins" the competition adapts towards the selected input while the other sensor adapts more slowly towards the input.

4.2 Specialization in metaphorical space

This second type of simulation involves agents specializing over a different kind of space, similarity space. Inspired by self-organizing neuronal sensors (Von de Malsburg 1973), the Sensors and Inputs simulation shows how initially homogenous sensors — sensors that react similarly to all inputs — become specialized to a certain range of inputs. The simulation is based on Rumelhart and Zipser's competitive learning algorithm (1985) used to find clusters of patterns in neural network inputs. They provide a geometric construal of pattern learning that is useful to review here. Imagine each input as a vector in a multidimensional feature-space (vector endpoints are illustrated in Figure 4 in a hypersphere). Inputs that share many features, a classic view of similarity, have endpoints that are close together and dissimilar inputs are far apart. Sensors start off with random feature values (feature weights in the original competitive learning algorithm), in other words

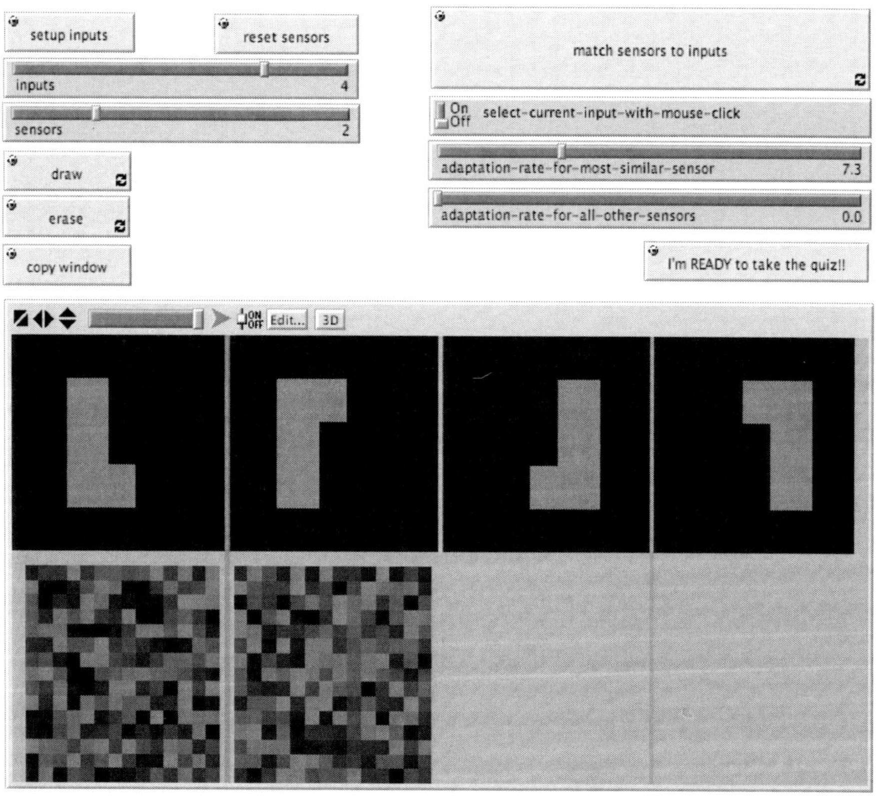

Figure 5. Screenshot of Sensors and Inputs simulation. Four input pictures (top row) have been drawn by the user and the two sensors (bottom row) are initialized with random pixel values.

as random points in the high-dimensional space. Applying the rules of competitive specialization, (1) an input is randomly presented, (2) the sensor that is most similar is chosen as the winner, and (3) the winner adapts a large amount towards the presented input and the losers adapt by a small amount.

This technique roughly produces sensors that capture general similarities among groups of instances (for improvements to this algorithm, see Goldstone 2003). Specialized sensors react to inputs that are close in multidimensional space just as the specialized ants in the previous section react to points of food that are close in 2-dimensional space. Although this simulation was created based on this more abstract conceptualization of spatial proximity, the user-interface only indirectly reflected this (see Figure 5). A sensor adapting toward an input, distance reduction in the high-dimensional space, merely looks more similar to the input, and does not actually move towards the input.

In the simulation, inputs are drawn in on the first row and sensors are randomly initialized on the second row. Inputs are defined as arrays of pixels such that inputs that are "close" in multidimensional space have many overlapping pixels and look like each other. As the sensors are adapted towards inputs, they come to share more pixels and look like them. The key parameters in the Sensors and Inputs simulation are 'adaption-rate-for-most-similar-sensor' and 'adaption-rate-for-all-other-sensors' (which we will refer to as the most-similar and other rates).

Students can control these parameters, draw inputs, set the number of inputs and sensors to explore the simulation. Once again, the rules governing the system were explicated to students in a worksheet (worksheet and simulation available for download) and they were told that the command 'match sensors to inputs' would execute the rules iteratively. Students were generically asked to think about how sensors could become specialized for similar inputs by following the three rules. Unlike the simulations for specialization in literal space (i.e., ants and food), this simulation did not have a series of exercises mapped out for students. They were allowed to freely explore this simulation.

Consider Figure 5's set of initial input patterns drawn by a user and two random sensors. Figure 6 demonstrates how changing the two critical adaptation parameters result in varying degrees of specialization. If only the sensor most similar to a randomly selected input pattern adapts and the other does not adapt at all, the sensor that starts off a bit more similar to the patterns becomes even more similar to the inputs (which happen to be similar to each other by virtue of their black backgrounds). This sensor reacts to all inputs and comes to looks like all the inputs superimposed on top of each other, while the other sensor never reacts to any input. If all sensors (the most similar and others) adapt at the same rate, they all react to all inputs, again a sub-optimal solution. Specialization occurs when the most-similar sensor adapts at a faster rate and the others adapt more slowly. Even

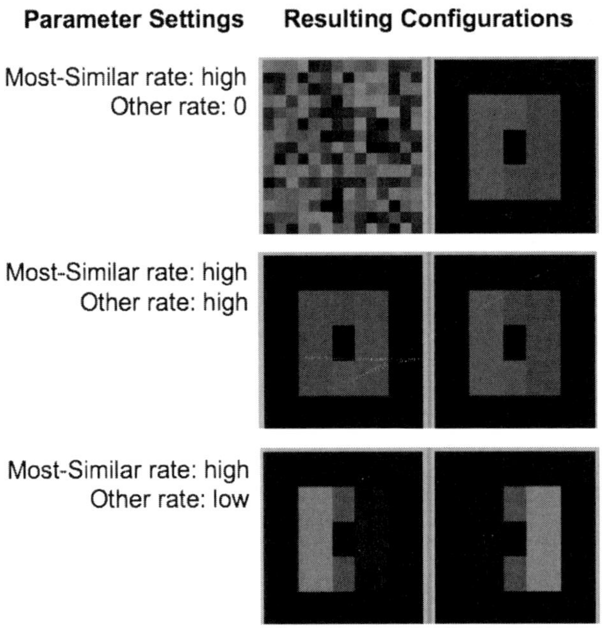

Figure 6. Resulting sensors from various parameter settings of the Sensors and Inputs simulation. Optimal covering of the sensors to the input patterns is achieved only when the sensor most similar to a randomly selected input pattern adapts quickly and the other sensor adapts slowly. In this case, when an optimal covering is found, the sensors spontaneously group the input patterns into subsets according to their similarity.

though one sensor might start off adapting towards all four inputs, the other will also be adapting toward them. Eventually, the closer, winning sensor, by virtue of adapting to one of the inputs, will be pulled away from the other inputs. The other, losing sensor can then adapt quickly, because it is the most-similar sensor to these inputs. The resulting sensors are each similar to some subset of the inputs, and these subsets form groups according to similarity. These three combinations of adaptation rates show results that are analogous to the literal-space parameter results shown in Figure 2. These instances from both literal-space and metaphorical-space are equivalent under the abstract description of competitive specialization. Our studies examine the conditions under which students can come to appreciate this equivalence.

5. Experimental findings

Two situations being analogous does not predict whether students will be able to appreciate the analogy. However, in education the aim is two-fold: To help students appreciate the relations *between* phenomena, the analogies, but also deeply understand the phenomena themselves, the individual analogs. Although concreteness typically leads to good understanding of particular situations, it often endangers transfer between them (Bransford, Brown, and Cocking 1999). Idealization has been characterized as necessary for transfer (Singley and Anderson 1989) but may not provide enough understanding to transfer in the first place. There is an inherent tension between these two design directions, but the potential for grounded understanding that transfers has been tempting enough to draw several theoretical attempts to put together the advantages of concrete situated contexts with idealized, generalizable abstractions. These combination attempts range from "situated abstraction" (Noss, Hoyles, and Pozzi 2002) and "situated generalization" (Carraher, Nemirovsky, and Schliemann 1995) to "abstraction in context" (Hershkowitz, Schwarz, and Dreyfus 2001).

Despite the implications of empirical research that shows promise for combining concreteness and idealization, there have been few attempts to find design principles that emphasize the advantages of each. We will summarize several previously published studies examining the effects of graphical concreteness and idealization. Then we present three new studies examining the effect of concretely intuitive versus idealized descriptions and the best way for combining concrete/idealized graphics and descriptions.

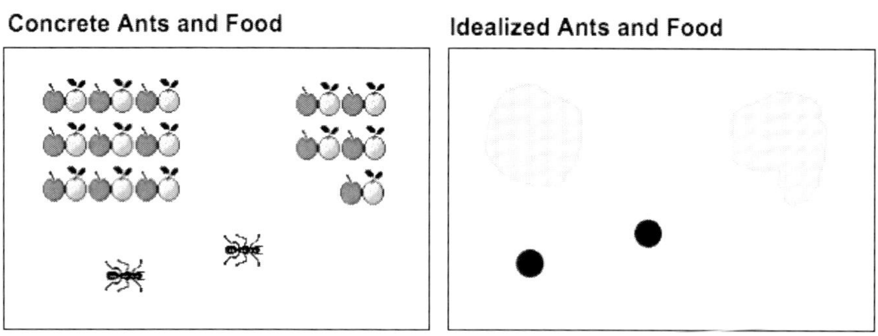

Figure 7. Graphical concrete/idealized manipulations used in the Ants and Food simulations (Goldstone and Sakamoto 2003; Goldstone and Son 2005).

5.1 Perceptual concreteness and idealization

Our initial foray into teaching competitive specialization to undergraduates was simply to examine whether there was an effect of training with concrete or idealized graphics on transfer (Goldstone and Sakamoto 2003; Goldstone and Son 2005). All participants were trained in an earlier version of the Ants and Food simulation with concrete graphics (black ants and small fruit) or idealized elements (black dots and green blobs) as shown in Figure 7. Afterwards they were able to explore the Sensors and Inputs simulation. Participants answered multiple-choice questions after each simulation that probed their knowledge of the embedded competitive specialization principles. Although these questions were always written in context-specific terms (i.e., "when the ant moves towards the food", "when the sensor adapts towards the input"), they could only be answered correctly by applying the principles of competitive specialization. These questions were written to be analogous across the two contexts (ants and sensors) and examples are provided in the Appendix. This procedure helps distinguish the effect of perceptual concreteness on both initial learning (Ants and Food simulation) and transfer (Sensors and Input simulation).

Even these relatively minor manipulations of concreteness — after all line drawings of ants are not that much more concrete than black dots — were found to have impact on both initial learning on the Ants and Food quiz and transfer to the Sensors and Inputs quiz. Participants in the concrete condition, with drawings readily perceptible as ants, showed better initial quiz performance than those in the idealized condition (39.8% and 33.8%, respectively). However, despite an initial disadvantage, the idealized condition showed better transfer to the Sensors and Inputs quiz (41.3%) than the concrete condition (36.4%). In particular, learners who had a poor understanding of the initial learning situation transferred better with idealized simulations.

These results can be described by the complementary advantages of concreteness and idealization. Although the concretely detailed ants and food graphics allowed students to learn effectively from that simulation, their knowledge may have been tied down to that domain. Students do well as long as they remain in the domain but fail to adapt their knowledge to new isomorphic situations. However, the idealized dots, because they were ambiguous and perhaps less intuitively connected to ants, had to be interpreted as ants, introducing difficulties in learning. However, this very ambiguity allows the idealized dots to serve as a useful representation for transfer, interpreted through the context of other isomorphic systems.

What is so striking about these results is how trivial the difference between conditions is. Looking from the ants and dots (Figure 7), the "idealization" seems insignificant. But in some sense, this physical change, stripping away the details such as ant legs and fruit stems to leave generic dots and blobs, is abstraction. Research from schema development (Fivush 1984) and the creation of mental models (Schwartz and Black 1996) suggest that the psychological process of forgetting or removing details creates structural representations. An external training that mimicked such processes might act as an aid to structural transfer.

Our first effort to combine the advantages of both concrete and idealized graphics was "concreteness fading," to start users with concrete graphics that transition into more abstract idealizations. Given that concrete similarities to corresponding real-world elements may have helped users gain an advantage in initially comprehending the simulation, concrete graphics are introduced first. But after this link has been established, the ants shift to dots and the fruit patches shift to blobs as a means of "fading" out the details that may have initially helped but also hurt transfer to new domains. We compared fading to "concreteness introduction," where the idealized simulations became more detailed over time. Both of these conditions could potentially promote transfer because it is frequently advantageous to introduce multiple versions of the same analog (Gick and Holyoak 1980,

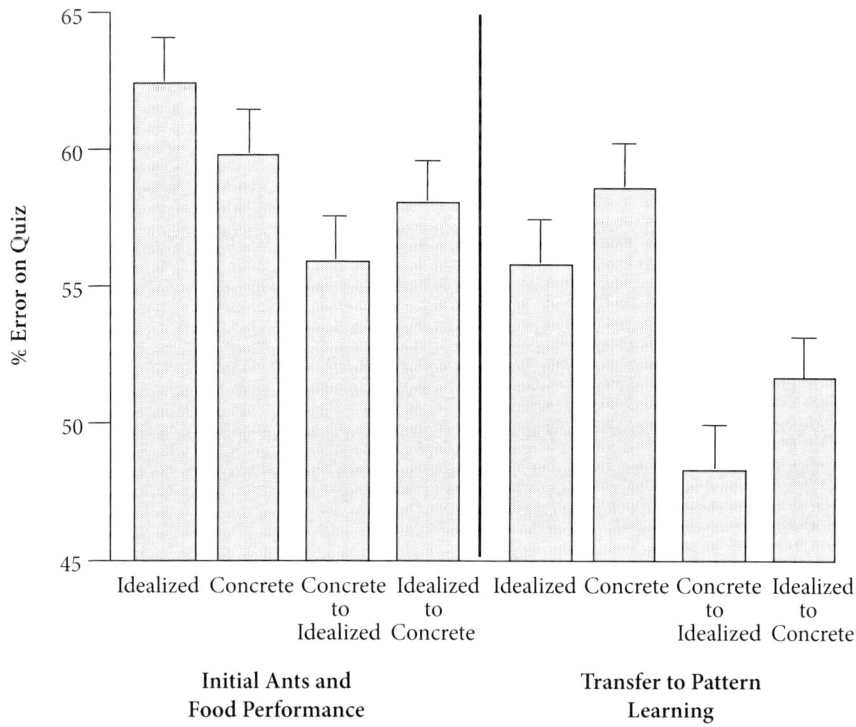

Figure 8. Results from Experiment 1 reported in Goldstone and Son (2005).

1983; Reeves and Weisberg 1990). To examine the effect of variability, consistent conditions (only concrete or only idealized) were also included in the experiment.

The same simulations from Goldstone and Sakamoto (2003) were used for teaching and probing transfer. In variable conditions, such as concreteness fading, 10 minutes after participants explored the concrete ants and food simulation, this message appeared, "We are now changing the appearances of the food and ants, but they still behave just as they did before." Then the alternative graphics appeared for another 10 minutes before the participants took the ants and food quiz. The concreteness introduction condition received 10 minutes of the idealized simulation, followed by the concrete one. There were no switches in the consistent conditions that received 20 minutes of the concrete simulation or 20 minutes of the idealized one.

The results revealed several informative aspects of presenting both concrete and idealized graphics. By combining concreteness fading and introduction conditions into a "variability" condition and the idealized and concrete conditions into a "consistency" condition, we found an aggregate advantage of variability over consistency for both learning (61.3% to 56.8%, respectively) and transfer (57.5 to 50.1%, respectively). In addition, there was a more pronounced advantage when the variation in graphics was in the direction from concrete to idealized than vice versa (shown in Figure 8). A second experiment showed these effects in two measures of comprehension, quiz scores as well as problem-solving within the simulation environment.

The advantage of variability fits with theoretical intuitions that both concreteness and idealization contribute to learning and generalization. It is often difficult to focus on structure apart from rich details (Ratterman and Gentner 1998) or the context it is embedded in (Catrambone and Holyoak 1989; Holyoak and Koh 1987). Knowledge has even been characterized as completely dependent on these contextual details (Lave 1988; Lave and Wenger 1991). Researchers have documented housewives and fishermen carrying out complex mathematical computations for problems in familiar contexts without being able to demonstrate these skills in less familiar settings (Nunes, Schliemann, and Carrahar 1993). These results have been interpreted as evidence for domain-specific knowledge of mathematics. Concrete graphics might represent a situation where both structure and concrete context are present to support learning. However, this can produce a contextually tied construal helpful for understanding the presented situation. Idealized graphical representations cut those ties, enabling the learning experience to transfer to new situations.

Being exposed to both construals seems to be additively advantageous because both concreteness fading and introduction conditions experience benefits to both learning and transfer. It seems as though participants in the variable condition were given a clue as to the more abstract commonality between the two spatial instances (ants and dots) of competitive specialization. Furthermore, even though informal interviews suggest that participants easily treated these instances as the "same thing" (Goldstone and Son 2005, 100), this practice in expanding their equivalence class of competitive specialization exemplars may have played a significant role in promoting the noticing of structural similarities. Several studies from analogical and symbolic reasoning have shown that comparison between two highly similar instances enhances attention to relational information (Loewenstein and Gentner 2005; Markman and Gentner 1993).

Although having both concrete and idealized graphics are better than just one or the other, the distinctive advantage of concreteness fading indicates an additional advantage of positioning concrete graphics first. One of the disadvantages, and advantages, of idealized simulations is that they can be multiply interpreted. This is advantageous in transfer since the idealized learning can be re-used for new interpretations. But this ambiguity makes initial learning difficult. Presenting concrete graphics first is beneficial because ambiguous objects are interpreted in light of previously seen unambiguous objects (Leeper 1935; Medin, Goldstone, and Gentner 1993; Moore and Engel 2001). The perceptual scaffolding provided by concrete details provides a link between real world elements and the elements of the model. Stripping away seemingly unimportant elements of that scaffolding helps learners become more sensitive to the scaffold itself.

5.2 Intuitive concreteness

Our characterization of concreteness fading largely depends on the idea that the influence of concreteness comes from activating past knowledge to provide an intuitive basis for comprehending new material. If this is indeed the case, intuitive concreteness does not have to be instantiated purely perceptually. After all, the verbal description of "ants and food" provides a concrete situational interpretation for the perceptual elements of a simulation. One of the advantages of concrete pictures is that they match with their concrete interpretations. However, just as these matching intuitions might facilitate comprehending the current domain, we wondered if the complementary disadvantage to transfer might also result from this intuitive background.

In an attempt to separate the effects of a concrete description with an intuitive one, we changed the contextual descriptions applied to the spatial covering simulation. Although ants covering food is a concrete example of agents efficiently covering space, competitive specialization is not a very common way of understanding

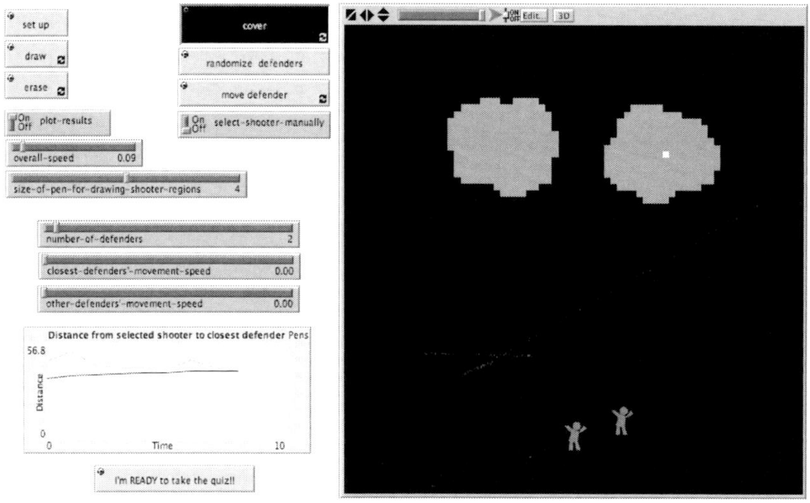

Figure 9. Screenshot of Defenders and Shooters simulation.

ant behavior. However, a highly intuitive example comes from the sports domain: Zone defense, a strategy in soccer or basketball where players defend zones of a playing field. The same general rules for competitive specialization can be described in the zone defense context: A shooter is randomly selected from the available shooting regions, the closest defender moves towards the selected shooter quickly while all other defenders move more slowly. Figure 9 shows the ants and food simulation modified to reflect zone defense. These rules seem to genuinely reflect what players might actually do on the soccer field (the defender closest to a shooter should run quickly towards that player!) rather than being abstract rules imposed upon a system. A poor soccer team has one player that defends the entire field while the rest of the defenders sit by. Conversely, a whole team of individuals trying to pursue every shooter is not very good either, as any parent of a six-year old soccer player will attest. Only when individuals specialize does the entire team cover the entire field. Experiment 1 examined whether these intuitive descriptions enable understanding and/or foster transfer, and Experiment 2 incorporated idealization to make better use of intuitions. Experiment 3 further examined the interpretability of idealized graphics.

6. Experiment 1

Space frequently provides a perceptual metaphor for understanding more abstract structures (Gardenfors 2000; Goldstone and Barsalou 1998) so both ant and defender simulations might foster good understanding of competitive specialization. Highly intuitive examples might foster even better understanding of competitive specialization. However, if the goal of CAS simulations is to produce *transferable* understanding, will these intuitive construals transfer to highly dissimilar situations? Does spatially grounded learning transfer to non-spatial situations?

6.1 Method

Participants. Thirty-seven undergraduates from Indiana University participated in this experiment for credit. Participants were randomly placed in one of two learning conditions: 18 received Concrete descriptions ("ants and food") and 19 received Intuitive descriptions ("defenders and shooter zones").

Materials and Procedure. All of our simulations were instantiated in NetLogo and are described more fully in Section 4. Both of the learning simulations were instantiations of specialization over physical space while the transfer simulation was over similarity space. The "Ants and Food" simulation was a combination of concrete and idealized graphical elements used in previous studies (Goldstone and Sakamoto 2003; Goldstone and Son 2005) with line drawings of ants as agents and blobs depicting the food regions. In the "Defenders and Shooters simulation", defenders were depicted as stick figures and blobs depicted shooter regions. Participants received a packet of instructions and were given examples of configurations. They were guided through several combinations of parameters to help them discover the settings that would result in efficient specialization. After participants explored the first simulation, they took a seven-question multiple-choice quiz modified from previously used quizzes.

The transfer simulation was the Sensors and Inputs simulation shown in Section 4. There was a handout of instructions but no guidance as to useful parameter settings. Participants were instructed to explore this simulation before going on to a seven-question quiz with elements comparable to the learning quiz. All materials (including the NetLogo simulations) are available on our website (http://www.calstatela.edu/centers/learnlab/simulations). Afterwards, participants were debriefed and asked whether they were familiar with zone defense.

6.2 Results

Because our manipulation of "intuitiveness" hinges on whether students were already familiar with zone defense, we used the debriefing question to determine whether it was a known concept. Zone defense seems to be a general concept among our undergraduates because only one person in our Intuitive condition and three in the Concrete condition reported that they did not know what a zone defense was.

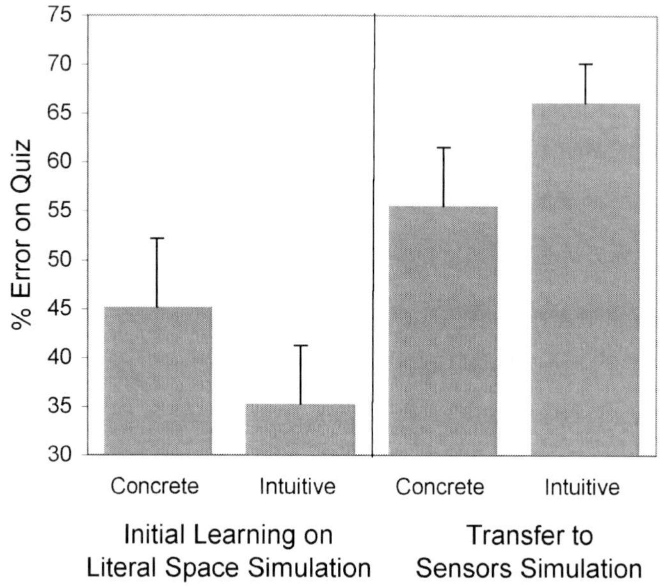

Figure 10. Results for Experiment 1. The intuitive condition does well (few errors) on the initial simulation, but shows less transfer to an analogous situation than does the concrete condition.

The quiz results are shown in Figure 10 and were analyzed with a 2 (quiz-type: learning, transfer) x 2 (description condition: Concrete, Intuitive) repeated-measures ANOVA. There was a significant effect of test, $F(1, 35) = 21.40$, $p < .001$, and an interaction between test and description, $F(1, 35) = 5.27$, $p < .05$. A paired T-test revealed that the average score on the learning quiz (59.9%) was significantly higher than the transfer quiz (39%), $t(36) = 4.43$, $p < .001$. Closer examination of the interaction revealed that this was mostly caused by the Intuitive condition which performed 30.8 percentage points better on learning than transfer, $t(18) = 5.05$, $p < .001$. On the other hand, the concrete condition did not show a significant difference, only 10 percentage points better on learning than transfer tests, $t(17) = 1.60$. Although T-tests between the two description conditions were not significant, $p > .15$, it seems that whatever learning the intuitive condition might have shown did not come across for transfer performance.

To further examine this possibility, we examined the correlations between test scores between the two training conditions and the transfer test. The concrete condition showed a significant correlation between learning and transfer performance across participants, $r = .53$, $p < .05$, suggesting that those who understood the Ants and Food simulation well also did well on the Sensors and Inputs quiz. However, the intuitive condition's training and testing quiz scores were not sig-

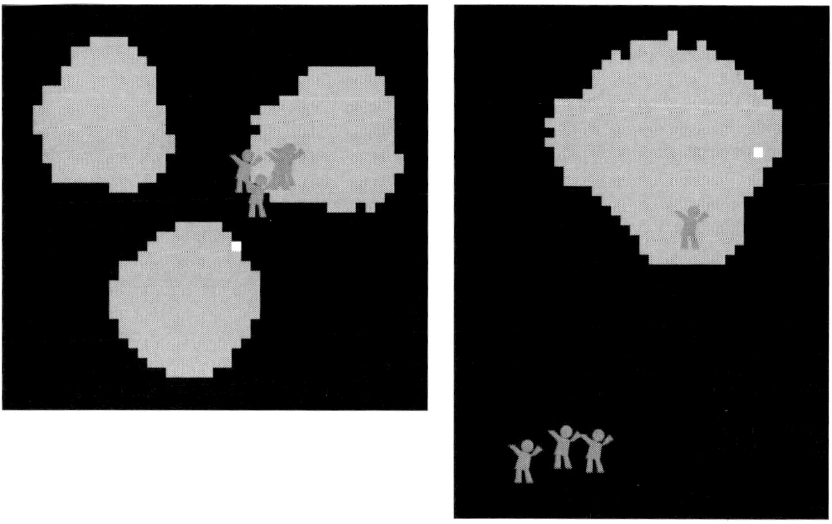

Figure 11. (a) This state on the left is the result of all defenders moving at the same rate. (b) The state on the right is the results of only the closest-defender moving at all. These results were described in sports-specific terms such as "bunch ball" or "shooters being wide open," respectively.

nificantly correlated, $r = .38$. This, combined with the paired T-test results, suggests that what students learned during training in the intuitive condition did not transfer well to the analogous but superficially unrelated simulation.

These results are interesting because defender and shooter are relational terms and zone defense is a structurally proper instantiation of competitive specialization. Additionally, through this simulation participants can invoke other context-specific intuitions that support this structure. Informal observation of written notes on the instruction packets showed that participants in the Intuitive condition used sports-specific terms to describe particular states of the system. For example, when describing the "clumping" that happens when all agents move at the same rate (see Figure 11), participants called this "bunch ball" and when describing a state where some defenders are not covering anything, participants used descriptions such as "shooters [are] being left wide open" or "inefficient block." Contrast this to the domain-specific comments made by those in the concrete condition: "the rest stay hungry", "ants dying out", "ended up on the grass", "wiggle around", "chewing food". These statements neither describe competitive specialization nor are related to particular parameter settings. This contrast illustrates one of the learning benefits from intuitive simulations — that the relation between the world and the model becomes transparent thus allowing domain-specific intuitions from the world to help students interpret the model. However, taken to the extreme, these benefits can also become detrimental, particularly for transfer.

When situations are too intuitive and the model-to-modeled-world link too transparent, the model ceases to become a general representation of the rules of competitive specialization. Instead the model simply provides an interpretation of zone defense. This learning example strongly tied to the sports domain allows learners to use their intuitions about sports to answer the learning quiz questions, but without the support of domain specific knowledge, they did not have any previous learning that could help them in a dissimilar transfer situation. All of this supporting contextualization that helped during the learning quiz may have acted as a crutch rather than a scaffold (Pani, Jeffres, Shippey, and Schwartz 1996). By drawing upon so much rich knowledge, participants may not have learned anything new about the competitive specialization principles underlying zone defense. In some sense, the relations were so deeply embedded in the zone defense context that participants could not separate them out.

Another way to construe this tight model-to-modeled-world link is that although zone defense clearly demonstrates this link, it also prevents learners from making the model-to-*modelable*-worlds link. This link requires learners to understand the model's potential referents beyond merely understanding the model itself. Here it may be useful to invoke DeLoache's dual-representation hypothesis (1995) which proposes that transfer between a model and a referential object comes from understanding two things: (1) the model itself as well as (2) the model's referential role. DeLoache's studies (1995, 2000) examine children's use of scale models as maps for larger rooms. In these studies, young children are shown a small Snoopy doll hidden under a small piece of furniture in a small model room. They are taken to a larger room that is set up in the same way and asked to find big Snoopy in the corresponding location. Typically 2.5-year-olds have trouble using the model while 3-year-olds use the model location to find Snoopy. DeLoache (2000) proposes that in order to transfer information from the model to the larger room, children must represent both the shown location as well as the referential relation between the model and the room. Thus, when younger children are shown the model behind a pane of fiberglass, strengthening the model's referential role, they make better use of the model in the finding task. Distance from the model directs more attention to the room that is being modeled rather than the model itself. Additionally, if the older children are given an opportunity to play with the model before the finding task, weakening the referential understanding by making the model an interesting object in its own right, their ability to use the model declines.

Our intuitiveness manipulation may have similarly weakened the referential role by making the model itself an object with interesting properties. This probably contributed to increases in actual understanding of the model as well, as shown in Experiment 1. Following DeLoache's lead, one solution for making effective use of

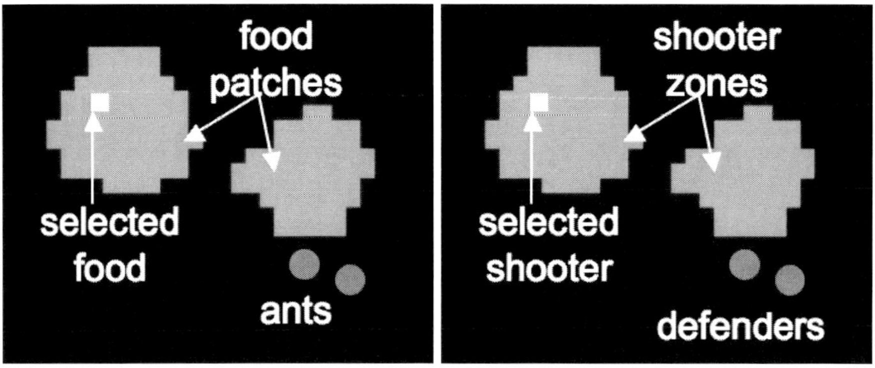

Figure 12. Pictures from the instruction packets of Experiment 2.

intuitive models might be to make the model less interesting as a domain in and of itself, and strengthen the model-to-modelable-worlds link. Experiment 2 is an attempt to put our own "fiber glass" in front of the model.

7. Experiment 2

Experiment 2 is an effort to make the zone defense simulation less evocative of real-life zone defense in order to foster improvements in generalization. We used the insight from previous studies on perceptual idealization and created a generic spatial covering simulation in NetLogo with dots and blobs. Dots can be described as people, animals, defenders, or oil drills so the two descriptions ("defenders" and "ants") from Experiment 1 were each applied to the dot simulation. This experiment thus distinguishes whether the differences found between concrete interpretations and intuitive ones are mediated by their matching pictures or solely by these descriptions. If intuitive descriptions are always detrimental to transfer, we should see the same pattern of results as Experiment 1. If they are not detrimental when applied to idealized dots, this provides further support for the benefits of idealized simulations.

7.1 Method

Participants. Forty-seven undergraduates from Indiana University participated in this experiment for credit. Although all participants learned with a simulation that had dots and blobs, they were described in two ways: 22 had Concrete descriptions ("ants and food") and 25 had Intuitive descriptions ("defenders and shooter zones").

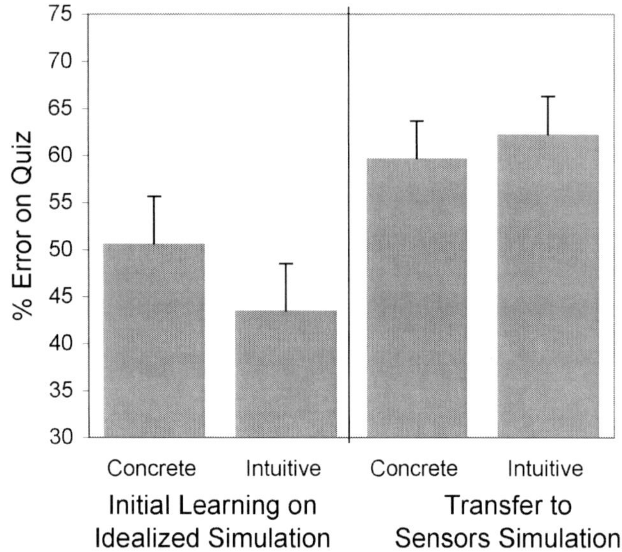

Figure 13. Results from Experiment 2. The graphical elements for all participants were idealized, but the descriptions associated with these elements could either be concrete (e.g., ants) or intuitively related to competitive specialization (intuitive). Pairing idealized graphics with the intuitive defenders background story yields good understanding of the training simulation (low error rate on quiz), and equivalent transfer to the concrete story.

Materials and Procedure. The procedure is identical to that of Experiment 1. The only change is in the elements depicted in the learning simulations. The ants in the Ants and Food simulation were changed to dots and the people in the Defenders and Shooters simulation were also changed to dots (Figure 12). Transfer was measured with the Sensors and Inputs simulation used previously.

7.2 Results

There were several participants who reported that they did not know zone defense (6 in the Intuitive condition and 5 in the concrete condition) but this was not a significant factor by any analysis. The main quiz results are shown in Figure 13 and were analyzed with a 2x2, quiz-type (learning, transfer) x description condition (Concrete, Intuitive) repeated-measures ANOVA. There was a significant effect of test, $F(1, 45) = 45.00$, $p < .001$, but no effect of description, $F(1, 45) = .171$, nor interaction, $F(1, 35) = 1.78$. A paired T-test revealed that scores on the learning quiz were 14.2% higher than on the transfer quiz, $t(46) = 3.88$, $p < .001$. Collapsing across concrete and intuitive conditions, scores on the two quizzes were correlated across participants, $r = .38$, $p < .01$. Although the intuitive condition still performed significantly better on learning than transfer (18.8%), $p < .001$, their scores on these two quizzes are now also significantly correlated, $r = .51$, $p < .01$. On the other hand, the concrete condition's 9% difference between the tests was not reliably difference, $t(21) = 1.60$, nor were participants' training and test scores correlated, $r = .28$. T-tests between the two description conditions were not significant for either quiz, $p > .30$.

In Experiment 1, intuitive descriptions seemed to have value for learning but was devastating for transfer. By using idealized simulations, the major disadvantage of using intuitive descriptions, lack of transfer, seems to have been mitigated. There were two reasons that intuitive stories hurt transfer in Experiment 1: (1) by embedding the rules of competitive specialization too deeply in one domain and (2) by weakening the model's referential role. Idealized pictures could help alleviate both of these effects on transfer. By being visually less similar to the zone defense context, idealized graphics may have forced students to work harder to make the link between the simulation elements and zone defense, but this effort could enable more transfer. Turning defenders into more context-neutral dots gave students practice with interpreting rich and complex scenarios using the lens of competitive specialization. This practice is helpful when students are then given the sensors simulation because it employs competitive specialization in an even subtler manner. By this account, students benefit not only from exposure to clear principles, but perhaps even more importantly by receiving training in the critical cognitive skill of interpreting model elements according to the principles. This suggestion is consistent with Bransford and Schwartz's (1999) framing of transfer in terms of giving students skills for future learning. Additionally, by virtue of being interpretable in more ways, simple dots are more applicable to the wide variety of competitive specialization instances than little people.

However, idealized simulations also seem to compromise some of the advantages of using concrete descriptions. Concrete visual situations described concretely have a strong model-to-modeled-world link providing a frame for the abstract principles of competitive specialization. Idealized graphics reduces this meaningful link, thus reducing the amount of learning in the initial simulation. This may have contributed to a similar level of decrease in transfer.

A priori, an important design aspect seems to be how simulations get linguistically described. They typically can be described in a number of ways and some of these descriptions may be more helpful for later needs than others. According to constructivist theories of learning, most notably Piaget (1980), knowledge is constructed by coordinating multiple instances or representations. With the rise of multimedia educational tools, there is a greater need for understanding the integration of both visual information and linguistic descriptions (Mayer 1993; Schnotz 1993). There are several theories posing a form of dual coding (e.g., Baddeley

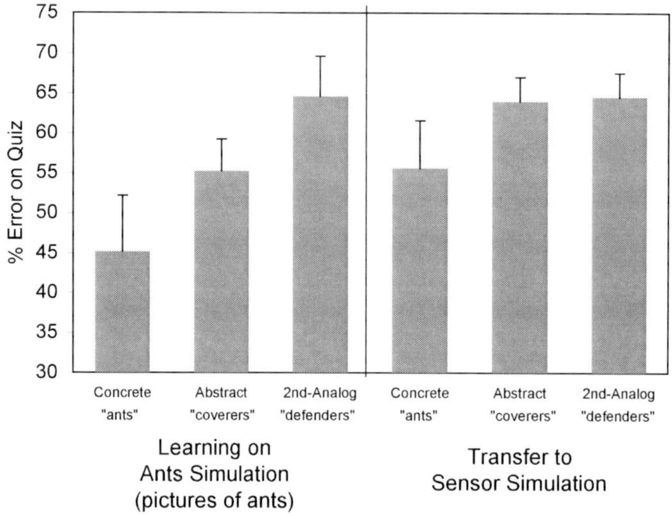

Figure 14. Results of pilot studies on abstract descriptions. The graphical elements for all participants were ants, but the descriptions associated with these elements could be either abstract (e.g., "coverers") or a second analog (e.g., "defenders"). These descriptions yield generally poor understanding of the training simulation (high error rate on quiz) and similarly poor transfer.

1992; Mayer 1992; Paivio 1986; Schnotz 1993) that suggest that these two streams must be coordinated with each other for effective learning (Clark and Paivio 1991; Mayer 1984). Paivio (1986) referred to a process of "building referential connections" that may be relevant to the linguistic interactions with concrete and idealized graphics. Although descriptions that match their perceptual elements have strong referential connections already (i.e., "ants" is strongly linked to pictures of ants), in order to foster generalizable knowledge, we need to create a new link, not to ants but to "originally homogenous agents that become specialized." Ambiguous visual stimuli weaken the referential link to ants per se but may allow this more abstract class to be formed instead. An interesting prediction might be that using these ambiguous visual stimuli with multiple linguistic descriptions (e.g., first calling the elements "ants" and then "defenders") might result in better internalization of the underlying principle.

Although the studies reported here examine the impact of using concrete and intuitive linguistic descriptions to understand multiply interpretable perceptual events, it is possible that there is a way to use abstract linguistic descriptions to interpret concrete perceptual events. We have made several unsuccessful attempts to find ways to build this referential connection in the opposite direction. Pilot studies have examined the effects of describing the concrete depictions of ants in abstract ways, such as "coverers and resources," with the aim of combining graphical concreteness and linguistic idealization. We have even tried teaching with two analogs simultaneously by showing pictures of ants but describing them as "defenders and shooters." However, both of these training conditions result in marginally detrimental effects on both learning and transfer. Pilot results from abstract and second-analog description conditions are shown in Figure 14. As of yet we have not found a successful way of combining concrete pictures with abstract words, in contrast to the beneficial effects of idealized pictures with concrete and intuitive descriptions shown in Figure 14. Through these failed attempts, we realize how difficult it is to create words that helpfully capture the wide array of agents that can take part in competitive specialization. One way of "abstracting" without being abstract per se is to describe perceptual ants as "insects" or "animals." Although we have not tested such descriptions, this may be able to foster a wider appreciation for the types of things that could be agents of competitive specialization. However, it may be more effective to teach with idealized images describable in multiple ways than to have one abstract description applied to multiple concrete instances. Although scientific efforts for universal principles are typically aimed towards the latter, the pedagogical aims of teaching science may be better achieved through the former.

8. Experiment 3

Experiment 3 may more clearly illustrate the benefit of idealized images to take on a broad range of descriptions. In an effort to come up with a general but meaningful term to capture agents that 'cover' both physical and metaphorical space, the simulation depicting ants was modified in terms of "lids specializing over pots." The same descriptive modifications were made to the idealized dot simulation. For both ant and dot depictions, the rules of competitive specialization are described as follows: A pot is randomly selected, the closest lid moves towards it with one rate, while all other lids move toward it with a different rate. "Lids and Pots" is not at all an intuitive cover story but it is a concrete one. Lids and pots are about physical covering situations and are relatively concrete simple objects. There is no a priori reason to believe that this description should help anyone understand competitive specialization, much less show transfer to the domain of sensors and inputs, and this was true for those who received the ants simulation described as "lids".

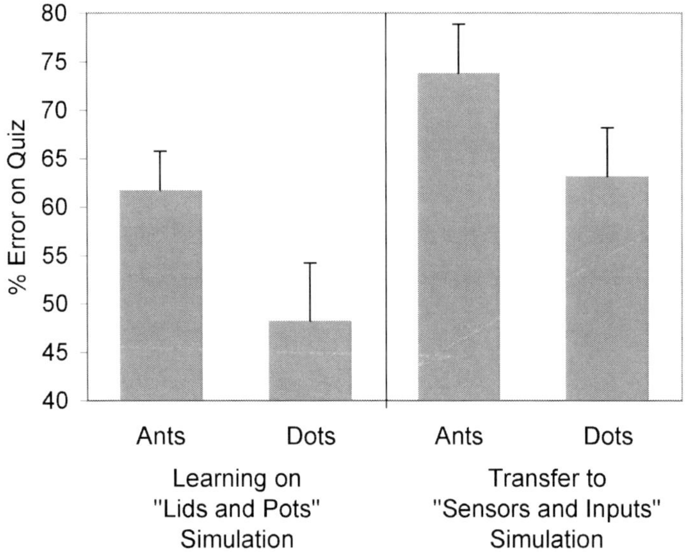

Figure 15. Experiment 3 results illustrating the flexibility of idealized depictions of simulation elements. The two graphical conditions, ants versus dots, represent the depicted elements in the learning simulation described as "lids and pots." However, as odd and unintuitive as this description may be, the idealized graphics allow students to learn and transfer better than concrete graphics.

8.1 Method

Participants. Thirty-one undergraduates from Indiana University participated in this experiment for credit. Although all participants learned with a simulation described as "lids covering pots," this was applied to two different graphics: 12 participants learned with Concrete ants and 19 with Idealized dots.

Materials and Procedure. The procedure is identical to that of Experiment 1 and 2. The elements depicted in the learning simulations were literal space instantiations of competitive specialization with element depicted as either ants or dots. Both were (somewhat oddly) described as "lids". The Sensors and Inputs simulation provided a measure of transfer.

8.2 Results and discussion

The main quiz results are shown in Figure 15 and were analyzed with a 2x2, quiz-type (learning, transfer) x learning graphics (Concrete ants, Idealized dots) repeated-measures ANOVA. There was a significant effect of test, $F(1, 29) = 10.15$, $p < .01$, and a significant effect of graphical elements, $F(1, 29) = 4.93$, $p < .05$, but no interaction, $F(1, 29) = .11$. A paired T-test revealed that scores on the learning quiz were 13.8% higher than on the transfer quiz, $t(30) = 3.40$, $p < .01$, and these scores were significantly correlated, $r = .46$, $p < .01$. Learning with ant graphics resulted in significantly worse performance on both learning, $t(30) = 5.44$, $p < .05$, and transfer quizzes, $t(30) = 4.4$, $p < .05$. Describing idealized dots as "lids and pots" allowed participants not only to learn and transfer better than those who were shown concrete ants, but also to learn and transfer at levels comparable to participants from Experiment 2 who had more meaningful descriptions applied to the dots.

Considering how odd the description of "lids covering pots" is (at least compared to ants covering food and defenders covering shooters), it is surprising that any graphical elements could allow participants to learn competitive specialization from it. This is a demonstration of the advantage of idealized graphics. Their flexibility, to be interpreted in multiple ways, gives them an advantage over more specific and less interpretable concrete graphics. Whereas participants were confused when a line drawing of an ant was called a "lid", they were apparently more amenable to calling an idealized dot a "lid".

9. Some design principles for interactive simulations

With regard to concreteness and idealization, as well as an eye on both learning and transfer, there are a few design principles that emerge from these experiments:

Get the best of both worlds

Both educators and cognitive scientists have realized the advantages that come from both concrete learning instances as well as abstract representations of structure. A simple design suggestion is to present multiple instantiations of the same idea in easily relatable ways. In many ways, presenting students with multiple linked representations is not a new idea; however, our research suggests some strategies for traversing across the different types of representations. For example, although sparse equations and highly concrete instantiations of them are relatable, one problem is that they are too different from each other to reconcile properly. Simulations can range over a continuum of concreteness, from virtual reality all the way down to simple dots. Learners may benefit by taking small manageable steps across that continuum. Highly concrete simulations invite learners to involve their past knowledge and intuitions. Shifting those simulations towards increasingly idealized forms may help by providing connection to that past knowledge while removing some of the irrelevant specific details.

Be wary of too much concrete intuition

Although highly intuitive learning situations seem to be easier for learners to grasp, educators should be aware of the potential detriment to transfer. Intuitions that are highly tied to a context may only be effective in that context. One danger is that these intuitions often allow students to excel in domain-specific tests of knowledge, where intuitions are consistent with the correct answer (Dror, Peron, Hind, and Charlton 2005). The disadvantage is only seen in tests of transfer to dissimilar contexts. Thus, students and teachers may feel that students have learned more with a model grounded in intuition, but the student may be less able to apply their knowledge to new analogs. Scientific simulations should be designed with the primary goal of *fostering* scientific intuitions rather than simply *depending* on these intuitions. This emphasis on creating new ways of seeing and interpreting situations implicates being able to transcend specific contexts. So it is important to test the effectiveness of simulations for later transfer as well as immediate performance (see also Bransford and Scwhartz 1998). However, combining intuitions with other more abstract design elements, such as idealized graphics, allows students to use their intuitions more effectively for transfer.

When in doubt, idealize perceptual elements

Perceptual simulations instantiate models. Experience with simulations may potentially provide building blocks for mental models and idealized elements may provide particularly efficient building blocks that can be used to model a variety of situations. This effective portrayal may also be the advantage of extreme or caricatured examples which exaggerate critical features (Dror, Stevenage, and Ashworth 2008). Furthermore, idealized perceptual elements, by being less connected to specific real-world categories, can illustrate a greater diversity of contextually specific descriptions than concretely similar elements. In this way, idealized simulations appear to provide effective mental manipulatives for building future models.

Additionally, since it is rather difficult to find abstract descriptions that students immediately grasp, using idealized graphics can draw upon their already well-developed perceptual capabilities. Idealized graphics seem relatively resilient to the dangers of intuitive descriptions, while more concrete elements must be described in particular ways to be effective.

10. Conclusions

For a long time, scientific models were visually presented by the insertion of pictures or graphs in text. The possibilities present in complex interactive simulations for radically affecting science as well as science education are enormous. However, to make use of all of that potential, we must design simulations that respect psychological, not just technical, constraints. The psychology of analogical problem-solving and other forms of relational reasoning often draws evidence from mathematical and scientific learning because these domains are aimed at precisely encapsulating structure, stripping away irrelevant details. Scientific explanations, by using the same mathematical or formal abstractions, reflect a level of description useful for problem-solving in a variety of situations, thereby allowing these disparate situations to be similar. We propose that simulations may be able to help students create models that explain a wide variety of phenomena. However, there is always the danger that learners will deal with these learning technologies in superficial or otherwise inadequate ways, so research on relevant aspects of design aspects is vital.

The interesting claims that come out of science can be counterintuitive. Complex systems have that flavor because most people assume that in order to explain high-level behavior, one must have a high-level plan (Chi 2005). In trying to foster the opposite intuition, that some high-level phenomena can have low-level emergent solutions, educational technologies will play an important role in helping create new intuitions. Combining the advantages of seeing appropriate simulations with compelling intuitive explanations may be an efficient way of using available resources to create effective learning opportunities.

References

Anderson, J.R., Greeno, J.G., Reder, L.M., and Simon, H.A. 2000. "Perspectives on learning, thinking, and activity". *Educational Researcher* 29: 11–13.

Anderson, J.R., Reder, L.M., and Simon, H.A. 1996. "Situated learning and education". *Educational Researcher* 25: 5–11.

Bransford, J., Brown, A.L., and Cocking, R.R. (eds). 1999. *How People Learn: Brain, Mind, Experience, and School.* Washington, D.C.: National Academy Press.

Baddeley, A. 1992. "Working memory". *Science* 255: 556–559.

Ball, P. 1999. *The Self-Made Tapestry.* Oxford: Oxford University Press.

Bar-Yam, Y. 1997. *Dynamics of Complex Systems.* Reading, MA: Addison-Wesley.

Barnett, S.M. and Ceci, S.J. 2002. "When and where do we apply what we learn? A taxonomy for far transfer". *Psychological Bulletin* 4: 612–637.

Barsalou, L.W. 1999. "Perceptual symbol systems". *Behavioral and Brain Sciences* 22: 577–660.

Bassok, M. and Holyoak, K.J. 1989. "Interdomain transfer between isomorphic topics in algebra and physics". *Journal of Experimental Psychology: Learning, Memory, and Cognition* 15: 153–166.

Batty, M. 2005. *Cities and Complexity: Understanding Cities with Cellular Automata, Agent-Based Models, and Fractals*. Cambridge, MA: The MIT Press.

Beals, R., Krantz, D.H., and Tversky, A. 1968. "Foundations of multidimensional scaling". *Psychological Review* 75: 127–142.

Bentley, W.A. and Humphreys, W.J. 1962. *Snow Crystals*. New York: Dover.

Bransford, J.D. and Schwartz, D.L. 1999. "Rethinking transfer: A simple proposal with multiple implications". In A. Iran-Nejad and P.D. Pearson (eds), *Review of Research in Education* 24: 61–101.

Brooks, R.A. 1991. "Intelligence without representation". *Artificial Intelligence* 47: 139–159.

Carraher, D.W., Nemirovsky, R., and Schliemann, A.D. 1995. "Situated generalization". *Proceedings of the 19th Annual Meeting of the International Group for the Psychology of Mathematics Education* (Vol. 1). Recife: Universidade Federal de Pernambuco, 234.

Carraher, D. and Schliemann, A.D. 2002. "The transfer dilemma". *The Journal of the Learning Sciences* 11: 1–24.

Casti, J.L. 1994. *Complexification*. New York: HarperCollins.

Casti, J.L. 1997. "Would-be worlds: Towards a theory of complex systems". *Artificial Life and Robotics* 1: 1433–5298.

Catrambone, R. and Holyoak, K.J. 1989. "Overcoming contextual limitations on problem-solving transfer". *Journal of Experimental Psychology: Learning, Memory, and Cognition* 15: 1147–1156.

Clark, J.M. and Paivio, A. 1991. "Dual coding theory and education". *Educational Psychology Review* 3: 149–210.

Chi, M.T.H. 2005. "Commonsense conceptions of emergent processes: Why some misconceptions are robust". *Journal of Learning Sciences* 14: 161–199.

Chi, M.T.H., Feltovich, P., and Glaser, R. 1981. "Categorization and representation of physics problems by experts and novices". *Cognitive Science* 5: 121–152.

Dede, C. 1995. "The evolution of constructivist learning environments: Immersion in distributed, virtual worlds". *Educational Technology* 35: 46–52.

DeLoache, J.S. 1995. "Early understanding and use of symbols: The model model". *Current Directions in Psychological Science* 4: 109–113.

DeLoache, J.S. 2000. "Dual representation and young children's use of scale models". *Child Development* 71: 329–338.

DeLoache, J.S., Kolstad, D.V., and Anderson, K.N. 1991. "Physical similarity and young children's understanding of scale models". *Child Development* 62: 111–126.

DiFonzo, N., Hantula, D.A., and Bordia, P. 1998. "Microworlds for experimental research: Having your (control and collections) cake and realism too". *Behavioral Research Methods, Instruments, and Computers* 30: 278–286.

Dixon, J.A. and Bangert, A.S. 2004. "On the spontaneous discovery of a mathematical relation during problem solving". *Cognitive Science* 28: 433–449.

Dror, I.E., Stevenage, S.V., and Ashworth, A.R.S. 2008. "Helping the cognitive system learn: Exaggerating distinctiveness and uniqueness". *Applied Cognitive Psychology* 22: 573-585.

Dror, I.E., Peron, A.E., Hind, S.-L., and Charlton, D. 2005. "When emotions get the better of us: The effect of contextual top-down processing on matching fingerprints". *Applied Cognitive Psychology* 19: 799–809.

Duschl, R.A. 1990. *Restructuring Science Education.* New York: Teachers College Press.
Flake, G.W. 1998. *The Computational Beauty of Nature.* Cambridge, MA: The MIT Press.
Garcia-Ruiz, J.M., Louis, E., Meakin, P., and Sander, L.M. 1993. *Growth Patterns in Physical Sciences and Biology.* New York: Plenum Press.
Gardenfors, P. 2000. *Conceptual Spaces.* Cambridge, MA: The MIT Press.
Gentner, D. and Rattermann, M.J. 1991. "Language and the career of similarity". In S.A. Gelman and J.P. Byrnes (eds), *Perspectives on Language and Thought: Interrelations in Development.* Cambridge: Cambridge University Press, 225–277.
Gentner, D. and Toupin, C. 1986. "Systematicity and surface similarity in the development of analogy". *Cognitive Science* 10: 277–300.
Gick, M.L. and Holyoak, K.J. 1980. "Analogical problem solving". *Cognitive Psychology* 12: 306–355.
Gick, M.L. and Holyoak, K.J. 1983. "Schema induction and analogical transfer". *Cognitive Psychology* 15: 1–39.
Goldstone, R.L. 2003. "Learning to perceive while perceiving to learn". In R. Kimchi, M. Behrmann and C. Olson (eds), *Perceptual Organization in Vision: Behavioral and Neural Perspectives.* Mahwah, NJ: Lawrence Erlbaum, 233–278.
Goldstone, R.L. and Barsalou, L. 1998. "Reuniting perception and conception". *Cognition* 65: 231–262.
Goldstone, R.L., Landy, D., and Son, J.Y. 2008. "A well grounded education: The role of perception in science and mathematics". In M. de Vega, A. Glenberg, and A. Graesser (eds), *Symbols, Embodiment, and Meaning.* Oxford: Oxford University Press, 327-355.
Goldstone, R.L., Medin, D.L., and Gentner, D. 1991. "Relational similarity and the nonindependence of features in similarity judgments". *Cognitive Psychology* 23: 222–264.
Goldstone, R.L. and Sakamoto, Y. 2003. "The transfer of abstract principles governing complex adaptive systems". *Cognitive Psychology* 46: 414–466.
Goldstone, R.L. and Son, J.Y. 2005. "The transfer of scientific principles using concrete and idealized simulations". *Journal of the Learning Sciences* 14: 69–114.
Grady, S.M. 1998. *Virtual Reality: Computers Mimic the Physical World.* New York: Facts on File.
Heim, M. 2000. *Virtual Realism.* New York: Oxford University Press.
Hershkowitz, R., Schwarz, B.B., and Dreyfus, T. 2001. "Abstraction in context: Epistemic actions". *Journal for Research in Mathematics Education* 32: 195–222.
Holyoak, K.J. and Koh, K. 1987. "Surface and structural similarity in analogical transfer". *Memory & Cognition* 15: 332–340.
Jackson, S., Stratford, J., Krajcik, S., and Soloway, E. 1996. "Making system dynamics modeling accessible to pre-college science students". *Interactive Learning Environments* 4: 233–257.
Kaminski, J.A., Sloutsky, V.M., and Heckler, A.F. 2005. "Relevant concreteness and its effects on learning and transfer". In B. Bara, L. Barsalou, and M. Bucciarelli (eds), *Proceedings of the XXVII Annual Conference of the Cognitive Science Society.* Mahwah, NJ: Erlbaum, 1167–1172.
Kaminski, J.A., Sloutsky, V.M., and Heckler, A.F. 2006. "Do children need concrete instantiations to learn an abstract concept?". In R. Sun and N. Miyake (eds), *Proceedings of the XXVIII Annual Conference of the Cognitive Science Society,* Mahwah, NJ: Erlbaum, 411–416.
Kirkpatrick, S., Gelatt, C.D., and Vecchi, M.P. 1983. "Optimization by simulated annealing". *Science* 220: 671–680.
Klahr, D. and Carver, S.M. 1988. "Cognitive objectives in a logo debugging curriculum: Instruction, learning, and transfer". *Cognitive Psychology* 20: 362–404.

Lave, J. 1988. *Cognition in Practice: Mind, Mathematics, and Culture in Everyday Life*. New York: Cambridge University Press.
Lave, J. and Wenger, E. 1991. *Situated Learning: Legitimate Peripheral Participation*. Cambridge, MA: Cambridge University Press.
Lederman, N.G. 1992. "Students' and teachers' conceptions of the nature of science: A review of the research". *Journal of Research in Science Teaching* 29: 331–359.
Leeper, R.W. 1935. "A study of a neglected portion of the field of learning — The development of sensory organization". *Journal of Genetic Psychology* 46: 41–75.
Levin, J.R. and Mayer, R.E. 1993. "Understanding illustrations in text". In B. Britton and A. Woodward (eds), *Learning from Textbooks: Processes and Principles*. Hillsdale, NJ: Erlbaum, 95–134.
Markman, A.B. and Gentner, D. 1993. "Structural alignment during similarity comparisons". *Cognitive Psychology* 25: 431–467.
Mayer, R.E. 1992. "Guiding students' cognitive processing of scientific information in text". In M. Pressley, K.R. Harris, and J.T. Guthrie (eds), *Promoting Academic Competency and Literacy in School*. San Diego: Academic, 243–258.
Mayer, R.E. 1984. "Aids to prose comprehension". *Educational Psychologist* 19: 30–42.
Mayer, R.E. and Anderson, R.W. 1992. "The instructive animation: Helping students build connections between words and pictures in multimedia learning". *Journal of Educational Psychology* 84: 444–452.
Medin, D.L., Goldstone, R.L., and Gentner, D. 1993. "Respects for similarity". *Psychological Review* 100: 254–278.
Miller, C.S., Lehman, J.F., and Koedinger, K.R. 1999. "Goals and learning in microworlds". *Cognitive Science* 23: 305–336.
Moore, C. and Engel, S.A. 2001. "Neural response to perception of volume in the lateral occipital complex". *Neuron* 29: 277–286.
Narayanan, N.H. and Hegarty, M. 1998. "On designing comprehensible interactive hypermedia manuals". *International Journal of Human-Computer Studies* 48: 267–301.
Noss, R., Hoyles, C., and Pozzi, S. 2002. "Abstraction in expertise: A study of nurses' conceptions of concentration". *Journal for Research in Mathematics Education* 33: 204–229.
Nunes, T., Schliemann, A.D., and Carraher, D.W. 1993. *Mathematics in the Streets and in Schools*. Cambridge: Cambridge University Press.
O'Reilly, R.C. 2001. "Generalization in interactive networks: The benefits of inhibitory competition and Hebbian learning". *Neural Computation* 13: 1199–1242.
Paivio, A. 1986. *Mental Representations: A Dual Coding Approach*. Oxford: Oxford University Press.
Pani, J.R., Jeffres, J.A., Shippey, G.T., and Schwartz, K.J. 1996. "Imagining projective transformations: Aligned orientations in spatial organization". *Cognitive Psychology* 31: 125–167.
Penner, D.E. 2001. "Complexity, emergence, and synthetic models in science education". In K. Crowley, C.D. Schunn, and T. Okada (eds), *Designing for Science*. Hillsdale, NJ: Erlbaum, 177–208.
Rattermann, M.J. and Gentner, D. 1998. "The effect of language on similarity: The use of relational labels improves young children". In K. Holyoak, D. Gentner, and B. Kokinov (eds), *Advances in Analogy Research: Integration of Theory and Data from the Cognitive, Computational, and Neural Sciences*. Sophia: New Bulgarian University, 274–282.

Reeves, L.M. and Weisberg, R.W. 1994. "The role of content and abstract information in analogical transfer". *Psychological Bulletin* 115: 381–400.
Resnick, M.R. 1994. *Turtles, Termites, and Traffic Jams.* Cambridge, MA: The MIT Press.
Resnick, M.R. and Wilensky, U. 1998. "Diving into complexity: Developing probabilistic decen tralized thinking through role-playing activities". *Journal of Learning Sciences* 7: 153–172.
Rumelhart, D.E. and Zipser, D. 1985. "Feature discovery by competitive learning". *Cognitive Science* 9: 75–112.
Schank, R.C. and Farrel, R. 1988. "Creativity in education: A standard for computer-based teaching". *Machine Mediated Learning* 2: 175–194.
Schnotz, W. 1993. "On the relation between dual coding and mental models in graphics comprehension". *Learning and Instruction* 3: 247–249.
Schwartz, D.L. and Black, J.B. 1996. "Shuttling between depictive models and abstract rules: Induction and fallback". *Cognitive Science* 20: 457–497.
Shepherd, R.N. 1958. "Stimulus and response generalization: Tests of a model relating generalization to distance in psychological space". *Journal of Experimental Psychology* 55: 509–523.
Singley, M.K. and Anderson, J.R. 1989. *Transfer of Cognitive Skill.* Cambridge, MA: Harvard University Press.
Smith, L.B. and Gasser, M. 2005. "The development of embodied cognition: Six lessons from babies". *Artificial Life* 11: 13–29.
Turing, A.M. 1952. "The chemical basis of morphogenesis". *Philosophical Transactions of the Royal Society of London* B 327: 37–72.
Uttal, D.H., Liu, L.L., and DeLoache, J.S. 1999. "Taking a hard look at concreteness: Do concrete objects help young children learn symbolic relations?". In L. Balter and C. Tamis-LeMonda (eds), *Child Psychology: A Handbook of Contemporary Issues.* Philadelphia: Psychology Press, 177–192.
Uttal, D.H., Scudder, K.V., and DeLoache, J.S. 1997. "Manipulatives as symbols: A new perspective on the use of concrete objects to teach mathematics". *Journal of Applied Developmental Psychology* 18: 37–54.
Wilensky, U. 1997. *NetLogo Traffic Basic Model.* Center for Connected Learning and Computer-Based Modeling, Northwestern University, Evanston, IL. http://ccl.northwestern.edu/netlogo/models/TrafficBasic.
Wilensky, U. 1999. NetLogo (and NetLogo User Manual). Center for Connected Learning and Computer-Based Modeling, Northwestern University, Evanston, IL. http://ccl.northwestern.edu/netlogo/
Wilensky, U. and Resnick, M. 1999. "Thinking in levels: A dynamic systems perspective to making sense of the world". *Journal of Science Education and Technology* 8: 3–18.
White, B.Y. 1993. "ThinkerTools: Causal models, conceptual change, and science education". *Cognition and Instruction* 10: 1–100.
White, B.Y. and Fredericksen, J.R. 1998. "Inquiry, modeling, and metacognition: Making science accessible to all students". *Cognition and Instruction* 16: 3–118.
Willows, D.M. and Houghton, H.A. 1987. *The Psychology of Illustration.* New York: Springer.
Winn, W. 2003. "Learning in artificial environments: Embodiment, embeddedness, and dynamic adaptation". *Technology, Instruction, Cognition and Learning* 1: 87–114.

Appendix

Selected questions from Ants and Food Quiz

1. To make the ants as a population spread out evenly over the food, which strategy is best:
   a. Have all the ants move as quickly as possible.
   b. Make the ant that is closest to a piece of food move more quickly than all the other ants.
   c. Make the ant that is closest to a piece of food move more slowly than all the other ants.
   d. Early on, make the closest ant move more quickly than the others, but later on, make the closest ant move more slowly.

2. Why don't the ants cover the food well if the closet ant and all of the other ants all move with the same speed?
   a. The closest ant will quickly cover food but the other ants will have to quickly find other food that needs covering.
   b. If other ants move as fast as the closest ant, then when a piece of food is selected, all of the ants, close and far, will move towards it. The ants will all be covering the same piece of food.
   c. If all the ants move with the same speed, then they will all get an equal opportunity to cover food but there is a limited supply of food for everyone.
   d. If the closest ant moves as fast as the other ants, then it will get to the food first, and will prevent the other ants from covering it. The other ants will only cover food after the closest ones have finished.

3. To have the ants cover the food well, it is necessary to have the ants become specialized for particular food patches. Which action most directly allows for this specialization?
   a. Make sure that there are not very many ants on the field. That way, no matter what speed they are moving at each ant can be far away from other ants.
   b. Make sure that there are many ants on the field. That way, no matter what speed they are moving at each ant become specialized for a tiny patch.
   c. Make the ant that is closest to the chosen piece of food move quickly to the food, but other ants should only move slowly towards it.
   d. Make the ant that is closest to a chosen piece of food move slowly to the food, but other ants should move more quickly towards it.

4. If there are two equally sized patches of food and only one ant, what usually happens after a long time?
   a. The ant will alternate between the patches, but only if it moves very slowly.
   b. Pieces from both food patches will be randomly chosen so ant will end up halfway between the two patches.
   c. Pieces from both food patches will be randomly chosen so the ant will have to select one of the patches and stay there.
   d. The ant will not move toward either of the patches unless it is very close to them in the first place.

Selected questions from Defenders and Shooters Quiz (Analogous questions to Ants and Food Quiz)

1. To make the defenders as a population spread out evenly over the shooters, which strategy is best:
   a. Have all the defenders move as quickly as possible.
   b. Make the defender that is closest to a shooter move more quickly than all the other defenders.
   c. Make the defender that is closest to a shooter move more slowly than all the other defenders.
   d. Early on, make the closest defender move more quickly than the others, but later on, make the closest defender move more slowly.

2. Why don't the defenders cover the shooters well if the closet defender and all of the other defenders all move with the same speed?
   a. The closest defender will quickly cover shooters but the other defenders will have to quickly find other shooters that need covering.
   b. If other defenders move as fast as the closest defender, then when a shooter is selected, all of the defenders, close and far, will move towards him. The defenders will all be covering the same shooter.
   c. If all the defenders move with the same speed, then they will all get an equal opportunity to cover shooters but there is a limited number of shooters for everyone.
   d. If the closest defender moves as fast as the other defenders, then he will get to the shooters first, and will prevent the other defenders from covering them. The other defenders will only cover shooters after the closest ones have finished.

3. To have the defenders cover the shooters well, it is necessary to have the defenders become specialized for particular shooters. Which action most directly allows for this specialization?
   a. Make sure that there are not very many defenders on the field. That way, no matter what speed they are moving at each defender can be far away from other defenders.
   b. Make sure that there are many defenders on the field. That way, no matter what speed they are moving at each defender become specialized for very few shooters.
   c. Make the defender that is closest to the chosen shooter move quickly to the shooter, but other defenders should only move slowly towards him.
   d. Make the defender that is closest to a chosen shooter move slowly to the shooter, but other defenders should move more quickly towards him.

4. If there are two equally sized regions of shooters and only one defender, what usually happens after a long time?
   a. The defender will alternate between the regions, but only if he moves very slowly.
   b. Shooters from both regions of shooters will be randomly chosen so defender will end up halfway between the two regions.
   c. Shooters from both regions of shooters will be randomly chosen so the defender will have to select one of the regions and stay there.
   d. The defender will not move toward either of the regions unless he is very close to them in the first place.

Selected questions from Sensors and Inputs Quiz (Analogous questions to Ants and Food Quiz)

1. To make the sensors best represent the natural groups in a set of inputs, you should:
   a. Have the sensors adapt as quickly as possible.
   b. Make the sensor that is most similar to a selected input adapt more quickly than all the other sensors.
   c. Make the sensor that is most similar to a selected input adapt more slowly than all the other sensors.
   d. Early on, make the most similar sensor adapt more quickly than the others, but later on, make the most similar sensor adapt more slowly.

2. Why aren't specialized sensors formed if all of the sensors (the most similar and the others) all adapt equally quickly?
   a. The most similar sensor will quickly become responsible for inputs but the other sensors will have to quickly find other inputs that need matching.
   b. **If other sensors adapt as quickly as the most similar sensor, then when a new input is selected, then all sensors will adapt to it. The sensors will all try to match the same input.**
   c. If all of the sensors adapt with the same speed, then they will all get an equal opportunity to look like the selected input but there is a limited number of inputs available for matching.
   d. If the most similar sensor adapts as quickly as the other sensors, then it will match the input first, and will prevent the other sensors from matching it.

3. To create sensors that can accommodate the whole range of inputs naturally, it is necessary to have the sensors become specialized for different inputs. Which action most directly allows for this specialization?
   a. Create just a few sensors. That way, no matter the rate of adaptation each sensor can be very dissimilar from the other sensors.
   b. Create more sensors than there are inputs. That way, no matter the rate of adaptation each sensor can become very specialized.
   c. **Make the sensor that is most similar to the selected input adapt quickly to that input, but the other sensors should only adapt slowly to it.**
   d. Make the sensor that is most similar to the selected input adapt slowly to the input, but the other sensors should adapt quickly to it.

4. There are two inputs and only one sensor, what usually happens?
   a. The sensor will alternate between matching the two inputs, but only if it adapts very slowly.
   b. The sensor will be a blend of the two inputs, highlighting parts shared by the inputs.
   c. The sensor will become specialized for one of the inputs only.
   d. The sensor will not become adapted to either input, unless it is highly similar to them in the first place.

Attention management for dynamic and adaptive scaffolding*

Inge Molenaar and Claudia Roda
University of Amsterdam / American University of Paris

Many pedagogues have argued that learners should shape their own learning experience whilst tutors should facilitate this process of knowledge construction. Digital environments have been often used in an attempt to scaffold learning in these innovative learning settings. However the results obtained have been mixed both in terms of learning achievements and learners' satisfaction. We argue that this is due to the fact that scaffolds are often implemented in a too static and generic manner, and attention-related, fine-grained aspects of timeliness and fitness are normally disregarded. We propose that dynamic and adaptive scaffolds can be provided by observing and responding-to learners' attentional focus. We present a system that implements such attention-based scaffolding. We indicate how learners' attentional states may be detected and how several categories of interventions may scaffold learning in a timely and appropriate manner. Finally, we report the results obtained in system tests which show an improvement in performance and motivation for students working with attention based scaffolding.

Keywords: adaptive scaffolding, attention, attention aware system, attention management system, e-learning system

1. Introduction

As digital learning environments become more ubiquitous, it is also becoming obvious that a more accurate application of pedagogical theories is needed in order to overcome some of the problems that many learners experience in such environments. Classic learning challenges are accompanied by challenges proper to the usage of digital tools; the former have been increasingly addressed with innovative pedagogical approaches including experiential learning, situated learning, and many others. Digital tools have been widely employed by teachers embracing these pedagogical approaches; those tools however, whilst providing access to a much larger and varied set of information, have generated a new set of difficulties for learners. In Roda and Nabeth (2005) we argue that many of these difficulties are due to the fact that current IT based learning environments are still mostly inspired by classic *lecture style* teaching which mainly emphasize the *presentation of information to learners.* In this framework the teacher selects the information to be presented and the mode of presentation. This selection happens in a static manner when teachers prepare their lectures and "configure" the digital tools for information presentation. Instead, innovative pedagogical approaches assume that learners can somehow shape their own learning experience (Papert and Harel 1991), and therefore information selection cannot happen statically and cannot be solely guided by the teacher. Learners should be free to access information and tools when and if they need them. Therefore, many instructors and learning systems simply provide as much access as possible to information and tools so that students can choose those best suited to their needs at any given time. Unfortunately, this frequently results in overwhelming environments where learners have difficulties finding information, selecting the appropriate course of action, and generally focussing their attention.

Ideally, learning support systems should help students to better control their own learning processes. It is important that learners are allowed to actively participate in setting their own learning agenda, which would result: (1) in their ability to self-regulate learning; (2) in gaining a better knowledge transfer due to a better connection between the prior knowledge and the learning content; and (3) in higher motivation of the students. Therefore, digital tools assisting learning environments must provide learners with the help necessary to direct and sustain attention to the appropriate tools and information; further, this support must evolve with the student's knowledge and skills. In educational psychology this evolving support to students is called *adaptive scaffolding*. In this paper we argue that in order to derive the information needed to provide adaptive scaffolding with diagnosis, calibration and fading — i.e., following the classic description originally proposed by Wood, Bruner, and Ross (1976) — e-learning systems must observe, and reason about, the learner's attention-allocation processes. We describe a system, AtgentSchool, in which attention management and scaffolding constructs are integrated to produce a dynamic and adaptive e-learning environment for school children.

In Section 2 we review several interpretations and implementations of scaffolding, we report on the main findings related to human attention and attention aware systems, and we describe how attention aware systems can provide the input needed to support adaptive scaffolding.

In Section 3 we describe a conceptual framework for attention aware scaffolding, and we detail a model in which scaffolding *interventions* are connected to different events tracking the learning environment. We claim that the model proposed is a generic attention-based model for scaffolding that can be applied to a variety of e-learning applications. In Section 4 we describe the implementation of the conceptual framework in the Atgentschool system. In Section 5 we report the results of a set of evaluation studies of the AtgentSchool system and of the effects of attention-based dynamic and adaptive scaffolding.

2. Relevant background

The next two sections provide a short introduction to scaffolding and attention aware systems. We restrict ourselves to the aspects most relevant to our work; this means that this section is by no means a full literature study of these two areas.

2.1 Scaffolding learning

Hadwin, Winn, and Nesbit (2005) provide an overview of the advancements and possibilities of software for the field of educational psychology. The broad theme addressed is the changing nature of instructional interventions, which refers to both the delivery of instruction and the use of computers to guide and tutor learning. The use of computers to guide and tutor learning is identified as an exciting line of investigation, which "could shape research that aims to study and improve instructional processes and scaffold learning" (ibid: 2). In recent years it has been often claimed that various digital tools could be used to scaffold learning. This is certainly the case, in the same sense in which a book, a drawing, and many other tools can, if appropriately employed, provide some support to scaffolding. Digital scaffolding however has presented several, difficult to address, problems; below we provide an overview of the interpretations of the term scaffolding and its use in digital environments.

The term *scaffolding* was introduced by Wood, Bruner, and Ross (1976). It is defined as providing assistance to a student on as-needed basis, fading the assistance as the competence increases. The general idea behind scaffolding is that some of the control within the learning environment is temporally transferred from the learner to another more experienced actor in order to support students in the acquisition of the abilities necessary to fully self sustain learning. *Scaffolds* support the execution of learning tasks difficult for the student and they are removed when no longer necessary. Several studies have provided evidence that students, learning about complex topics in computer based learning environments, experience various types of difficulties in absence of scaffolding. These studies show the students' poor ability to regulate their learning and their failure to gain a conceptual understanding of the topics (Azevedo and Hadwin 2005). In particular, within innovative learning arrangements, where student are provided with more control of both learning content and learning procedures, scaffolds can support students in dealing with this increased responsibility.

Three elements that were essential for scaffolding in Wood's traditional descriptions are *diagnosis*, *calibration* and *fading* (Puntambekar and Hübscher 2005). In this framework the abilities of the learner must be diagnosed continuously in order to define the appropriate scaffolding. This diagnosis supports the careful calibration of the scaffolds and eventual fading of the support provided. When the learner masters all aspects of the task the control is fully transferred to the learner.

In analyzing the literature and the application of Wood's theory in innovative learning arrangement, it is important to notice that the meaning associated to the term *scaffolding* has evolved over time. In recent literature the use of the term is often different from the traditional meaning. Puntambeker and Hübscher (2005), for example, refer to the modern scaffolding approaches as *blanket support*. The amount and type of support is fixed and not adjusted on the basis of an observation and diagnosis of the learner. Frequently, the support is the same for all students and no adaptive tuning of the support to the changing needs of the individual student is offered. Adaptive scaffolding directed at the dialogue between the learner and the tutor has been reduced to passively setting the scaffolds. The fading of the scaffolding is not in place; the scaffolds are permanent and unchanging.

On the basis of the above analysis two types of scaffolding have been specified: *Fixed scaffolding* is defined once, and it is the same for all students (e.g., one may provide a list of instructions that helps users to perform a learning activity). *Adaptive scaffolding* entails pedagogical agents which diagnose, calibrate, and provide support to learning in an individualized manner; such agents are capable of fading or adapting as the learners' abilities and confidence increase. Whilst fixed scaffolding appears to produce mixed results, adaptive scaffolding has been shown to benefit several aspects of students learning (Aleven and Koedinger 2002; Chi, Siler, Jeong, Yamauchi, and Hausmann 2001). Scaffolding has two main functions: the immediate intent to support knowledge construction, and the long term intent to develop heuristics to support future independent learning (Holton and Clarke 2006). These two functions connect closely to the benefits of more constructive learning environments as mentioned in the introduction.

Different techniques for scaffolding within computer based environments exist. Among others: prompts and question prompting (Ge, Chen, and Davis 2005; Kauffman 2004); expert modeling (Schoenfeld 1985); guided peer questioning (King 1991); process models (Lin and Lehman 1999); support lists; representations; and reports. Process models, support list, representations, and reports represent mostly fixed scaffolding techniques. Prompts and question prompts can be provided to the user as adaptive forms of scaffolding. Prompts are statements provided to the user to highlight specific elements in the learning environment. Questions prompts are questions posed to elicit responses from the user. Prompts and question prompts have been found to support students' structuring of problem solving (King 1991); reasoning and justification process (King 1992; Lin and Lehman 1999); self monitoring and strategic studying (Kauffman 2004); problem representation, developing solutions, making justifications, and monitoring and evaluation (Ge and Land 2003). These prompts and question prompts are generated based upon the answers students give to questions asked in the learning systems. This is adaptive in form, but we cannot speak of agents that diagnose, calibrate and fade their interventions. Below we propose to use attention and attention aware systems to support adaptive scaffolding.

2.2 Attention and attention aware systems

Systems capable of adapting to, and supporting, human attentional processes have been called Attention Aware Systems (Roda and Thomas 2006; Roda and Nabeth 2007). In this section we very briefly review the vast literature that has aimed at defining what attention is and how it is controlled, and we highlight the findings that are most relevant to the design of Attention Aware e-learning Systems (for a more thorough review see Roda and Thomas 2006).

Human *attention* is normally understood as the set of processes that enable us to cope with our limited cognitive abilities; these processes guide the selection of incoming perceptual stimuli (Driver 2001: 53; Lavie and Tsal 1994: 183; Posner 1982). What we see, hear, and generally perceive around us (in the physical world) exceeds, probably by several orders of magnitude, what we are actually capable of processing. Chun and Wolfe propose that "First, attention can be used to select behaviorally relevant information and/or to ignore the irrelevant or interfering information. [...] Second, attention can modulate or enhance this selected information according to the state and goals of the perceiver. With attention, the perceivers are more than passive receivers of information. They become active seekers and processors of information, able to interact intelligently with their environment" (Chun and Wolfe 2001: 273).

In the cognitive psychology literature, there is a general agreement that attention can either be controlled voluntarily by the subject, or it can be captured by some external event (Arvidson 2003; Posner 1980; Yantis 1998). Voluntary control is referred to as *endogenous*, *top-down*, or *goal-driven* attention. Attention captured by external events is referred to as *exogenous*, *bottom-up*, or *stimulus-driven* attention. For example, if one reads some text, one applies endogenous attention, however a sudden noise may attract attention and create an exogenous process.

Chun and Wolfe indicate that these two mechanisms have different characteristics, "endogenous attention is voluntary, effortful, and has a slow (sustained) time course; […] exogenous attention draws attention automatically and has a rapid, transient time course" (Chun and Wolfe 2001: 279). The two mechanisms (exogenous and endogenous) are strongly related (Yantis 2000). In fact the endogenous mechanisms in place (e.g., what one is looking for in a visual field, and how this search is performed at the voluntary level) seem to determine whether one will automatically be able to ignore certain stimuli; in other words "the guidance of attention is determined by interactions between the bottom-up input and top-down perceptual set" (Chun and Wolfe 2001: 280).

In modern learning settings the strategy used to "set off" the learning process provides for the top-down attention allocation processes, i.e. the student is given the motivation necessary to pay attention to certain information and tools. Scaffolding provides for guiding the learner's attention to the most relevant items often using both endogenous (motivational) mechanisms, and exogenous (perception-related) mechanisms.

Several researchers have aimed at clarifying how endogenous and exogenous processes may interact in the environment and which role these processes may play in the pre-attentive and attentive stages. Treisman (1960, 1969) has suggested that non-attended stimuli may be elaborated at the attentive stage if they are particularly significant in someone's current environment or personal experience. This partially explains the different reactions of individual students to the same scaffold.

Hillstrom and Chai (2006) review the main factors intervening in retaining/distracting visual attention in computer interaction. They analyze how the direction of attention may be influenced by the distinctiveness of stimuli in the visual scene, the observer's intentions, memory of what has been attended in the past, and the perceptual organization of the display. Several theories relate attentional mechanisms to personal experience and current environment in an attempt to explain *interference effects* (delays in the processing of stimuli due to unwanted stimuli called *distractors*). Interference effects would be responsible for situations in which we are unable to keep attention on a target stimulus or to avoid distractors. For example, stimuli that have been actively ignored in preceding trials are more difficult to select (negative priming) (Allport 1989; Tipper 1985); distractors with features similar to the features currently prioritized generate more interference (Folk, Remington, and Johnston 1992); and stimuli related to familiar and recent foci may cause greater disruption to the user's current activity (Rafal and Henik 1994; Rogers and Monsell 1995). The history of the learner's interaction with the learning environment (including the tutor and the learner's peers) and with previous learning environments impacts on the effect that a new stimulus (possibly a scaffold) will have on that learner.

In terms of e-learning systems design the above findings imply that the impact of interventions on the learner cannot be evaluated statically (at design time), but it varies and depends on the recent activities and goals of the learner. For example, one could expect that if a learner is working at a team project, the notification of an email from a team member is more likely to attract the learner's attention than any message unrelated to recent activities. This is confirmed by experimental results by research in change blindness (the phenomenon by which significant changes in the visual field may go unnoticed) which demonstrate that attention is highly selective and information is extracted only "just in time" if relevant to the current task (Hayhoe 2000; Triesch, Ballard, Hayhoe, and Sullivan 2003). This corroborates the fact that endogenous and exogenous attentional processes interact to define what we perceive. The selective nature of vision has been demonstrated by several other works in inattentional blindness (Mack and Rock 1998; Rensink 2000) and inattentional amnesia (Rensink 2000; Woolfe 1999), whilst other experiments emphasize involuntary attention-capture related to visual context (Jiang, Chun, and Olson 2004; Wells and Olson 2003) rather than to task. Historically, the study of change blindness has significantly contributed to the understanding of attention and its relations to memory and awareness, some reviews (Durlach 2004; Rensink 2002) report on the many situations in which observers fail to detect significant changes in their visual field. Simons and Rensink (2005) explain that in all these situations the localization of the motion signals that accompanied the change was impaired, which suggests that "attention is needed for change perception, with change blindness resulting whenever the accompanying motion signals failed to draw attention" and that "these effects are even stronger when the changes are unexpected" (ibid: 16). See, for example, the surprising results on unexpected changes (Levin and Simons 1997; Levin, Simons, Angelone, and Chabris 2002; Simons and Levin 1998), which somehow contradict our naïve understanding of what would draw attention. Although all the results above refer to the visual modality, what we can abstract is that, given the selective nature of attention allocation processes, scaffolds have a much better chance to be effective in environments in which the learner is strongly motivated and if they are proposed just-in-time, i.e. when the learner is in need of the knowledge being scaffolded.

Some research has aimed at building overall models of attentional processes within the frame of other cognitive processes. Grossberg (1976a, 1976b, 1999), for example, proposes a model addressing learning and conscious experience, and explains how intentions may guide attention in two ways. First, intentions reflect expectations of events that may (or may not) occur. Second, intentions help monitoring sequences of events that should take place in order to satisfy behavioral goals. In this manner "we can get ready to experience an expected event so that when it finally occurs we can react to it more quickly and vigorously, and until it occurs, we are able to ignore other, less desired, events" (Grossberg 1999: 12). Grossberg's theory hints that since users' attention will be focused on information that matches their momentary expectations, understanding users' intentions (both in the sense of behavioral goals, and in the sense of events likelihood) is essential in supporting attentional processes. Therefore, the diagnosis phase proposed by Wood should include the assessment of the learner's expectations in terms of his/her intentions. Furthermore, one way of directing and maintaining learners' focus is to act at the level of intention.

Several experiments (and common experience) reveal however that intentionality may not always result in attending appropriate events: sometimes, relevant cues are ignored and irrelevant ones are attended. Kruschke (2001, 2003) explains the above phenomena stipulating that in order to achieve rapid error reduction in the selection of the cue to attend, we learn to attend to certain cues (learned attention — highlighting) and to ignore others (learned inattention — conditioned blocking). A similar model, where attention to cues that have been learned to be relevant increases, whilst attention to cues that have been learned to be irrelevant decreases, had been already proposed (Mackintosh 1975). We seem to apply these strategies all the time both at the macro level (e.g., we establish *trusted* learning resources), and at the micro level (we disregard information displayed in certain areas of the screen if we have often experienced the area as irrelevant to our current activity). An initial analysis of how these processes may be modelled within an interactivist model of learning is proposed in Roda (2007). In terms of automatic scaffolds this entails that the calibration phase should take into consideration the history of the interaction of the learner with previously proposed scaffolds and enough variety should be available to be able to cope with learned attention and learned inattention especially.

Multi-tasking, which regularly occurs in human activity, adds complexity to the understanding of attention allocation. How do we manage to switch our attention from one task to another? Under which conditions can we do this most efficiently? What are the effects on task performance and learning? Based on a computational model addressing these issues, the EPIC architecture, some studies (Kieras, Meyer, Ballas, and Lauber 2000; Rubinstein, Meyer, and Evans 2001) have proposed that two distinguishable sets of processes control the execution of consecutive tasks: *executive control processes*, and *task processes. Task processes* control performance of the individual tasks and *executive control processes* control task switching. In this model endogenous control prepares, in a top-down manner, for the next task; and exogenous control, triggered by the onset of the next task stimulus, completes the preparation for the task. The authors explain delays occurring in task switching condition by the fact that "if a switch occurs from one task to another, there is a pause between the end of stimulus identification and the beginning of response selection for the current task […]. This pause is used by an executive control process whose operations enable the subsequent response selection stage to proceed correctly" (Rubinstein, Meyer, and Evans 2001: 770). This model seems to match several experimental results. First it models appropriately the fact that the difference in performance time for task repetition and task alternation increases with the complexity of the tasks (Jersild 1927). Second, under the assumption that task cueing may facilitate the executive control process selecting the next task, the model explains the fact that task switching times may be significantly reduced if visual cues are provided about the task to be performed next (Spector and Biederman 1976). Third, under the hypothesis that endogenous processes initiate preparing for the next task only if the Response Stimulus Interval (RSI) is predictable, the model explains why, under certain conditions, increasing the length of RSI decreases switching times costs only if the RSI is constant (Allport, Styles, and Hsieh 1994; Rogers and Monsell 1995).

The findings reported in this section have three important implications on the design of Attention Aware e-learning Systems. First, **there is always a cost associated with switching attention** from one task to another and this cost is **related to the complexity of the tasks involved**. In order to design systems supporting the learning process, it is necessary to identify the parameters that define task complexity and evaluate the cost of focus switching on the basis of these parameters. It seems likely that both general and learner-related parameters will contribute to the evaluation of task complexity (intuitively we can define the level of complexity of a task both "in a general sense" and "for a specific person"). An example of the application of the evaluation of task switching cost is the case in which the system has some project-relevant information and should decide whether to interrupt the student activity in order to provide the information.

Second, results on task cueing in task alternation hint that **systems capable of providing cues about the task to be performed next would reduce cognitive load for the learner**. Further it seems likely that, in the case of task resumption, providing cues about the context of interrupted work would reduce cognitive load. For example, in a word processor, task cues may provide information about which part of a document was last edited, and about the context in which that editing took place (e.g., after opening a certain web page and reading a certain email).

Third, in relation to interruptions, it appears that increasing the time between attention switches will not reduce users' cognitive load per se. A system aimed at supporting users' attentional processes should instead **allow the user to predict interruption times.**

2.3 Attention awareness for adaptive scaffolding

The system and methodology described in this paper are based on the observation that an essential element required for providing adaptive and dynamic scaffolding is the management of the learners' attentional state.

In their original work, Wood and his colleagues stated, "The actual pattern of effective instruction then, will be both task and tutee dependent, the requirements of the tutorial being generated by the interaction of the tutor's two theories" about the task and how it may be completed, and about the performance characteristics of the tutee. (Wood, Bruner, and Ross, 1976: 97) Unfortunately, within e-learning research and applications, the "theory of performance characteristics of the tutee" (Wood, Bruner, and Ross 1976: 97) has often been interpreted (or implemented) through static models of the tutee performance. Such models are normally static both from a temporal and an ontological point of view. *Temporally static* models represent the performance characteristics of the tutee once-for-all and do not take into account the changes that intervene during the learning experience. *Ontologically static* models define the learning-relevant characteristics of the tutees once-for-all and, although the "values" associated to these characteristics may vary over time during the learning process, it is not possible to introduce new ontological categories adapted to the specific learning experience and tutee. For example, the fact that a tutee is (or is not) a *good programmer* may not be part of the categories originally defined as describing his/her performance. Such category may however become relevant for certain learning projects, or for certain strategies chosen by the tutee in order to work on a learning project. While the dynamic creation of ontological categories is desirable, in this research we concentrate on temporally dynamic and ontologically static, but configurable (for the specific learning application) user/tutee models. We propose that the problem of having static ontological models may be (for the time being) addressed by a continuous tracking of the tutee attention allocation associated to an evaluation of his/her performance on the selected foci. In this manner for example, although being a good/bad programmer may not be part of the tutee profile, one is able to detect whether the attention allocated to a certain activity (programming) actually results in the tutee moving closer to the problem solution or not. Within our framework the **diagnostic phase** is based on the detection of the learner current attentional focus and an evaluation of whether the user performs as expected (based on the task model and the tutee model) on the associated task. **Calibration** corresponds to *intervening* with the learner in a manner that is *adapted* to both his/her current attentional focus and characteristics (e.g., history of interaction, needs, abilities, etc.); intervening with the learner amounts to either supporting the learner's current attentional focus or proposing alternative ones. **Fading** results from the adaptation process of calibration.

Good tutors are not only able to select the appropriate scaffolds for students, but they can also choose, in a very precise manner, the **best time and modality for providing those scaffolds.** This aspect, which has been often neglected in systems aimed at scaffolding learning, emerges naturally from the model we propose of attention-based scaffolding.

3. Conceptual framework for attention-based scaffolding

Our objective is to model the attentional state of a learner on the basis of system-observable ***events***, and select appropriate ***interventions*** to either support such state or guide the learner towards a different attentional state. Consequently, the input to our model will be a set of *events*, and the output of the model will be *interventions*. Because our model aims at being *temporally dynamic*, the generation of interventions is based both on current *events* and on the memory of past events. The memory of past events is maintained in a learner description, called ***learner model***, which subsumes the previous activity of the user in the environment. Because interventions on the attentional state of the learner must also be based on some knowledge of the task being performed by the user, the model also includes a ***task model*** describing in some detail the structure that users' activities may have within the learning environment. Below we describe the different components (events models; learner model; task model; intervention model) of our conceptual framework. In Section 4 we will describe how such framework can be implemented in a system supporting dynamic and adaptive scaffolding.

3.1 Model input: Events

Below we use a simple grammar to describe only the main elements of our model, the complete grammar is not reported for sake of brevity. The grammar we employ here is similar to a BNF (Backus–Naur form) and supplies derivation rules, written as LHS ::= RHS where LHS is a non-terminal symbol of the grammar that can be substituted with one of the OR separated expressions on the RHS (OR is indicated by the vertical bar |). Terminal symbols are enclosed in triangular brackets (e.g., <this is a terminal>). Optional items are enclosed in square brackets (e.g., [this is an optional item]). Items repeating 0 or more times are suffixed with an asterisk *.

Events reveal either the current attentional focus of the learner (e.g., the learner is working on a certain exercise, or is typing in a certain window) or items that may be relevant foci for the learner in the future (e.g., an email that has arrived for the learner, a lecture on the same subject of the exercise the learner is working on). We have defined three types of events: *Application events*, *User events*, *Tracking events*.

(1) EVENT ::= APPLICATION_EVENT | USER_EVENT | TRACKING_EVENT

The three sections below describe each one of these events in more detail. A complete description of the model's events is out of the scope of this paper and the interested reader should see Roda (2006) for the complete events taxonomy.

3.1.1 *Application events*

Application events reveal the activity of the user within a software application. We assume that e-learning applications are capable of supplying information about the learner's activity to the model. This information may include:

- Explicit actions of the learner (e.g., the user starts reading Chapter 1, the user has completed exercise 1); we call these events *user-applications events.*
- Changes in the application environment (e.g., a new chapter is available, the teacher has corrected the exercise); we call these *environment-application events.*

(2) APPLICATION_EVENT ::= USER_APPLICATION_EVENT | ENVIRONMENT_APPLICATION_EVENT

User-application events reveal the current focus of the learner, whilst Environment-application events reveal possible alternative foci for the learner. Table 1 provides some examples, of application events.[1]

Table 1. Examples of application events (these are the events that the e-learning application sends to the model)

APPLICATION EVENTS (Events generated by the application)		
Event name	**Description**	**Examples / Comments**
	User-Application Events	
Start event	User starts a new task	student starts *exercise 1*
Continue event	User switches sub-task continuing on a super-task	student accesses a text describing *exercise 1*
Complete event	User has completed a task	student has completed *exercise 1*
Resume event	User resumes a task previously interrupted	student re-starts *exercise 1* after an interruption
Initiating event	User enters the application	
Stop event	User leaves the application	
	Environment-Application Events	
New information available event	The application recognizes that the user could focus on newly available information	Arrival of an email message from the teacher

3.1.2 *User events*

In most cases learners are the best judges of their own characteristics, preferences, and needs; user events represent the cases in which the users directly supply some input to the model. This can be in the form of:

- Information about their attentional preferences and constraints such as the maximum frequency of interruption, the preferred method of interruption, tasks deadlines, or how long they will be available until the next off-line interruption. We call these *user-information-supply events*
- Requests of services such as: notification of events, context restoration for a task, help in interacting with the model. We call these *service-request events*
- Feedback on the model's interventions by for example explicitly accepting or dismissing them. We call these *feedback events*

(3) USER_EVENT ::= USER_INFORMATION_SUPPLY_EVENT | SERVICE_REQUEST_EVENT | FEEDBACK_EVENT

Table 2 provides some examples, of user events.

3.1.3 *Tracking events*

It is assumed that attention-related events may also result from either tracking application-independent user activities or changes in the environment.

- User-tracking events report on the user's states by either directly observing the user through psycho-physiological measures (e.g., gaze, facial expression, body posture, etc.) or by tracking the user activity on the devices. Examples of these events include: *idle input events* generated when the user has not provided input for a time longer than a specified time (normally dependent upon the current user task), or *low input frequency events* generated if the user becomes too slow in his/her activity (also user and task dependant).
- Environment-tracking events report on the environmental states that might affect the user attentional state. This tracking may include the observation of the computing environment (e.g., the user being active in a different application) or the overall environment (e.g., the phone ringing, a person entering the room)

(4) TRACKING_EVENT ::= USER_TRACKING_EVENT | ENVIRONMENT_TRACKING_EVENT

Table 2. Examples of user events (these are the events that the user sends to the model)

USER EVENTS (Events generated by the user)		
Event name	**Description**	**Examples / Comments**
	User-Information-Supply Events	
Set time available event	User indicates a time when he will interrupt the activity	User indicates that he has a meeting in 30'
Set task priority event	User indicates the priority that he assigns to a certain task	User indicates that the task *review for exam* has the highest priority
Set task deadline event	User indicates a deadline for the task	User indicates that *exercise 1* should be finished by Tuesday
Set interruption frequency event	User indicates the maximum frequency of interruptions	User indicates that interruptions should only be presented at 10' intervals
	Service-Request Events	
Notify me event	User informs the agents about events for which he wants to receive notification	User asks to be notified about any email received from the teacher
Resume task event	User requests to set the context in order to resume a task that was previously interrupted	User asks that the context of *exercise 1* be restored so that he can restart working at it
Help event	The user requests help on the current task	User asks further explanations for *exercise 1*
	Feedback Events	
Dismiss suggestion event	User indicates that a suggested focus should not be further suggested	Following a suggestion to restore the context for *exercise 1*, the user indicates that it is obsolete
Accept suggestion event	User indicates that a suggestion is accepted	Following a suggestion that the user works at *exercise 1*, the user accepts the suggestion
Mood event	The user indicates his/her level of satisfaction with the system behavior	The user indicates that he/she is happy/neutral/unhappy about the suggestion generated by the system

Table 3 provides some examples of tracking events.

Table 3. Examples of user events (these are the events that the user sends to the model)

	TRACKING EVENTS (Events generated by tracking devices)	
Event name	**Description**	**Examples / Comments**
	User-Tracking Events	
Idle-input event	User has not performed any input activity for longer than a given expected reaction time	No keyboard, nor mouse activity
Low input frequency event	User is providing input at a rate slower than expected	Slow keyboard or mouse activity
Foci sequences event	A pattern is recognized in the sequence of user's foci	After accessing an exercise the learner always accesses the related lecture
Low alertness event	The user appears tired	Events generated by psycho-physiological measurements
	Environment tracking	
Idle application event	The application has been idle for a certain amount of time	The user has temporarily left the application
Physical event event	Tracking devices report changes in the physical environment that may indicate a switch in the user's attentional state	The phone rings, someone walks in the room
Copy and past event	Reports copy and paste operations between the window(s) of the current task and other windows	Allows to associate windows from other applications to the context of the current task

3.2 Learner model

The learner model serves as a memory storing information about the characteristics, experience, and progress of the learner over time. The information stored in the learner model forms the basis for the assessment of the learner's attentional state, for the evaluation of possible alternative foci, and for the definition of appropriate scaffolding interventions. A complete description of the learner model is out of the scope of this paper; below we briefly describe the information maintained in the learner model that is most crucial for the following discussion of scaffolding:

- The learner's current focus and foci history — these describe the current and past activity of the learner and allow to infer the learner's advancement on the learning activities based on the events information
- The learner's characteristics, e.g., expertise level, learning preferences

- A list of alternative foci — these are activities that the learner is not currently focussing on but that could, in the future, constitute relevant foci. Alternative foci may be foci that have been suspended by the user (e.g., foci related to interrupted task) or that have been evaluated as relevant but have not yet been considered by the learner (e.g., a new important email, a task related to the learner's current activity). Alterative foci represent possible activities and scaffolds for the tutee that can be activated on an as-needed basis
- User preferences — A set of declared preferences including: maximum frequency of interruption, no-interruption times, notification modalities, tasks that shouldn't be interrupted, etc.
- Reactions to previous interventions — This information allows the fine-tuning of interventions to the specific users

LEARNER_MODEL ::= LEARNER_MODEL_ELEMENT*
LEARNER_MODEL_ELEMENT ::= CURRENT_FOCUS | PREVIOUS_FOCUS | ALTERNATIVE_FOCUS | LEARNER_CHARACTERISTIC | LEARNER_PREFERENCE | LEARNER_FEEDBACK
LEARNER_CHARACTERISTIC ::= EXPERTISE_LEVEL | LEARNING_PREFERENCES
EXPERTISE_LEVEL ::= <new user> | <known user> | <frequent user> | <expert user>

Within the conceptual framework it is possible to express *conditions on the learner state* by indicating what the content of certain fields of the learner model should be at a certain time using the following grammar:

LEARNER_STATE ::= LM_CONDITION*
LM_CONDITION ::= LM[LEARNER_MODEL_ELEMENT = LEARNER_MODEL_ELEMENT_VALUE] where the LEARNER_MODEL_ELEMENT_VALUE is a possible value for the corresponding LEARNER_MODEL_ELEMENT.[2]

For example, within the conceptual framework it is possible to indicate that a certain type of scaffolding action should take place only for new users by using the condition:

LM[EXPERTISE_LEVEL=new user].

3.3 Task model

The ***task model*** (Laukkanen, Roda, and Molenaar 2007) describes the tasks that the learner may perform within the e-learning application. Tasks are organized in hierarchies, may be defined at different levels of granularity, may be ordered, and may be either mandatory or optional. For example, the task *complete class project 1* may be organized in sub-tasks *read preliminary information* and *build object X* where the subtask *read preliminary information* is optional, and the subtask *build object X* is mandatory.

Task structure however, may not provide sufficient information to reason about the attention allocation processes of a learner who is performing or is about to perform the task. As discussed in Section 2, the specific characteristic of the task with respect to the user and his previous activity play an important role in attention allocation and eventually in the choice of the scaffolding necessary to support the learner in performing the task. For this reason, in our framework we associate to each task a set of properties including:

- The *resources needed* for the task — this allows to avoid proposing to a learner to perform a task for which the resources are currently unavailable.
- The *time on task* — the total time the learner has spent on the task. This indicator, together with the *expected* duration indicator, allows an evaluation of the *progression state* of a task. The progression state of a task is important in the management of focus switches, for example one may want to avoid interrupting a task that is very close to completion, or one may want to suggest completing an interrupted task that is close to completion. Further, knowledge of the progression state may help in deadlines management, and in the evaluation of achievements over time.
- The *deadline for completion* of the task — this allows generating interventions reminding the user to attend those tasks that are close to the deadline. As described in Roda and Nabeth (2007), in situations of frequent interruption and multitasking, deadline management may impose high levels of cognitive load therefore the model aims at providing support that may reduce this load.
- Some *keywords* describing the task — these allow recognizing similarities between tasks.
- The *maximum time the learner could be idle* on the task — this allows intervening with learners that remain idle for too long on a task. This indicator is necessary to distinguish tasks that may result in the user being *apparently* idle (e.g., a learner is reading a long text on screen), from tasks that require obvious learner's activity (e.g., answering to a short question).
- The *expected duration* of the task — this indicator is used in combination with the *time on task* indicator in order to evaluate the *task progression state.*
- The *people* associated with the task — this allows recognizing when interventions (e.g., emails) from certain people may be relevant to the task.
- The *difficulty level* of the task — as discussed in Section 2, this indicator may be necessary for the evaluation of the cost of interrupting the task. This indicator

may also allow defining the level of support that one may want to provide for the task.

- The *task activity* — this allows to define task specific parameters. For example, for a task that involves typing some text in a text-field, it allows to indicate how much text has been entered in the text-field. This indicator, together with the *time-on-task* indicator allows one to obtain a good evaluation on the state of advancement of the task.

In our model it is also possible to associate *help tasks* or *help messages* to a task. Help task and help messages basically provide the different types of scaffolding that can be associated to a task. Help tasks and messages belong to one of three categories: Pre-task support, on-task support, and post task support indicating the time when the scaffold applies: As the learner is about to perform the task, when the learner is performing the task, and as the learner completes the task.

(5) TASK_MODEL ::= TASK _MODEL_ELEMENT*

(6) TASK _MODEL_ELEMENT ::= RESOURCES_NEEDED | TIME_ON_TASK | TASK_DEADLINE | TASK_KEYWORDS | MAXIMUM_TIME_IDLE | EXPECTED_DURATION | TASK_PEOPLE | DIFFICULTY_LEVEL | TASK_ACTIVITY | PRE-TASK_SUPPORT | ON-TASK_SUPPORT | POST-TASK_SUPPORT

Within the conceptual framework it is possible to express *conditions on the state of a task* by indicating what the value of certain task elements should be using:

TASK_STATE ::= TASK_CONDITION*
TASK_CONDITION ::= task(TASK_MODEL_ELEMENT = TASK_MODEL_ELEMENT_VALUE][3]

For example, within the conceptual framework it is possible to indicate that a certain type of scaffolding action should take place only if the task is a difficult one, by using the condition:

task(DIFFICULTY_LEVEL=high)

3.4 Model output: Interventions

The set of possible interventions provided to the user could be very situation and domain dependent. The objective of our work has been the creation of a general model of interventions applicable to many learning situations and largely independent of the learning domain at hand.

Originally six types of scaffolding support were defined in Wood, Bruner, and Ross (1976): Recruiting the child's interest, reducing the degrees of freedom by simplifying the task, maintaining direction, highlighting the critical task features, controlling frustration, and demonstrating ideal solution paths. Scaffolding can be directed at different instructional targets: Learning domain knowledge; learning to regulate one's own learning; learning about using an electronic learning environment; learning how to adapt to particular instructional context (Azevedo and Hadwin 2005). Interventions can be provided towards the development of declarative, procedural, conceptual, or metacognitive knowledge. We have categorized our interventions following the classic model of support to self regulated learning (Zimmerman and Chrunk 2001) which distinguishes 4 levels, namely cognition, metacognition, motivation, and behavior. *Cognition* has a focus on thinking, *metacognition* is focused on monitoring and evaluation, *behavior* is focused on doing, and *motivation* is directed towards feelings (Hadwin, Wozney, and Pontin 2005).

Cognitive interventions support the users' learning process during the execution of a learning activity, and they are directed at activating cognitive behavior. Cognitive interventions support actions with respect to content and context of the learning task and they are direct at the level that Nelson (1996) referred to as the object level, as opposed to the meta level, which refers to the metacognitive activities. Cognitive interventions provide the knowledge and skills necessary to perform the task (Garner 1987).

Metacognitive interventions support users in the regulation of the learning process by helping them understand how the learning process is developing. This form of support is directed at activating metacognitive behavior. Meijer, Veenman, and van Hout-Wolters (2006) define the following metacognitive activities: Orientation, planning, execution, monitoring evaluation and reflection. Metacogntive interventions help learners become aware of different metacognitive activities. The literature reports that learners with low self regulation skills do not perform metacognitive activities during their learning process. This results in less efficient learning and a strong dependence of the student on external regulation by the teacher (Zimmerman 2002).

Motivational interventions support the users' motivation to work on the task and they are directed at increasing the drive of the students. Motivation strongly influences learning activities (Boekarts 1999).

Behavioral interventions support the users' in effectively working with the environment. These interventions, which target the learner's actions in the environment, are directed at supporting the users' in effectively moving between activities.

In this section we first briefly describe the case-study analysis that has guided the specification of each intervention category in intervention types. We then detail the interventions types derived for each main category and how they may be generated on the basis of the attention-based input events.

3.4.1 *Case studies analysis for identifying scaffolding cases*

3.4.1.1 *Context.* The case study was undertaken within the context of the Ontdeknet e-learning system (Molenaar 2003), an electronic learning environment for students aged 7 to 16. This environment supports students in maintaining a virtual learning relationship with a human *expert* on the subject of an assigned project. Students work in small groups collaborating with the expert in order to learn from his/her expertise. Students control the learning content by asking questions and requesting information about project-related topics. Teachers act as facilitators. Earlier research has shown that students are motivated to work with Ontdeknet and that this environment promotes transformative use of ICT in education (Molenaar 2003). Ontdeknet is often used to support students' vocational orientation, for example, a student consults a lawyer, a chemist, or a carpenter about their daily activities, schooling, schedules, payment and career paths as well as finding out about technical issues such as instruments and procedures used in the profession. Several hundreds experts, representing many professions, are available for consultancy. In order to support the collaboration between the student and the expert, collaboration scripts (Dillenbourg 1999) are embedded in the environment. A script is defined as a didactic scenario that structures the collaborative learning activities, specifying the roles, subtasks and deadlines. In Ontdeknet a script is provided to the learner in the form of a project screen which consists of: (1) a main assignment, (2) an overview of the learning activities supporting the main assignment, (3) a description and connection to the expert, (4) an overview of the team, and (5) a planner. The Ontdeknet system has been used for several years in many schools in the Netherlands.

3.4.1.2 *Procedure.* The purpose of the case studies was to asses the basic framework for the interventions by the agent, i.e. we wanted to understand if and how learning within the Ontdeknet system could be scaffolded by an attention aware system. To achieve this we have observed how teachers intervened with students working with Ontdeknet. We have observed and recorded the dialogues of 4 groups of 3 students working with the Ontdeknet system for a period of 6 hours per group. Two groups were formed by eight years old students; and two groups were formed by twelve years old students. Groups were formed by teachers and each group included three students, each with a different recommendation for their high school education; one student with good reading abilities; one student with good computer skills; and a mix of boys and girls. Students were asked to write a paper about a profession with the help of an expert. In order to complete the assignment, the groups worked in a computer lab, one hour per week, for a period of six weeks, under thc supervision of one of the authors. The groups of three students worked together on one computer. During each one-hour session, children received instruction at the beginning of the session and were then asked to work independently and only ask for support if they really did not know what to do anymore. The project within Ontdeknet was organized in five learning activities (tasks) for the students: (1) *introduction* of the team to the expert, (2) *presentation of the assignment* to the expert, (3) *selection of the expert,* (4) creation of a *mindmap* based on the expert input, (5) writing the *paper* and asking questions to the expert.

Table 4. Examples from case study for intervention definitions

Observation of the task introduction
Group 1 (8 years old): Students read the explanation and they understand the *introduction* task immediately and start with it. 1a. After a while they do not know what to add anymore Intervention teacher: the teacher suggests writing their hobbies and age. SCAFFOLDING CASE: model input: low activity. Model output: help with task, e.g., suggest topics to write about 1b. Students asks: "What else can we write?" Teacher responds: "Nothing we are done" SCAFFOLDING CASE: model input: finishing of an activity. Model output: provide feedback on task
Group 3 (11 years old) 3a. Students are making jokes while reading the explanation. Then they do not know what they have to do. Students; What do we have to do? Intervention teacher: what does it say in the explanation? Students: That we have to introduce ourselves Intervention teacher: what do you think our expert wants to know about you? Students: we introduce ourselves to your expert. Now students start to work SCAFFOLDING CASE: model input: students are lost (e.g., idle input, off-task activity; request for help). Model output: provide explanation for task 3b. Finish: Intervention teacher: time is up, please save. SCAFFOLDING CASE: model input: approaching end of time available. Model output: notify students and ask to save

3.4.1.3 *Results.* Within the observation data and the dialogue protocols, we analyzed occurrences where the teacher interfered with the children activity and cases where the students were in need of additional help. For each one of these occurrences we defined a "scaffolding case" describing the types of intervention that could support the students in the specific situation. We collected all the interventions made by teachers in order to specify the four intervention categories further into different interventions types. Table 4 reports two examples of the observations and scaffolding cases.

3.4.2 *Definition of interventions on the basis of scaffolding cases*

The analysis of the case studies allowed us to identify the interventions needed to support the learning process. Table 5 exemplifies the interventions derived from the sample case studies shown in Table 4. The first column of Table 5 refers to the case study that prompted the intervention, the second column indicates the conditions under which the model would generate the intervention, the third column indicates the intervention category and type, and the fifth column gives an example of the specific content for the intervention. The conditions indicated in the second column are expressed using the grammar specified in Sections 3.1–3.3.

In a similar manner we continued for all the learning activities included in the assignment. These interventions were classified along the four main interventions categories: Metacognitive, cognitive, behavioral and motivational support. The total intervention model after this study consisted of 39 intervention types, 16 of which were implemented in the system described in Section 4.

3.4.3 *Presentation of interventions to the user: Timing and modality*

Although in this paper we concentrate on the discussion of how one may appropriately select the *content* of scaffolding interventions (i.e., what one would say to a student to provide such scaffolding), two other aspects are important: *Timing* and *mode* of presentation. Some aspects of intervention timing are discussed above (in particular those related to the synchronization with the appropriate tasks), more fine aspects of such timing are only very briefly touched upon in this paper with respect to *breakpoint* selection (see Section 4.1), a more detailed discussion can be found in (Laukkanen, Roda, and Molenaar 2007).

The choice of *how* to present interventions may also impact on the learners activity at various levels: It may go completely unnoticed, it may smoothly integrate with their current task, or it may capture their attention and cause a temporary or durable focus switch. We assume that each intervention may be presented as text only, audio only, a combination of the two, or through an *embodied agent*.

Within these main modalities it is possible to identify further sub-modalities related, for example, to the size on screen of the intervention, the possible choices in

Table 5. Sample interventions derived from the case study shown in Table 4

Activity	Input events / State	Intervention Category	Intervention Content
Case 1a	IDLE_USER_EVENT LM[current focus = task(name = introduction)] LM[experience = new users] LM[current focus = task(timeActive = 15')] LM[current_focus=task(Amount of text in fields = large)]	Cognitive / C_support	"Did you include the following topics?" Show a checklist
Case 1b	START_TASK_EVENT(task(name=save page_introduction)) LM[current focus = task(name = introduction)] LM[experience = new users] LM[current focus = task(timeActive = 15')] LM[current_focus=task(Amount of text in fields = large)]	Metacognitive / MC_monitoring	"Quite a story you wrote, good to meet you!.
Case 3a.	HELP_EVENT LM[current focus = task(name = introduction)] LM[experience = new users] LM[current focus = task(timeActive = 2')] LM[current_focus=task(Amount of text in fields = empty)]	Metacognitive / MC_orientation	Please start with introducing yourselves to your expert.
Case 3b.	START_TASK_EVENT(task(name=fill form introduction)) LM[current focus = task(name = introduction)] LM[experience = new users] LM[current focus = task(timeActive = 30')] LM[current_focus=task(Amount of text in fields = medium)]	Behavioral / support	Please save, the lesson is almost over.

terms of colors, tone of voice, loudness, text size, and many others. In order to control complexity within the conceptual framework we have chosen to provide as output of the model three parameters: The *modality* (text, sound, or embodied agent), the *mood* (happy, angry, neutral), and the *strength* (*strong, neutral*, and *weak*). We assume that a dedicated component will be responsible for the implementation of the three parameters in appropriate interactions with the user (see Section 4.4).

Modality selection is based at least on two parameters: The characteristics of the intervention, and the learner's preferences. The characteristics of the intervention include the complexity of the message that needs to be transmitted to the user, the urgency of the intervention, the level of certainty of the proposed intervention (this is related to "how much better" the agents believe the proposed focus is with respect to the current one). The learner's preferences include preferences on modalities explicitly declared by the user (through the set preferences event) and inferred preferred modalities (either by observation of the user, or as a result of a feedback event). The choice of modality, mood, and strength is guided by rules similar to those presented in column 2 of Table 5.

3.5 Attention based approach to scaffolding

In this section the three essential elements of scaffolding — diagnosing, calibration and fading — are explained in the light of the conceptual framework just described.

3.5.1 *Diagnosis*

Diagnosing is defined as the ongoing measurement of the students' current level of understanding (Wood, Bruner, and Ross 1976). This entails the evaluation of users' progress during the learning activities. Two main processes are distinguished: The development of knowledge over the learning domain, and the development of the performance characteristics of the student. In our model the progress of the students is diagnosed based on the attention-relevant events occurring in the learning environment, the task model and the learner model. User-application events are particularly important for diagnosing because they provide a real-time description of the learner's activity within the learning domain. Additional information is supplied by *environment-events* tracing the overall behavior of the learner, and *user events* which allow a direct interaction with the learner. This information enables the attention management system to go beyond the level of involvement in the learning application, by also measuring the activities of the students in the overall environment. This environmental information provides the context necessary to the model for reasoning about a more complete set of the learner's activities rather than just those within the individual e-learning application. With respect to the development of the **performance characteristics** of the students, the learner's experience and progress are always accessible within the learner's model and can be incorporated in the diagnosis. For example, if a learner is using the concept map tool in the learning application proceeding quickly, filling-in different fields, and continuing with the selection of different fields accordingly; then, this information is stored in the learner's model and it may be subsumed by an indication that the learner is capable of appropriately using the mind-map tools. Our model currently does not provide for a description of the development of the **knowledge over the learning domain,** to this end, either diagnostic tests or semantic reasoning on the content provided by the users would be needed and could be included in the framework in the future.

3.5.2 *Calibration*

Calibration is directed at selecting the right interventions and providing it to the user at the right time. This entails that both the selected intervention as well as the timing of the interventions can be different for different students, but also for the same student over a period of time (Puntambekar and Hübscher 2005). Calibration also reflects the adaptive and dynamic aspects of scaffolding. The dynamic aspect implies adjusting the timing and selection of the interventions to the progress and current activity of the learner (e.g., when a student starts a task for the first time the system provides an explanation of the task). The adaptive aspect implies the selection of the right intervention for the advancement of a particular student taking into account his/her personal characteristics (e.g., adjusts the explanation to the intellectual level of the particular student say, giving a more elaborated explanation for a slow learner than for a quick learner). In our model, calibration is obtained through the appropriate selection of the amount, form, and timing of interventions. The question of when to send an intervention is largely determined by the evolving activity of the student and reflects the dynamic aspect. The questions of *what* interventions to give and *how* to communicate them are determined by the characteristics of the learner and therefore are more adaptive in nature.

3.5.3 *Fading*

The final important element of scaffolding is fading. Gradually as the user is becoming more experienced the scaffolds should be reduced. The task model and the learner model register the advancements of the user which provide the main input for the fading of the interventions in this system. The user's characteristics play an important role in the decision towards fading. For example, a user that is registered as a low ability user and has performed a task well two times before, will receive more interventions than a user that is registered as high ability user that has performed the same task well only once. The fading decision of the system take into account different types of information collected in the learner model and will act accordingly. As soon as the diagnostics of the system and the learner model contradict each other the fading will be reduced, and possibly the learner model will be updated. For example, if the learner model indicates that the user is an experienced user, and the diagnostics of the system show that the user does not perform the task in the right way, the system will reduce the fading and send the supporting intervention to the user.

3.6 Discussion of the framework

The framework described shows how, by detecting and reasoning about the attentional state of the learner, it is possible to provide scaffolding interventions that better reflect the traditional approach. Diagnosis, calibration and fading processes are, in fact, appropriately implemented by selecting suitable intervention and the most appropriate timing and mode for their presentation.

Furthermore, the model allows taking into account the limitation of human cognitive abilities as discussed in Section 2. For example, in order to limit task-switching costs, it is possible to track the task the learner is currently focusing on and, depending on its level of complexity, evaluate the best time for intervening (see Section 4.1). This type of behavior allows fine-tuning of the introduction of scaffolds so as to lower the risk of increasing cognitive load. Another example of cognitive support is related to cueing. As discussed in Section 3.3, Atgentive's task model includes the possibility to associate *help tasks* and *help messages* to tasks. Some of this help is explicitly defined as *pre-task* help which may take the form of cues to the learner about the next task to be performed, so as to reduce cognitive load (e.g., metacognitive orientation interventions described in Section 4.5.1).

4. A system for adaptive scaffolding supported by an attention aware system

The framework described in Section 3 was partially implemented in a system that we describe in this section. The system is composed of three reusable components: The reasoning module, the environment tracking modules, and the embodied agent module. These components are customized to serve an application, in this case the Ontdeknet e-learning environment (see 3.4.1.1). The application is, in turn, augmented with an interface to the reusable components. The complete system was called AtgentSchool. On the basis of the observation of the learners' actions, the system proposes *interventions* aimed at supporting the learning.

Figure 1 depicts a generic Atgentive system. The overall system monitors the environment of the learner and reasons towards scaffolds that are supportive for the learning process of a specific learner in a specific context. In the center of the image is the application independent attention management component, the

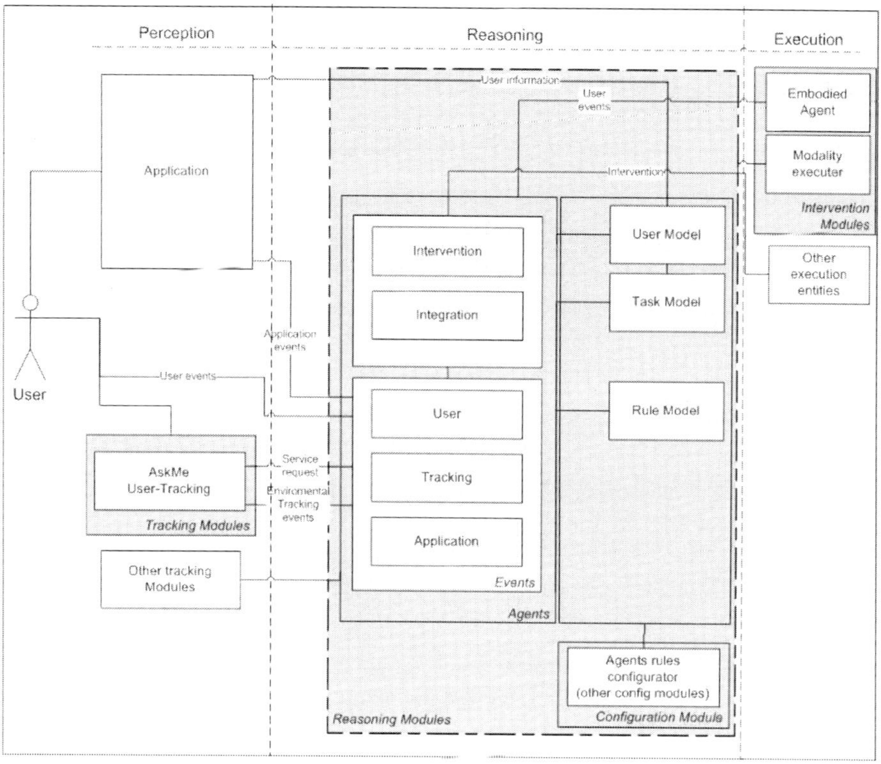

Figure 1. Generic Atgentive System

Reasoning Module. The **Reasoning Module** is employed to diagnose the situation of the learner, calibrate the support to the current situation, and fade the support when the learner is capable of self sustaining his/her learning. The Reasoning Module enables the selection of the **appropriate interventions**, of the correct **timing** for the interventions, and of the correct **form** for communication to the user. Another application independent module, the **embodied agent module** (on the right of Figure 1), is used to communicate the interventions to the user(s). The left side of Figure 1 shows the *perception* components: The (Atgentive enabled) **application**, and the **AskMe** tracking module; these components provide input to the reasoning module. The users' attentional choices, preferences, and possible future foci, are revealed by *events* (depicted as lines from input components to reasoning module in Figure 1) that are then analyzed in the Reasoning Module. This analysis results in *interventions* depicted as a line from the Reasoning Module to the *execution* components.

4.1 The reasoning module

The Reasoning Module is composed of a set of ***Agents*** (shown on the left-hand side of the Reasoning Module component in Figure 1). These agents base their reasoning on the input received by the perception modules, on the content of the user/learner model, of the task model (shown on the right-hand side of the Reasoning Module component in Figure 1). The agents may also update the content of the user/learner model and task model as they acquire information about the learners' activity and the environment. *Event agents* (user, tracking, and application) are capable of reasoning about *events* describing the learner's attentional state and generate hypothesis on the current learner's focus as well as possible alternative foci. The *integration agent* mediates the hypothesis generated by the event agents and creates a prioritized list of the most suitable foci for the learner. Finally, the *intervention agent* decides when and how (time and modality) to intervene with the learner and generates the appropriate *interventions.*

The rules guiding the agents' reasoning are customisable through a configuration module (shown on the bottom-right side of the Reasoning Module component in Figure 1) and form the *rule model.*

In the current implementation *event agents* are capable of processing a subset of the events described in the conceptual framework. In particular all *application events* listed in Table 1, except the *resume* and *continue* events, are managed; amongst the *user events,* the *set time available*, the *help event*, and the *mood event* listed in Table 2 are managed; finally for the *tracking events,* only the *idle input* event is managed.

We have chosen to start with the implementation of these events for several reasons. The fact that we planned to test our application with children has influenced the choice in two manners. First, we have chosen to implement only those *user-tracking events* that, given the current technologies, could have been realized with un-intrusive interfaces (i.e., we have avoided all tracking that would have required the children to wear special devices). Second, we have chosen to delay the implementation of *user events* that would have required the children to provide complex input (i.e. many of the *user events* have not been implemented); and for the implemented *user events* a simple interface is provided that allows children to request for help (*help event)* by clicking on a question mark button, and generate *mood events* by clicking on smiley faces (see Figure 4). Also, because the surrounding environment for the students did not provide particular distractions such as telephones, or people entering the room, we have not implemented the *environment tracking* devices and events.

The processing of each of the implemented events enables several of the scaffolding behaviors described earlier. The implementation of the *event agents* amounts to the implementation of a set of rules similar to those exemplified in Table 5. For example for case 1a in Table 5, when the AskMe module signals that the user is idle (*idle-input event*), the *tracking agents* consider information such as what is the level of experience of the learners, how long they have been active on the task, and how much work they have already performed; and if appropriate, generate the proposal for a new focus that eventually will trigger the cognitive interventions simulating the behavior of a teacher who would intervene with scaffolding actions for students who are taking too long to complete a task or get distracted.

Event agents are mainly responsible for the generation of possible foci for the learner. Subsequently the *integration agent* and *intervention agent* will actually generate the interventions. For example, on the onset of a *user-application event*, the objective is to determine whether there are alternative foci for the learner. If this is the case, the agents decide how to best propose such alternative foci to the learner.

The handling mechanism for *user-application events* follows a five steps process (in brackets are indicated the agents responsible for the processing):

1. If the event reports a focus switch, the context of the interrupted task is saved to allow for easy resume. (*event agents)*
2. The list of alternative foci in the *learner model* is updated (*event agents).*
3. The current learner's focus is evaluated against the alternative foci taking into consideration the complexity and advancement state of the current task and the likelihood that the focused task will be completed within the available time (*integration agents*)
4. The best time for intervention is determined on the basis of the urgency of the focused task, the progression state of the task, and the complexity of the focused task. As a result the system will either immediately propose an intervention or wait for a *breakpoint.* A *breakpoint* is a natural pause caused by some change in the learner's activity. It has been demonstrated that interruptions presented at breakpoints are less disruptive for the user (Bailey and Konstan 2006) and the system uses both task structure and sensory based input to detect breakpoints (Laukkanen, Roda, and Molenaar 2007) (*intervention agent*).
5. Determine the best modality for intervention on the basis of the user preferences, the current task, and the intervention type (*intervention agent*).

4.2 The tracking modules

In Section 3.1.3 we have introduced the assumption that some attention-related events may result from tracking application-independent user activities or changes in the environment. This requires two types of tracking modules: *Environment-tracking modules* capable of tracking changes in the environment (e.g., a person enters the room, an email arrives, the telephone rings, etc.) and *user-tracking modules* capable of detecting user cognitive and physical state or activity (e.g., the user is typing, or he/she is talking to someone). Currently, only one of the many possible tracking modules has been implemented: The AskMe module (depicted on the left-hand side of Figure 1). This module tracks mouse and keyboard activity. Currently, only one of the events generated by this module is processed, the *idle input event* (the user has not produced any input for a certain amount of time).

4.3 The e-learning application

Existing **e-learning applications** (top-left of Figure 1) can use the services of the Reasoning Module by implementing an *Interface to the Atgentive system,* which sends events describing the user activity in the application, and receives proposed interventions. In the specific case of the system described in this paper the e-learning application is the OntdekNet application which has been augmented with an interface to the Atgentive system. The augmented application generates all the events listed in Table 1 except the *resume* and *continue* events. Currently AtgentSchool is available in three languages Dutch, Czech, and English. The AtgentSchool system (both the Reasoning Module and the augmented Ontdeknet learning application) was developed in an incremental manner and on the basis of recurrent formative evaluation studies, i.e. studies that allowed us to feedback the results of the system evaluation in its conceptualization, design and implementation.

4.4 The embodied agent

In Section 3.4.3 we have briefly indicated how, associated to each intervention, the model generates a suggestion of modality, mood, and strength for presentation of the intervention. In the current implementation, we only generate intervention in the *embodied agent* modality (this is because children find it more difficult to read text as compared to listening to a message spoken by an embodied agent). The system includes an **embodied agent module** (on the right hand side of Figure 1) that is capable of implementing presentations of interventions in different *moods* and *strengths* using predefined scripts selected at run-time (Clauzel, Roda, Ach, and Morel 2007). As a result, in the Atgentive system the scaffolder is an embodied character (shown in the center of Figure 2) that communicates the interventions to the learner. This character is a three dimensional animated character, which speaks to the user with a human language; it shows emotions and moves across the screen and is powered by Living Actor© technology.

Figure 2. Example of metacognitive orientation support

4.5 Intervention model

Below we describe the 16 intervention types within the four different intervention categories that were actually implemented in the system. Each section details an intervention category; we provide examples of the different intervention types and the relation with the events model as they were implemented.

4.5.1 *Metacognitive interventions*

Our system aims at dynamically providing metacognitive interventions at the appropriate moments to help students become aware of the metacognitive activities that could help them regulate their learning. The following intervention types are implemented in the first version of the system (see also the left column in Figure 4);

1. *Metacognitive orientation interventions* introduce learners to a new task. Experts are known to spend more time in orientation on a task than novices (Schmidt and Boshuizen 1993). A better orientation on the task allows for a better comprehension of the tasks elements which influences the time and performance on the task. An example of an orientation intervention introducing a new task is illustrated in Figure 2 and generates the following message to the learner: *Your expert would like to know what your learning goal is, could*

you tell him? Please click here to write your learning goal. These interventions are provided to the users in the project screen overview just before the user is about to commence working on the task (pre-task support).

2. *Metacogntive explanation interventions* exemplify the task for the learner. This is expected to help students in the effective execution of the task. An example of explanation intervention for the "introduction" task is the following message to the learner: *Here you will introduce yourself, I will give an example: "My name is David, I live in Prague, I am 16 years old. My hobbies are skating and chatting. I have one older brother named Karl."* These interventions are provided to the user right after the task page is opened (on task support).
3. *Metacognitive monitoring interventions* clearly indicate to the user that the current task is finished and reassert what the system or the expert will do with the provided information. The clear closure on the task helps students continue on the next task. Monitoring interventions are provided right after saving the task (post-task support). An example of a monitoring intervention after the completion of the "learning goal definition" task is the following: *I'll directly go to your expert and explain what you would like to learn.*

To summarize, we anticipate that the agent's interventions on the level of metacognition will help students become aware of the metacognitive activities that can be performed around different learning tasks. We expect that the help on this level will support students in constructing a better understanding of tasks and their relation with the main assignment.

4.5.2 *Cognitive interventions*

These interventions are specifically adjusted to the learning activity at hand to support the learner with the current task (see lower right section of Figure 4). Cognitive interventions are triggered by *idle user* events generated by the ASKME module, or by *help events* generated by the user clicking on the question mark icon. There are two types of cognitive interventions implemented in the system: *Cognitive support interventions* and *cognitive resources interventions. Cognitive support* is directed at helping the learner with the current learning activity, whereas *cognitive resource interventions* provide students with links to resources in the learning environment that can help them perform the task. For example, a cognitive support intervention for the activity concept map (students have to write down all topics that are related to the subject that they are studying) may say: *What do you already know about the subject you are going to study?* An example of a cognitive resource for the same learning activity would be: *Need some ideas? You can read the introduction diary of the expert.* These interventions are given to users when they become idle within a learning task or when they click on the question mark when they are working on a learning task.

Cognitive interventions are designed to support the thinking process of the students in relation to the task they are performing. We expect that learners will perform the tasks more successfully after receiving the cognitive interventions.

4.5.3 *Motivational intervention*

Motivational interventions support the motivation of the user. There are four types of motivational interventions implemented in the system: *Motivational support, emotional support happy, sad and neutral.* They are triggered by two events: The *idle user* event and the *mood* event. When the user has become idle in a task and there are no more cognitive interventions for this user, the motivational interventions will be shown. An example is: *You can do it! Just start writing.* The user can indicate his current emotional state with the smileys: Happy, neutral, and sad which results in *mood* events. When the user clicks on the emoticons the agents mirrors the state of the user showing an animation and expression resembling the state of the user. These three emotional feedback lead to three emotional support interventions with the embodied agent responding to a user notification of an emotional state: Sad, happy, and neutral; an example of *emotional support* intervention is shown in Figure 3 mirroring the user state sad.

Figure 3. Example of motivational intervention

The motivational interventions are expected to increase the motivation of the learners who receive them.

4.5.4 *Behavioral interventions*

Behavioral interventions are directed towards simple behavioral user actions. Two types of behavioral interventions are implemented in the system: *External events notifications* and *navigational support.* External events notifications are generated by *new information available* events, e.g., "*Your expert has answered your question*". *Navigational support* interventions are simple navigational statements that direct the user to certain elements in the system for instance "*click here to go back to the project screen*".

The effect of behavioral interventions is difficult to predict. We expect that external events communicated to the user will enhance the virtual communication with other users, the expert and the teacher. We do not anticipate an effect of the navigational support interventions because these are only provided in exceptional cases when users are not showing any pattern in their behavior.

Table 6. A summary of the intervention categories

Category	Type	Description
Metacognitive	MC orientation	Introduces the activity to the user
Metacognitive	MC explanation	Explains the activity to the user, preferably with an example
Metacognitive	MC monitoring	Provides general feedback to the user about the finished activity
Cognitive	Cognitive support	Provides additional explanation with respect to content issues to the user
Cognitive	Cognitive resources	Provides additional explanation by redirecting the user to an example of another user or additional information provided by another user
Motivation	Motivation support	Provides a motivational incentive to the user
Motivation	ES Happy	Reaction to happy user
Motivation	ES sad	Question to sad user
Motivation	ES neutral	Reaction to neutral user
Behavioral	External events notifications	Provides notification about an relevant external event plus the link
Behavioral	Navigational support	Provides support in navigation to certain learning activities

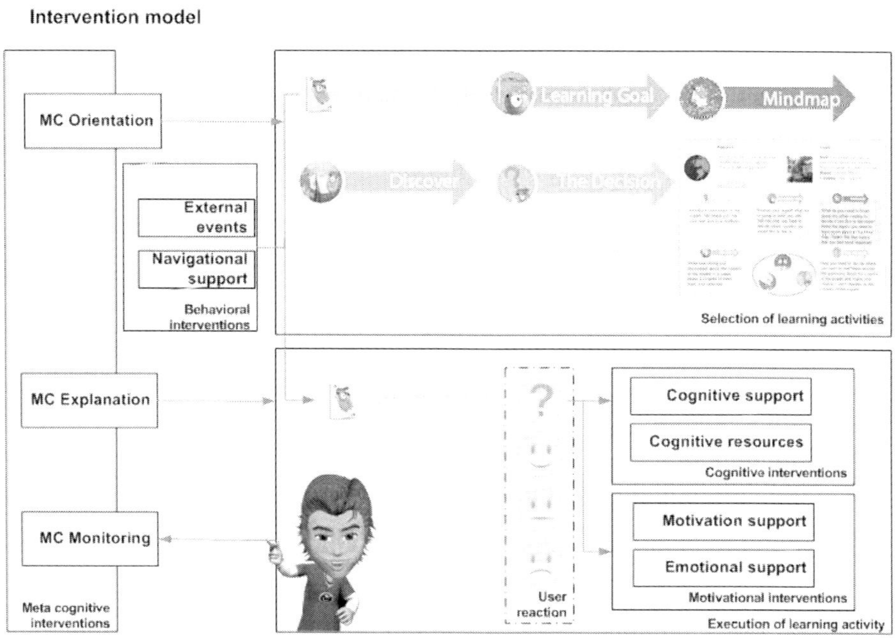

Figure 4. Overview of the Intervention Model

4.5.5 *Summary of the interventions by category*

The 4 intervention categories and 11 intervention types are summarized in Table 6.

Figure 4 below displays the relationships between the event information and the intervention categories and types. Metacognitive interventions may provide pre-task support, on-task support, or post task support. The positioning of these types of interventions is determined by the state of advancement of the learning process of the user. Metacognitive interventions are always related to a learning task and they communicate to the learner information related to this task. Cognitive and motivational interventions provide on-task support and they are always directly related to the learner's current task and current behavior. Behavioral interventions are not task related. However, the learner's current task determines the timing of these interventions.

5. Preliminary evaluation

The sections above explained how our attention aware system is giving form to dynamic scaffolding for the user. In this section we describe how adaptive scaffolding results from the interaction between the e-learning application and the Reasoning Module. Several assessment tools were employed to ensure that the resulting system would in fact provide dynamic and adaptive scaffolding on the basis of attention management. The adherence of the final system to these requirements is described in this section through the analysis of our two main assessment studies:, (1) classroom test runs and (2) the pilot study in Chzech Republic. The central question we addressed throughout the assessment process was if and how attention management was providing appropriate input for dynamic and adaptive scaffolding.

5.1 The test-runs: User perception

In order to test the stability and functioning of Atgentschool before the pilot in the Czech Republic, pre-pilot tests were run in 6 schools in the Netherlands. The main purpose of these tests was to ensure the proper functioning of the system with real users and a representative user load, as well as collecting preliminary results on how learners perceived working with the system.

5.1.1 *Context of the test runs*

These test-runs were one hour sessions in which children were asked to work on the project "Where do you want to live?' They worked on the project for 45 minutes, performing the following learning activities: 1. introducing themselves to the expert, 2. setting a learning goal, 3. filling in the concept map, 4. reading the first diary of the expert and 5. asking a question. This was a shorter version of the project later used in the pilot.

5.1.2 *Procedure of the test runs*

Six test-runs were performed with 108 students aged between 9 and 12. Students received a 5 to 10 minute introduction to the task as testers of AtgentSchool and to the project "where do you want to live?". During the sessions they were asked to use the smileys in the screen (happy, neutral, sad) to indicate how they felt about the agent. After their session they filled out a questionnaire about their perception of the agent and a short interview was conducted to further asses their perceptions of the system. In test-run 3, students were also shown interventions on a digital school board and they were asked to rate the interventions and to write down any comment they had.

The following measurements were analyzed after the test-runs:

- the log files of the students including feedback with the smileys,
- A questionnaire about the agent with 15 items,
- the discussion notes after the sessions,
- the class session rating and discussion of the interventions

Table 7. Judgement of the students of the Interventions shown.

Interventions shown	Cumulated average judgement of student
Metacognitive interventions	4.03 = good
Cognitive interventions	3.71 = good
Motivational interventions	2.70 = not good not bad

5.1.3 *Results of the test-runs*

We analyzed the logs of the sessions to confirm that all interventions selected conformed to the conceptual framework. A few interventions were studied in more detail and some debugging was done in relation to these findings. The children were asked to indicate how they felt with the smiley buttons. Unfortunately, these were used very little, because students were not able to attend a new task, read the interventions and act accordingly, and also indicate how they felt with the smileys. Based on these pilot-test findings, the feedback acquisition was redefined and we developed a session with children judging the interventions on the smart board in a classroom session after the test-run session. The students were asked to rate the interventions on a five point Likert scale and to write down their comments. The cognitive and metacognitive interventions were judged to be very good; the motivation interventions were judged neutral towards bad. See Table 7.

The analysis of the questionnaires produced very encouraging results. 90.5% of the children wanted to work with the agent Matthew again; 62% wanted to work with an agent more often; 9.5% would have liked to work with a different agent then Matthew. The agent provided good help according to 90% of the children, and the two students that disliked the agent found that more help could have been provided. Students gave Matthew a 7.5 average grade (girls a 8 and boys a 7).

5.1.4 *Conclusion*

Based on these test-runs we ensured the proper functioning of the software for the pilot. We improved the motivation interventions trying to address the children's feedbacks. We also adjusted some aspects of the original configuration of the motivational support and added the behavioral navigation support interventions as described in Section 4.5. The configuration of the metacognitive and cognitive support was judged positively by the users and therefore maintained. The agent Mathew (which had been developed within the Atgentive project with the purpose of supporting the AtgentSchool application) was well liked and accepted by the Dutch students.

5.2 The pilot

The pilot study was an experimental study in which the *experimental* group received scaffolds from the agent and the *control* group did not receive scaffolds. In order to prevent a Hawthorne effects, both groups had the agent in their screen. The main research question was: What is the effect of dynamic scaffolding based on the attention management system in the context of Atgentschool? We only briefly report the main effects below; the complete analysis will appear in a forthcoming publication.

5.2.1 *Context of the pilot*

This pilot study was conducted in 4 schools in the Czech Republic; a total of 134 Czech students aged 11 have used the system. The students worked in five 45 minute sessions in which they were asked to work on the project "Where do you want to live?". They were performing the following learning activities: 1. introducing themselves to the expert, 2. setting a learning goal, 3. filling in the concept map, 4. reading the diaries of the expert living in another country, 5. asking the expert questions, and 6. writing a paper and answering a questionnaire.

5.2.2 *Procedure of the pilot*

This study had an experimental design. The experimental group received interventions from the agent and a control group did not receive any interventions from the agent. Students worked on the project in groups consisting of 2 students. The groups of two students were randomly assigned to the conditions. This entails a within classes design controlling for in class differences. The experimental group consisted of 28 groups (56 students) and the control group of 27 groups (54 students).

The following measurements were taken before, during, and after the pilot run:

- Student questionnaires after 3 weeks and at the end of the pilot with questions measuring motivation and students' opinions about Atgentschool,
- Teacher questionnaires after 3 weeks and at the end of the pilot with questions measuring motivation of the teachers and the teachers' opinions about Atgentschool
- The log files of the students including feedback with the smileys,
- The structured diaries filled in after the lessons by the teachers,
- The work produced by the students,
- The blind assessment of the students' work by two graders,
- A discussion workshop with the teachers at the end of the pilot.

Table 8. The differences on task performance between the experimental and control group.

Independent Variable	Parameter Estimates	P-value
Intercept	−4.0116	0.3969
Introduction	−0.0787	0.6627
Setting a learning goal	1.3687	0.0926
Concept map	−0.0355	0.7758
Number of paragraphs in paper	−0.1831	0.4584
Quality of the paper	**0.9135**	**0.0506**
Questions asked	**0.4777**	**0.0491**
Questionnaire	−0.0999	0.3033

5.2.3 *Results of the pilot*

We only report the main results on student performance, learning and motivation in this section.

5.2.3.1 *Performance.* The performance of the experimental group and the control group was compared to see if there were significant differences between the performances of the students in the two conditions.

We first looked at the data evaluating the results obtained by groups of students on each one of the six tasks as described above. With respect to the paper, the length of the paper in the number of paragraphs was measured and the quality of the paper was judged (bad, medium or good).

A Logistic Regression Analysis on the data relative to the evaluation of the results obtained by students on the six tasks above revealed that **children in the Experimental group asked significantly more questions to the experts (P=0.0491) and produced papers of significantly better quality (P=0.0506) than children in the Control group** (see Table 8).

5.2.3.2 *Learning.* The students filled a 15 items pre- and post-test on their knowledge about the country studied. The means (using 0 as wrong and 1 as right) on the pre-test and post-test are displayed below in Table 9. We found a significant learning effect but no significant difference between the experimental and the control group.

Table 9. Learning results of control group and experimental group

Means	Pre test	Std. Deviation	Post test	Std. Deviation
Control group	0.42	0.38	0.70	0.41
Experimental group	0.40	0.40	0.72	0.37

5.2.4 *Discussion*

The results show performance differences on two out of six learning activities. These performance differences are particularly important, because they measure the direct effects of our attention-based scaffolding framework on the performance of the students (i.e. improvements can be seen in the experimental group but not in the control group). The two learning activities on which the effects were significant are the two activities students worked on the longest time during the project. The introduction, goal setting, concept map and the questionnaire are activities students only worked on for one consecutive session during the pilot. The paper and asking questions re-occurs for 4 sessions and constitutes the main and largest tasks the student performed during the project. These results indicate a more proactive attitude of learners supported by the adaptive and dynamic scaffolding. Finally, the results on overall learning do not show us a difference between the two groups. Both groups show a significant increase in factual knowledge about the country studied. If there are learning differences between the conditions, they are more subtle than the measurements means used can indicate.

As pointed out in the introduction, we expected students to show a more positive development on the ability to self-regulate the learning; better knowledge transfer due to a better connection between the prior knowledge and the learning content; higher motivation of the students. We can confirm that the higher quality of the papers of the experimental group indicates a better knowledge transfer. This pilot did not collect any data on the self-regulations, but the teachers in the workshop indicated that the experimental group asked far less for help and was more actively engaged in the pilot than the control group. This would indicate a better ability to self-regulate learning.

The attention management system based on the model proposed seems to be a powerful tool towards adaptive scaffolding. The encouraging results of the design and effect studies of the AtgentSchool system give us reasons to believe that attention management is an adequate basis for providing adaptive and dynamic scaffolding to learners.

6. Conclusions

The fundamental hypothesis of our research has been that scaffolds support learning by steering the tutee's attention to the appropriate information and tools, and that the selection of the appropriate scaffolds may be based on the knowledge of the history of the tutee attention allocation processes.

In this framework, the main elements of scaffolding as described in the classic literature (diagnosis, calibration and fading) are all immediately related to attentional processes. The progress of the students in diagnosis is based on the current and historical attention-relevant events occurring in the learning environment (where the history is subsumed in a learner model). Calibration is obtained by *intervening* with the learner in a manner that is *adapted* to both his/her current attentional focus and his/her characteristics (e.g., history of interaction, needs, abilities, etc.); intervening with the learner amounts to either supporting the learner's current attentional focus or proposing some more effective alternative foci. Fading results from the adaptation process of calibration. Furthermore, the timing of scaffolding interventions is evaluated on a very fine-grained scale in order to minimize disruption and maximize understanding of the scaffold. Both exogenous and endogenous attentional processes are taken into account in the selection and timing of scaffolding interventions in order to ensure that the learner correctly perceives the interventions and is motivated to exploit it.

Puntambekar and Hübscher (2005) have proposed a table summarizing the interpretation of scaffolding features in the modern and traditional environments. In Table 10 we extend Puntambekar and Hübscher's table to also include a comparison with our attention-aware scaffolding.

Although we have presented the implementation and evaluation of our framework within a specific e-learning system, the model we propose has been designed as a general purpose one for digital learning environments. The Reasoning Module, capable of tracking, modeling, and reasoning about events describing the

Table 10. Interpretation of scaffolding features in the modern, traditional, and attention-aware Atgentive system — extended from Puntambekar and Hübscher (2005)

Feature of scaffolding	Modern	Traditional	Attention-aware Atgentive system
Scaffolder	Tools and resources	Multimodal assistance provided by a knowledgeable human	Embodied agent
Diagnosis	Stable blanket	Adaptive support, sensitive to the needs of the student	Monitor of to personal behavior through attention-related events
Calibration	Passive support	Dynamic support tuned on ongoing assessment of the learner	Reacting on personal behavior and differences based on attention-related events
Fading	Permanent and unchanging	Fading reducing support over time	Monitor of personal advancement by event tracking and user model

attentional state of the learner is of general applicability (both its conceptualization and implementation). The interventions taxonomy organized in metacognitive, cognitive, motivational, and behavioral interventions, is designed to cover a wide range of scaffolding interventions in learning environments. The attention-based dynamic and adaptive scaffolding system we propose rests on a mapping of attention-related events to scaffolding interventions.

During the conceptualization phase we have run several formative evaluation studies (including case studies and test-runs) that have guided the design and development of the system. We have also run a pilot study that has allowed us to perform effect studies. The results obtained so far are encouraging and show that students supplied with attention-based scaffolding interventions produce better results, a more proactive attitude towards the learning activity, and a higher motivation.

The effects of our system on the learners need to be researched in more detail. Our future research will start by assessing if the interventions proposed cause the learning activities anticipated; i.e. behavioral interventions should initiate regulative learning activities; cognitive interventions should initiate cognitive learning activities; metacognitive interventions should initiate metacognitive learning activities. Another area of research will concentrate on a more detailed analysis of the effects of interventions "tones". Currently all our interventions have a directive tone (although they may be presented by the virtual agent using different strengths and moods). We will analyze the effects of using tones different from the directive one (e.g., suggestive or questioning). Overall, we are aware of the need to gain a better understanding of the results obtained and further refine the system, as well as implement those features that were not included in the first prototype. The results obtained so far however, demonstrate that attention based scaffolding has the potential to adapt better to the needs of learners, supporting motivation and performance on the more complex activities.

Notes

* The work described in this paper was partially sponsored by the EC under the FP6 framework project Atgentive IST-4-027529-STP. We would like to acknowledge the contribution of all project partners.

1. Note that the first column of Table 1 implies that

   USER_APPLICATION_EVENT ::= START_EVENT | CONTINUE_EVENT |
   COMPLETE_EVENT | RESUME_EVENT | INITIATING_EVENT | STOP_EVENT

For the sake of brevity we do not expand the grammar to this level of detail.

2. Note that this means that, following the given grammar, the LEARNER_MODEL_ELEMENT_VALUE can correctly replace the LEARNER_MODEL_ELEMENT.

3. Note that this means that, following the given grammar, the TASK_MODEL_ELEMENT_VALUE can correctly replace the TASK_MODEL_ELEMENT.

References

Aleven, V. and Koedinger, K. 2002. "An effective metacognitive strategy: Learning by doing and explaining with a computer-based cognitive tutor". *Cognitive Science* 26(2): 147–181.

Allport, A. 1989. "Visual attention". In M. Posner (ed), *Foundations of Cognitive Science*. Cambridge, MA: The MIT Press, 631–681.

Allport, A., Styles, E., and Hsieh, S. 1994. "Shifting intentional set: Exploring the dynamic control of tasks". In C. Umiltà and M. Moscovitch (eds), *Attention and Performance XV: Conscious and Nonconscious Information Processing*. Cambridge, MA: The MIT Press, 421–452.

Arvidson, P. S. 2003. "A lexicon of attention: From cognitive science to phenomenology". *Phenomenology and the Cognitive Sciences* 2(2): 99–132.

Azevedo, R. and Hadwin, A. F. 2005. "Scaffolding self-regulated learning and metacognition — implications for the design of computer-based scaffolds". *Instructional Science* 33: 367–379.

Bailey, B.P. and Konstan, J.A. 2006 . "On the need for attention aware systems: Measuring the effects of interruption on task — performance, error rate, and affective state." *Computers in Human Behavior* 22(4): 685–708.

Boekaerts, M. 1999. "Motivated learning: Studying students's situation transactional units". In M. Boekaerts and P. Nenniger (eds), *Advances in Motivation from the European Viewpoint*. Special Issue of *European Journal of Psychology of Education* 14(1): 41–55.

Chi, M.T.H., Siler, S., Jeong, H., Yamauchi, T., and Hausmann, R. 2001. "Learning from human tutoring". *Cognitive Science* 25: 471–534.

Chun, M.M. and Wolfe, J. 2001. "Visual attention". In E.B. Goldstein (ed), *Blackwell's Handbook of Perception*. Oxford: Blackwell, 272–310.

Clauzel, D., Roda, C., Ach, L., and Morel, B. 2007. "Attention based, naive strategies, for guiding intelligent virtual agents". *Proceedings of the 7th International Conference on Intelligent Virtual Agents* (Poster section), Paris.

Dillenbourg, P. 1999 "Introduction: What do you mean by "collaborative learning"?". In P. Dillenbourg (ed), *Collaborative Learning: Cognitive and Computational Approaches*. Amsterdam: Pergamon, 1–19.

Driver, J. 2001. "A selective review of selective attention research from the past century". *British Journal of Psychology* 92: 53–78.

Durlach, P. J. 2004. "Change blindness and its implications for complex monitoring and control systems design and operator training". *Human-Computer Interaction* 19(4): 423–451.

Folk, C.L., Remington, R.W., and Johnston, J.C. 1992. "Involuntary covert orienting is contingent on attentional control settings". *Journal of Experimental Psychology: Human Perception and Performance* 18: 1030–1044.

Garner, R. 1987. *Metacognition and Reading Comprehension*. Norwood, NJ: Ablex.

Ge, X., Chen, C., and Davis, K. 2005. "Scaffolding novice instructional designers' problem-solving processes using question prompts in a web-based learning environment". *Journal of Educational Computing Research* 33: 219–248.

Ge, X. and Land, S.M. 2003. "Scaffolding students' problem-solving processes in an ill-structured task using question prompts and peer interactions". *Educational Technology Research and Development* 51: 21–38.
Grossberg, S. 1976a. "Adaptive pattern classification and universal recoding. I. Parallel development and coding of neural feature detectors". *Biological Cybernetics* 23: 121–134.
Grossberg, S. 1976b. "Adaptive pattern classification and universal recoding. II. Feedback, expectation, olfaction, and illusions". *Biological Cybernetics* 23: 187–202.
Grossberg, S. 1999. "The link between brain learning, attention, and consciousness". *Consciousness and Cognition* 8(1): 1–44.
Hadwin, A., Winn, P.H, and Nesbit, J.C. 2005. "Roles for software technologies in advancing research and theory in educational psychology". *British Journal of Educational Psychology* vol. 75: 1–24.
Hadwin, A., Wozney, L., and Pontin, O. 2005. "Scaffolding the appropriation of self-regulatory activity: A socio-cultural analysis of changes in teacher–student discourse about a graduate research portfolio". *Instructional Science* 33(5–6): 413–450.
Hayhoe, M. 2000. "Vision using routines: A functional account of vision". *Visual Cognition* 7(1–3): 43–64.
Hillstrom, A.P. and Chai, Y.-C. 2006. "Factors that guide or disrupt attentive visual processing". *Computers in Human Behavior* 22(4): 648–656.
Holton, D. and Clarke, D. 2006. "Scaffolding and metacognition". *International Journal of Mathematical Education in Science and Technology* 37: 127–143.
Jersild, A. 1927. "Mental set and shift". *Archives of Psychology* 89 [Referenced in Rubinstein, Meyer, and Evans 2001].
Jiang, Y., Chun, M.M., and Olson, I.R. 2004. "Perceptual grouping in change detection". *Perception & Psychophysics* 66(3): 446–453.
Kauffman, D.F. 2004. "Self-regulated learning in web-based enviroments: Instructional tools designed to facilitate cognitive strategy use, metacognitive processing, and motivational beliefs". *Journal of Educational Computing Research* 30: 139–161.
Kieras, D.E., Meyer, D.E., Ballas, J.A., and Lauber, E.J. 2000. "Modern computational perspectives on executive mental processes and cognitive control: Where to from here?" In S. Monsell and J. Driver (eds), *Control of Cognitive Processes: Attention and Performance XVIII.* Cambridge, MA: The MIT Press, 681–712.
King, A.1991. "Effects of training in strategic questioning on children's problem solving performance". *Journal of Ecuational Pscychology* 83: 301–317.
King, A. 1992. "Facilitating elaborative learning through guided student-generated questioning". *Educational Psychology Review* 27: 111–126.
Kruschke, J.K. 2001. "Toward a unified model of attention in associative learning". *Journal of Mathematical Psychology* 45(6) : 812–863.
Kruschke, J.K. 2003. "Attention in learning". *Current Directions in Psychological Science* 12: 171–175.
Laukkanen, J., Roda, C., and Molenaar, I. 2007. "Modelling tasks: A requirements analysis based on attention support services". Proceedings of the Workshop on Contextualized Attention Metadata: Personalized access to digital resources CAMA 2007, at the ACM IEEE Joint Conference on Digital Libraries, Vancouver.
Lavie, N. and Tsal, Y. 1994. "Perceptual load as a major determinant of the locus of selection in visual attention". *Perception & Psychophysics* 56(2) : 183–197.

Levin, D.T. and Simons, D.J. 1997. "Failure to detect changes to attended objects in motion pictures". *Psychonomic Bulletin & Review* 4: 501–506.
Levin, D.T., Simons, D.J., Angelone, B.L., and Chabris, C.F. 2002. "Memory for centrally attended changing objects in an incidental real-world change detection paradigm". *British Journal of Psychology* 93: 289–302.
Lin, X. and Lehman, J.D. 1999. "Supporting learning of vaiable control in a computer-based biology environment: Effects of prompting college students to reflect on their own thinking". *Journal of Research in Science Teaching* 36(7): 837–858.
Nelson, T.O. 1996. "Consciousness and metacognition". *American Psychologist* 51: 102–116.
Mack, A. and Rock, I. 1998. *Inattentional Blindness*. Cambridge, MA: The MIT Press.
Mackintosh, N.J. 1975. "A theory of attention: Variations in the associability of stimuli with reinforcement". *Psychological Review* 82: 276–298.
Meijer, J., Veenman, M.V.J., and van Hout-Wolters, B.H.A.M. 2006. "Metacognitive activities in text-studying and problem; development of a taxonomy". *Educational Research and Evaluation* 12: 209–237.
Molenaar, I. 2003. "Knowledge exchange from citizens to learners through online collaboration". In D. Lassner and C. McNaught (eds), *Proceedings of World Conference on Educational Multimedia, Hypermedia and Telecommunications 2003*, Chesapeake, VA; AACE, 894–899.
Papert, S., and Harel, I. 1991. "Situating constructionism — Chapter 1". In S. Papert and I. Harel (eds), *Constructionism*. Norwood, NJ: Ablex Publishing Corporation, 1–11.
Posner, M. 1980. "Orienting of attention". *Quarterly Journal of Experimental Psychology* 32: 3–25.
Posner, M. 1982. "Cumulative development of attention theory". *American Psychologist* 37: 168–179.
Puntambekar, S. and Hübscher, R. 2005. "Tools for scaffolding students in a complex environment: What have we gained and what have we missed?". *Educational Psychologist* 40(1): 1–12.
Rafal, R., and Henik, A. 1994. "The neurobiology of inhibition: Integrating controlled and automatic processes". In D. Dagenbach and T. Carr (eds), *Inhibitory Processes in Attention, Memory, and Language*. New York: Academic Press, 1–52.
Rensink, R.A. 2000. "Seeing, sensing, and scrutinizing". *Vision Research* 40(10–12): 1469–1487.
Rensink, R.A. 2002. "Change detection". *Annual Review of Psychology* 53: 245–277.
Roda, C. 2007. "Supporting attention with dynamic user models (extended abstract)". *Proceedings Interactivist Summer Institute 2007*, Paris.
Roda, C. (ed). 2006. *Atgentive (ist-4-027529-stp) deliverable d1.3 — atgentive conceptual framework and application scenarios.*
Roda, C. and Nabeth, T. 2005. "The role of attention in the design of learning management systems". *Proceedings of the IADIS International Conference CELDA (Cognition and Exploratory Learning in Digital Age)*, Lisbon, 148–155.
Roda, C. and Nabeth, T. 2007. "Supporting attention in learning environments: Attention support services, and information management". In E. Duval, R. Klamma, and M. Wolpers (eds), *Creating New Experiences on a Global Scale. Proceedings of the Second European Conference on Technology Enhanced Learning, EC-TEL 2007*, Crete [= Lecture Notes in Computer Science (LNCS 4753); Springer, 277–291].
Roda, C. and Thomas, J. 2006. "Attention aware systems: Theories, applications, and research agenda". *Computers in Human Behavior* 22(4): 557–587.
Rogers, R. and Monsell, S. 1995. "Costs of a predictable switch between simple cognitive tasks". *Journal of Experimental Psychology: General* 124(2): 207–231.

Rubinstein, J.S., Meyer, D.E., and Evans, J. 2001. "Executive control of cognitive processes in task switching". *Journal of Experimental Psychology: Human Perception and Performance* 27(4): 763–797.

Rudman, P. (ed). 2007. *Atgentive (ist-4-027529-stp) deliverable d4.4 — Final evaluation report.*

Schoenfeld, A. 1985. *Mathematical Problem Solving*. Orlando, FL: Academic Press.

Schmidt, H.G. and Boshuizen, H.P.A. 1993. "On acquiring expertise in medicine". *Educational Psychology Review* 5: 1–17.

Simons, D.J. and Levin, D.T. 1998. "Failure to detect changes to people in a real-world interaction". *Psychonomic Bulletin & Review* 5: 644–649.

Simons, D.J. and Rensink, R.A. 2005. "Change blindness: Past, present, and future". *Trends in Cognitive Sciences* 9(1):16–20.

Spector, A. and Biederman, I. 1976. "Mental set and mental shift revisited". *American Journal of Psychology* 89: 669–679.

Tipper, S.P. 1985. "The negative priming effect: Inhibitory effects of ignored primes". *Quarterly Journal of Experimental Psychology* 37A: 571–590.

Treisman, A. 1960. "Contextual cues in selective listening". *Quarterly Journal of Experimental Psychology* 12: 242–248.

Treisman, A. 1969. "Strategies and models of selective attention". *Psychological Review* 76: 282–299.

Triesch, J., Ballard, D.H., Hayhoe, M.M., and Sullivan, B.T. 2003. "What you see is what you need". *Journal of Vision* 3: 86–94.

Wells, G.L. and Olson, E.A. 2003. "Eyewitness testimony". *Annual Review of Psychology* 54: 277–295.

Wood, D., Bruner, J., and Ross, G. 1976. "The role of tutoring in problem solving". *Journal of Child Psychology and Psychiatry and Allied Disciplines* 17: 89–100.

Woolfe, J.M. 1999. "Inattentional amnesia". In V. Coltheart (ed), *Fleeting Memories*. Cambridge, MA: The MIT Press, 71–94.

Yantis, S. 1998. "Control of visual attention". In H. Pashler (ed), *Attention*. London: University College London Press, 223–256.

Yantis, S. 2000. "Goal-directed and stimulus-driven determinants of attentional control". In S. Monsell and J. Driver (eds), *Attention and Performance* 18. Cambridge, MA: The MIT Press, 73–103.

Zimmerman, B.J. 2002. "Becoming a self-regulated learner: An overview". *Theory into Practice* 42(2): 64–70.

Zimmerman, B. and Schunk, D. 2001. "Theories of self-regulated learning and academic achievement: An overview and analysis". In B.J Zimmerman and D. Schunk (eds), *Self-regulated Learning and Academic Achievement* 2nd ed. Mahwah, NJ: Erlbaum, 1–37.

Social, usability, and pedagogical factors influencing students' learning experiences with wikis and blogs

Shailey Minocha and Dave Roberts
The Open University UK / IBM, UK

With a variety of technology-enabled tools and environments to choose from, it is increasingly difficult for educators to ascertain the factors that influence the quality of the students' learning experience and hence make appropriate choices for the use of technology. In this paper, we discuss the role of two technologies — wikis and blogs — in teaching and learning. We provide case studies of two courses at the Open Umiversity, UK and empirical evidence of students' experiences, perceptions, and expectations on these courses. We discuss the context of these courses and the usage of these technologies: The pedagogical underpinnings and the rationale for introducing these technologies; the intended learning outcomes from the usage of these tools; and the extent to which the activities based around these tools have enabled the intended learning and facilitated the learning process. We report on the social, usability, and pedagogical factors that have influenced the quality of students' learning experience. The research reported in this paper aims to provide guidance to course designers and educators for choosing tools, particularly wikis and blogs, for their contexts and for creating value and generating a positive student experience to engender student satisfaction and retention.

Keywords: blog, collaborative learning, computer mediated communications, on-line communities wiki, personal journal, virtual teams

1. Introduction

Web 2.0 technologies make it easy for users to contribute ideas and content to a community. There has been growing interest in Web 2.0 technologies in recent years. There are many popular examples, such as blogs and wikis, tagging and folksonomic tools, photo or social bookmark-sharing sites such as Flickr and deli.cio.us. Sites such as YouTube, Myspace and Facebook are part of a growing trend towards user-generated content and for sharing information and ideas via online communities and social networks. Using simple, web-based interfaces, users can build shared collection of resources such as links, photos, videos, documents and almost any kind of media. The sharing and social aspects of these user-centred technologies provide useful means for creative expression and offer great potential in the context of learning and teaching (Horizon Report 2007). For example, students can collaboratively create resources and materials on a group-project within a wiki environment. Photography students can use Flickr to post, organise, share and critique each other's contributions. There are several case studies and examples in the literature and on the Web about the usage of these technologies in education. However, it is still a significant challenge for educators to integrate them in their courses. Institutions are finding it difficult to make the choices and effectively link the technologies with the pedagogy and learning objectives of a particular course or discipline (e.g., Wilson 2005).

In this paper we discuss the role of two technologies in teaching and learning — wikis and blogs. Wikis help to facilitate student collaboration via co-production of text, and development of argument and consensus by communication of ideas through a shared online workspace (e.g., Parker and Chao 2007; Minocha et al. 2007). For example, a wiki could be used for collaboratively creating a glossary, co-authoring a paper, or writing an essay or a project report. As a result of several contributors adding material to the wiki, a wiki can grow and evolve and, therefore, can address pedagogical objectives such as student involvement, group activity, peer and tutor review, knowledge-sharing and knowledge creation.

Blogs provide a medium to write conversational entries in a Web-based environment which can be shared with its readers. A blog, therefore, facilitates collaborative learning through sharing of views and resources and giving comments on the blog posts. Group blogs, maintained by two or more bloggers on a project, are also common. A group blog can enable brainstorming, discussion on topic(s) of interest to the group (e.g., http://www.corante.com/, last accessed 13th March, 2008), and project management.

We provide case studies of two courses at the Open University, UK (OU) and empirical evidence of students' experiences, perceptions, and expectations in these courses. We discuss the context of these courses and the usage of these technologies; the pedagogical underpinnings and the rationale for introducing these technologies; the intended learning objectives from the usage of these tools; the extent to which the activities based around these tools have enabled the intended learning and facilitated the learning process; and the social, usability and pedagogical factors that influence the student's learning experience.

2. Blogs and wikis

Weblog (web-log) or 'blog' is a web-based publishing tool which consists of a series of posts by the author(s) on a personalised web page, with posts usually arranged in reverse chronology from the most recent post at the top of the page. Blogs are often created and maintained by one person, but they may also be done by small groups (group-blog), and some may involve large communities of people participating in a single blog (Bartlett-Bragg 2003). People blog for various reasons (Nardi et al. 2004), e.g. for sharing personal stories, events and activities; for facilitating reflective learning, through learning diaries and journals; and as a sometimes cathartic outlet for expressing commentaries, views, opinions, and insights, as well as thoughts, emotions and feelings.

Blogs differ from other forms of asynchronous personal-communication technologies for managing information and for knowledge sharing, such as e-mail and discussion forums (Du and Wagner 2007). E-mails are destined only for the designated receivers, while discussion forums could either be open to the public or only to registered members; the members are allowed to create posts and the forums are generally facilitated by administrator(s). Blogs and individual blog-posts can be open to the public or restricted to a few readers. Depending on the blogging software, users may add comments. However, new entries are only created by the blog owner(s), providing a sense of ownership or control towards the blog and its content. Blogs are, therefore, designed for self-publication and a medium for social sharing and collective sense-making (Oravec 2003; Du and Wagner 2007).

A wiki is an asynchronous collaborative authoring environment — a readable and writeable website in which potentially all the visitors to the site can create new pages or modify existing ones, with optional access control to set limits on authorship. Wikis, therefore, allow distributed teams to write and edit documents collaboratively over the Internet in a shared online workspace. The best known wiki is Wikipedia, an online encyclopaedia that has been written and maintained by thousands of contributors from around the world. The advantage of wikis, as demonstrated in Wikipedia, is that if a contributor makes an incorrect or inappropriate entry or change, other authors or editors can 'roll back' to a previous version or edit and keep the change.

In today's knowledge-based digital networked economy which is a shift from the traditional linear industrial-era models of mass-production and communication, there is an increasing importance of knowledge in economic activities. To prepare the students for the knowledge economy, it is important that they acquire skills of communication, collaboration, team-working and critical reflection. Thus there is a need to shift the pedagogical models from the traditional linear learning paradigms in education and training, to socio-constructivist pedagogical models (Bruns and Humphreys 2005). Socio-constructivism is a dimension of constructivist learning theory, which involves social, collaborative and problem-solving strategies in teaching and learning (Dougiamas 1998).

There are three main characteristics built into social constructivist scenarios: They use complex, realistic problems; they use group collaboration, interaction and cooperation; and learners are responsible for setting goals and learn through a process of shared understanding, while educators provide guidance (from Merriënboer and Pass 2003, quoted in Schneider et al. 2003: 36–37). Wikis and blogs enable the generation of social constructivist scenarios wherein a group of learners collaboratively construct shared artefacts, create a culture of dialogue, and negotiate meanings and take decisions. Educators are, therefore, realising the potential of blogs and wikis in learning and teaching, when they make use of these tools.

3. The context of the case studies

The Open University (OU) is the largest university in the United Kingdom and the UK's only university dedicated to distance learning with over 200,000 distance learners. The open source Virtual Learning Environment (VLE) Moodle (www.moodle.org, last accessed 13th March, 2008) has been adopted by the University and there has been an extensive development of this VLE to provide the required functionality for the OU. There is a range of ways in which the VLE tools and other web-based elements are being integrated into the courses at the OU:

- Courses which have paper-based materials but have a web-presence with resources, such as course-related web links, study calendar and downloadable (pdf) files of the course materials.
- Courses which have traditional paper-based materials and employ tools such as blogs or wikis in group-working and project work. These courses have an online forum for asynchronous communication with tutors and fellow-students.
- Courses where all the materials are online and students are provided with various tools such as wikis, blogs, e-portfolios and forums to support the communication and collaboration.

The wiki and blog case studied in this paper are situated in the second and third course types listed above, respectively. The post-graduate course 'Software Requirements for Business Systems' in the Department of Computing employs wikis for collaborative activities. The post-graduate course 'E-learning professional' in the Institute of Educational Technology is an online course employing blogs.

There are a number of social, pedagogical and technological challenges currently faced by institutions and educators in the era of technology-enabled learning. For example, students' perceptions of distance-education and the flexibility it offers in terms of learning in one's own time; unavailability of broadband/internet; hesitation and even resistance of students to participate in collaborative activities; issues such as, is there enough guidance for the course teams to integrate the usage of technology within the pedagogy of the course; how should the usage of technology on a course be justified to the students and tutors; how can the various tools be directly linked with the learning outcomes; how should the activities be designed using the tools to meet these learning outcomes; how effective will the activities in supporting the learning or the learning process be; how to design the assessment for on-line activities; and most importantly, ensuring that the technology is usable and accessible through extensive user-based evaluations before the technology is deployed. We will address some of these challenges in this paper.

3.1 An overview: Case studies of two courses at the OU

The course team of the course, Software Requirements for Business Systems, has been one of the early adopters of the VLE. The course involves teaching systematic elicitation, recording, and communication of requirements of software systems. On a software development project, the elicitation of requirements is generally carried out by a team of requirements engineers or system analysts. In software enterprises, requirements engineers often work remotely from one another and wikis are increasingly being used for collaboratively developing requirements specification documents (e.g., Farrell 2006; Decker et al. 2007). In this course, the wiki activities were introduced to provide students with the opportunity to engage in small-group collaboration to emulate Requirements Engineering (RE) practice. In this paper, we discuss the usage of wikis in RE practice, and the process of integrating collaborative-work and wikis on the RE course. We will draw on empirical evidence to discuss effectiveness of wiki in collaborative learning of the RE processes.

The blogging case study is from a year-long research project that we carried out to investigate the role of blogs in learning and teaching. Our research was student-centred in the sense that we primarily focused on investigating the student-experience of blogging, their perceptions of blogging, and for what purposes they use blogs for. In this paper, we will discuss our empirical investigations of the students' experiences on the 'E-learning professional' course in which a blog was a part of the web-based learning toolbox that is provided to the students (the other tools being wikis, podcasts, and forums). Blogging wasn't compulsory but there were activities in the course materials that suggested blogging and the usage of the blog. In Sections 4 and 5, we discuss the two case studies.

4. The approach to collaboration in wikis in the requirements engineering course

The RE course is a distance-learning course of five months duration. The course describes how to analyse a business problem, identify the stakeholders of the business problem, interact with the stakeholders and develop a requirements specification of a software system that can be used to determine an appropriate solution for a business problem. The course describes RE techniques and a disciplined approach to the RE process. The majority of the students on this course are software professionals who register on the course to update their skills in eliciting, analysing, communicating and agreeing requirements.

In practice, the RE processes of interacting with stakeholders, managing stakeholder conflicts, and removing conflicts, duplicates, and ambiguities from a set of requirements are generally performed by a small group of requirements engineers who discuss and reformulate the requirements in consultation with the stakeholders (Robertson and Robertson 2006). The aim of introducing collaborative activities in a wiki environment was to emulate this experience by enabling a group of students to take the roles of requirements engineers in a software development project. For example, the project (case study) could involve a dental practice setting up its website. The wiki activities involved a group of students contributing requirements to the group-wiki, discussing the requirements, identifying conflicts and ambiguities within the requirements, and resolving the conflicts through discussions from the perspectives of different stakeholders, to produce an unambiguous requirements specification. The wiki activities were designed to be self-managed by the students and required minimal or no intervention by the tutor and thereby avoided any significant increase in the tutors' workload.

4.1 Introducing wikis to students

The assessment on the course involves three tutor-marked assignments (TMAs) and an examination at the end of the presentation. Since not all students were expected to be aware of wikis and/or their role in RE practices, an introductory paper by Farrell (2006) on wikis was included as a part of the first TMA (the first TMA is due within the first month of the course).

In addition, many other introductory papers and web links related to wikis were placed on the course website to enable the students to familiarise themselves with wikis as collaborative authoring tools and specifically on the role of wikis in RE practice (e.g., Damian 2007; Decker et al. 2007), software development (Louridas 2006) and project management applications. It was important for the course team to convey to the students that the wiki activities fit within the pedagogy of the course, otherwise the wiki would have been perceived by students as yet another online tool that added to the workload on the course. In addition, two guidance documents were given to the students: (a) guidelines for using the wiki; and (b) guidelines for conducting the collaborative activities in the wiki, rules of collaboration on the course, and wiki-etiquette.

Students were asked to participate in their individual groups in an ice-breaker activity in first TMA. The ice-breaker had two objectives: To enable students to familiarise themselves with the wiki environment and to give them an opportunity to introduce themselves to their fellow group members. Each student was asked to do two tasks in this ice-breaker session; add a small biography to the wiki and enter a stakeholder type from a list of stakeholders in the case study. The exercise involved very little collaboration in the sense that little negotiation was required. Care was taken to ensure that there would be no advantage or disadvantage in choosing one stakeholder type rather than another. The choice of stakeholder type was a preparation for the second TMA where each student had been asked to discuss the requirements for the system in the case study from their chosen stakeholder's perspective. The evidence of their individual contributions was included in their TMAs by copying and pasting the log from the 'History' section of the wiki (the 'History' function in the wiki records all the changes and contributions made to a page in a wiki).

4.2 Collaborative requirements engineering

The wiki activities in the second and third TMAs were aimed to provide practical experience of requirements development to emulate real-practice. The activities had been designed around key course concepts so that students could develop shared understanding via collaboration. The second TMA involved each student (in the role of requirements engineer) in a group adding three requirements to the wiki from the perspective of the stakeholder chosen in the first wiki activity. Once all the students had entered their set of requirements, the collaboration involved discussing duplicates, conflicts, and ambiguities with the aim of achieving an agreed set of unambiguous requirements for the system in the case study. Students could also use the forum for discussion while performing this collaboration.

The collaborative activity in the third TMA involved each group checking the accuracy of the requirements developed in the second TMA and specifying a fit-criterion (a quantified measure) for each requirement. The development of suitable fit-criteria can be difficult if a requirements engineer is working on their own, and better quality fit-criteria can be obtained by a group of requirements engineers working collaboratively. Hence, the wiki activity asked the students to agree on a set of fit-criteria. The assessment was based on both the student's own contribution to the activity, as well as on the product of the activity which is reported in the TMAs. A significant advantage of the wiki is that it records each and every change to the document in the 'History', which means that there is evidence of each student's contribution.

4.3 Research questions

We were interested in the effectiveness of wiki as a tool for collaboration and collaborative learning. Further, we were interested in eliciting the factors that influenced the students' learning experiences. We focused on the following research questions:[1]

> Q1w: Did the wiki activities facilitate collaborative learning as intended?
> Q2w: How might the usage of wiki be integrated with other tools such as a scheduler for organisation, or a group-blog or forum for discussions during collaborative requirements development?
> Q3w: What are the challenges which students face in collaborative requirements development and specification? These challenges might include: Resolving conflicts in the perspectives of different team-members; building trust and shared values; establishing norms for communication; and assigning the roles of the team-members contributing to a wiki (authors, editors, readers, facilitators).

To address these research questions, a set of concrete questions were devised to elicit feedback from students. In the third TMA, the students were asked to report on the reflections that they had been recording in the reflection template throughout the course (Minocha et al. 2007). These reflective questions in the TMA are related to one or more of the research questions listed above:

> Where was your understanding of the RE process enhanced by your involvement in collaborative exercises? (to provide input for Q1w)
> What do you think of wiki as a medium for collaborative work on a distance education course? (for Q1w, Q2w and Q3w)
> Is a wiki a good medium for collaborative requirements development? (for Q1w and Q2w)
> Does collaborative authoring contribute to a better requirements engineering process? (for Q1w)

4.4 Data Sources and Data Analysis

Since the TMA questions (listed 1–3 in the previous section) had 15% marks allocated to it, the majority of students answered it (we had responses from 117 students).

Of these responses, we have analysed a random sample of 70 (60%). In this sample there were 13 (18.6%) females and 57 (81.4%) males compared with 20 (17%) females and 97 males in the full data set. All students on the course were adults studying part-time and most of them were professionals in the software industry.

Along with the reflective accounts in the third TMA, we collated and analysed discussions by students on the forum (70 in all), direct e-mails from students discussing their wiki experiences (15), and e-mails from tutors (14 — an average of 2 e-mails per tutor), discussing their perceptions of the wiki activities, and their experiences with students in their tutor-groups.

Using the research questions to guide us through the collated data, we (the first author and a colleague on the RE course) performed an inductive analysis of the various accounts of students' and tutors' experiences and their perceptions to identify the emerging themes, sub-themes and the inter-relationships between them. This involved:

- Collecting the forum discussions and e-mails from students and tutors pertaining to the wiki tool and collaborative activities into a Microsoft Word© document.
- Extracting the reflective accounts from the answers for each of the questions in the TMAs into a Word document.
- Reading the different sociological accounts in detail to gain an understanding of the positive accounts and the obstacles that had been described in the data.
- Identifying the emerging themes for both the positive accounts and obstacles, guided by the research questions. From these emerging themes, the top-level common themes were identified. The lower-level themes were found from multiple readings of the data.
- Analysing the accounts in e-mails and the discussion forum in a similar way.
- Identifying the themes and sub-themes in the sociological accounts derived from e-mails and forums.
- Validating the cataloguing scheme through dual-coding by the two independent researchers or coders in order to ensure that the sorting criteria were operationalised effectively and that the sorting process was consistent.

The process was iterative and the two researchers met to examine any discrepancies. These were resolved through discussion, and the sort criteria (the themes) were merged and documented. Following this, another subset of data was sorted independently using the agreed criteria. Again, any discrepancies were resolved, and the sort criteria were updated accordingly. This process was repeated one more time (three sorts overall) until discrepancies were minimised. Each time, the categories of themes and sub-themes became more concrete and more fully articulated. Finally, the entire data set was sorted using the stabilised sort criteria, and the two independent sorts were compared for consistency.

5. Evaluation of the wiki case study

The purpose of investigating the first research question (Q1w) 'Did the wiki activities facilitate collaborative learning as intended?' was to evaluate these key aspects:

- The pedagogical effectiveness of collaborative activities in a distance-learning environment;
- Whether and how the understanding of the RE process was enhanced; and
- The effectiveness of wiki as a tool for collaborative authoring.

We will now present the various themes and sub-themes that emerged from the data for each of the aspects of Q1w and of the other two research questions (Q2w and Q3w).

5.1 Collaborative learning

The following sub-themes for collaborative learning emerged for Q1w:

Understanding of the course concepts: There were several positive responses of which the following are representative of the benefits that the students have stated in terms of knowledge-sharing and learning:

> ...A more comprehensive list of requirements may be achieved as some will be included in the list that may not have been thought of by an individual. I realised a couple of requirements that I had not thought of myself when analysing the appointments system [the case study].
>
> ... The simple fact that my requirements were going to be viewed by other members helped me to think clearly about specifying my requirements. This, in turn, led to me writing less ambiguous requirements.

Peer review and feedback: The students mentioned benefiting from comments received from fellow students during the collaboration. The old adage 'two heads are better than one' is truly apparent during the collaborative exercise. This can be seen visibly when one author posts an item on the wiki and subsequently other authors make comments as to its correctness.

Clarification of own contributions and understanding: The inputs and views from fellow students facilitated the students to clarify their understanding of the course content related to the collaborative activity.

> ...Even though I understood exactly what I was trying to specify, it wasn't until I received feedback, and, indeed, gave feedback that I realised that some of what I had written was open to misinterpretation.

Re-interpretation and self-reflection of one's contributions: Students felt that peer-review and assessment helped them to re-assess their understanding of the course concepts and to reflect on their individual contributions and learning:

> ...The collaborative activity allowed me to see how the others addressed this question and evolve my own contribution and understanding based on these.

> ...The discussions from this activity helped me to reflect on my own views and potentially modify them (and the requirements).

Integration of multiple viewpoints: The students appreciated the role of multiple viewpoints in clarifying understanding:

> ...The collaborative approach incorporates more views; [if] properly managed, this usually leads to better results.

Aggregation of group knowledge: The students acknowledged the collaborative construction of knowledge within the group. The first quote also outlines the role of wiki in RE.

Anyone involved can submit new ideas, change existing content if incorrect and take issue with points raised. Because everyone's contribution is identified it empowers everyone involved. The group knowledge quickly becomes aggregated in one place instead of being dispersed throughout multiple communication channels. This improves requirements engineering since the quality and tempo of team interaction via the wiki has been enhanced.

However, students had mixed perceptions about collaborative activities: They were positive that collaborative activities were a way to bring students involved in distance-education together, but some perceived collaboration as being onerous and not in sync with OU's philosophy of flexible (open) learning and learning in one's own time.

5.2 Obstacles to collaboration

Loss of flexibility in study patterns: In a part-time distance-learning environment of the OU, students have the expectations of studying in their own time and any collaborative activity is considered to be a burden:

> ...I tend to study once every few weeks and do several chapters at once — basically, I organise my studying around my life. Now ... I'm being asked to organise my life around my studying.

Participants require prompting and organisation outside of the tool via group emails. Participants are not always available at convenient times e.g., holidays and business pressures. Enthusiasm to participate will drop when other work pressures are high and students may do as little as possible. When pushed for time, participants may not want to argue a point in order to finish the exercise quickly.

The following quote highlights several interesting aspects and is representative of several comments that we received on the loss of flexibility in part-time distance education due to collaborative activities that were assessed and had to be completed by some specified deadlines:

> ... The ethos of the Open University is that you can work in your own time, to your own time scales, in your own way (as long as the TMA deadlines are met). Forcing people into collaborative work produces a strait jacket that works against that flexibility.

Waiting for others to contribute: Collaborative activities on the course required everybody to contribute well before the deadline to give sufficient time for giving feedback to one another and achieving an agreement towards the final product the group has to produce. Waiting for others to contribute was one of the main obstacles in the positive experience of the students.

Non participation and late participation may have a negative effect on others within the group. Groups may split into early participating and late participating sub groups. On the other hand, some students felt that the asynchronous environment of wiki was an advantage in allowing group-members to contribute at a time that suits them:

> ... In terms of collaborating on an OU course, the benefits seem to outweigh the disadvantages; it is difficult for all people collaborating to be able to arrange a pre-determined time to collaborate, so using the wiki as collaboration medium is quite effective.

Then there were issues of peer-reviewing and critiquing (as is common in groupwork). Some students just weren't professional and felt they had the right to criticise other students work without being constructive.

5.3 Collaborative authoring

This account provides inputs for the second research question (Q2w): 'How might the usage of wiki be integrated with other tools such as a scheduler for organisation, or a group-blog or forum for discussions during collaborative requirements development?' The following sub-themes emerged in our analysis:

Availability 24x7: Students mentioned the advantages of wiki being web-based and accessible 24x7 which helps in supporting remote collaborations similar to other asynchronous tools such as forums and e-mail. The advantages are that it is easy to use (no training required), simple to access (you only need a basic pc), and available 24 hours a day 7 days a week, which makes it ideal for students who have to work at odd hours.

Group-work: Some students found that the wiki facilitated collaborative working:

> … It is difficult to see how our group could have produced and reviewed a set of requirements in the space of 2–3 weeks without the Wiki.

Saving costs of travel: Students mentioned how wiki-based collaboration can help reduce travelling costs for face-to-face team meetings in RE practice. Online wiki-based collaboration will be less expensive than hosting meetings at a site to which each travel member needs to travel (and possible stay in hotels).

History and evidence of contributions: The wiki has a history function that keeps a record of the changes that are made to the wiki by the different authors in the collaborative activity. This function has been particularly useful for assessment. Students were asked to post the entries on the History page as an evidence of their contributions towards the process and product:

> …With the ability to quickly assess the modification history, it is also possible to easily track changes.

> …It [wiki] allows a history and audit trail of documentation to be automatically maintained and referenced in the future therefore enabling traceability of requirements through to development.

While investigating research questions Q1w and Q2w, our analysis uncovered several technological obstacles with the wiki.

5.4 Technological and social obstacles

One of the obstacles was related to the usability of the user interface design of the wiki environment. The editing window in the wiki was small and couldn't be enlarged. The students reported that the small window didn't provide enough context and content for the document being edited. Students had to scroll the content up and down while they were entering text in the wiki via this editing window.

> … However, I feel that the wiki tool we used is quite limiting. The editing window was very small and it was difficult to get your formatting right.

The poor navigation within the wiki was another obstacle:

> … It is a time consuming tool to use, as navigation is poor, for example one must always return to the root before viewing another branch …

The students had to keep going back to the wiki to check if any new contributions by other group members had been made:

> … It would have been good to have some mechanism for requesting alerts on certain pages to save you constantly having to check.

> … It would have been useful to have perhaps an RSS feed, or e-mail notification option available which notified other users of changes.

This sociological account is representative of the various user interface design issues with the wiki environment:

> … I feel more effort should be invested in looking into how the user experience of the wiki can be improved.

Next, we analysed the data for (Q2w): How might the usage of wiki be integrated with other tools such as a scheduler for organisation, or a group-blog or forum for discussions during collaborative requirements development?

Lack of synchronous communications within the wiki environment: Over half the students in our sample mentioned the need to engage in some form of synchronous communication for discussion and debate ranging from face-to-face sessions to telephone conferencing. Many suggested the use of a forum so that there could be identifiable threads of communication. Indeed, some groups did engage in some form of synchronous communication:

> … It is slow as a communication medium…. A wiki is not a flexible discussion medium.

> … I do not believe that a Wiki can be used in isolation when collaborative working, rather it should be adopted alongside other more traditional methods e.g., telephone conferencing and face-to-face meetings.…face to face meetings should take place at various points in the requirements process in order to ensure that the process is managed correctly and difficult issues reviewed.

Thus, the students were generally in agreement with our own view and the views expressed by the tutors that while a wiki has strengths in recording decisions and for supporting collaborative authoring, it needs to be supported with a medium for synchronous discussion medium to facilitate timely decision making (face-to-face meetings are not possible in this distance-learning course).

In TMA 02 we had a split of the communication methods that the group members wished to use, half used messaging and half used the group discussion wiki. Members using the messaging would occasionally post comments on the wiki whilst doing the bulk of their work on messenger:

> … So I've learnt that you should pick the right method of collaborative communication in the right situation.

Perceived lack of socialisation: Another major obstacle was the relative lack of socialisation between group members. The students do not meet face-to-face in this course and, therefore, it is only through online socialisation activities that the students get to know one another. Whilst there was an 'ice-breaker' in the first TMA, this has proved to be inadequate and several students have commented on the difficulty of working with a group of relative strangers.

Where project teams already know and understand each other, electronic communication is fine. Where strangers do not, all non-verbal communication is lost, leading to misunderstanding and potential conflict.

Finally, some students felt that for a smooth process towards production of a consolidated artefact (a set of requirements), individual student members should have pre-defined roles.

To optimise collaborative authoring (and therefore the quality of the output), roles and responsibilities for authors are required, in order to ensure that issues such as identifying dependencies and conflicts between requirements can be fully resolved.

In spite of the obstacles, students felt that the wiki did meet their needs for collaborative requirements development:

> … It [wiki] centrally brings all the requirements together for all to see and update constantly. It allows more experienced Engineers to have an input in remote projects that in the past would have required reports to go back and forth, whilst losing time and competitive edge.

For the third research question (Q3w), 'What are the challenges which students face in collaborative writing and requirements development?', we uncovered a number of obstacles in the sociological accounts. The obstacles that the students experienced ranged from not having synchronous communication mechanisms which they felt were vital for negotiation and for arriving at a consolidated set of requirements in requirements development, to not having 'rules' for collaboration, and not having formal 'roles' in the group about managing the collaborative process:

> … A much better medium … would be a face to face meeting, as members of the group can discuss in real time and come to an agreement much more quickly.

As there is no specific owner for the collaborative work, there was a dependency on one person voluntarily pulling all the strings together, for example in TMA02 to incorporate all the suggestions into the final presentation. This is an extra burden for one person. Further, they felt that a wiki might become unusable and unmanageable for a large project:

> … The course wiki became difficult to follow at times so a project of any size would quickly become unusable. A moderator/administrator may be required if the project is large scale.

> … In medium or big ones [projects] one will probably lose the audit ability. There are missing some fundamental functions like a real professional version control, for example…

These observations by students are in sync with those reported in (Friske and John 2007) where wikis have only been suggested for early requirements elicitation. Therefore, this observation was an indication of students' understanding of the RE process and the role of wiki in collaborative requirements development.

In the next section, we discuss the students' perceptions and experiences with blogs in the second case study. The various factors which have influenced the pedagogical effectiveness of wikis and blogs and, therefore, students' learning experiences, will be summarised in the final section of the paper.

6. The use of blogs on the 'E-Learning Professional' course

The E-Learning Professional course is an on-line course designed for professionals engaged in post-school education and training, wanting to understand the issues involved in the evolving practices of e-learning and, in particular, personal and professional development using online tools, resources and e-portfolios. This course attracts a wide range of professionals from across the globe who work in education and who are keen to develop their professional expertise in e-learning. In the course the students examine debates about professionalism in e-learning practice and appraise the usefulness of tools for personal and professional development. They build an example e-portfolio to provide evidence of their own competencies. The key learning outcomes of this course are: Reflection on the role, practices and skills of teaching in e-learning, and on what constitutes good pedagogy; evaluation of specific technologies and their uses for learning and teaching; and developing the skill of reflection in the context of personal development.

6.1 Introducing blogs and other e-learning tools to the students

The students were presented with suggested reading resources, week by week, and the activities were designed to enable them to reflect upon their own practice in the light of what they had read. The course provided the students with various e-learning tools — blogs, podcasts, forums, wiki, and e-portfolio, but the course didn't prescribe a technology for a particular application. The students were provided with on-line documents guiding them on the usage of these technologies. One of the aims of the course team was that students evaluate the provided technologies for themselves and the students then decide on the applications of these technologies in their learning, teaching and training activities.

6.2 Reflective learning and blogging

Reflective learning and reflection-on-practice form the core themes of this course. Since the course is targeted for educators and trainers who have joined this course to become e-learning professionals, one of the learning outcomes of the course is to 'reflect on the role, practices and skills of teaching in e-learning, and on what constitutes good pedagogy'.

Reflection is the process of stepping back from an experience to ponder, carefully and persistently, its meaning to the self through the development of inferences; learning is the creation of meaning from past or current events that serves as a guide for future behaviour (Daudelin 1996). One of the goals of reflective learning is to encourage professionals to recognise the routine, implicit skills in their practice, which tend to be delivered without conscious deliberation or a deeper questioning of the wider situation or context within which the practitioner is operating.

The course suggests that reflection can be performed in the blog or in the forum. During the course, students completed three TMAs and also created and collected various pieces of evidence (e.g., personal reflections documented in Word© or their blog or in the forum) of their competencies in the areas of technology, communication, research, and practice on the course. The students were expected to assimilate evidence (from reflective accounts) towards these competencies in the e-portfolio which was submitted for end-of-course assessment.

Students were provided with a blog that was hosted on the OU server and visible to other students on the course, their tutor and anyone else to whom the student gave their URL. The blogs could not be located with an internet search engine. The content of the blogs was not assessed unless the student chose to submit some posts as part of their final e-portfolio. For some of the reflective activities on the course, capturing reflections in a blog were suggested on the course but not prescribed. The students could choose to reflect in word-processors on their own personal computers or keep a traditional paper-based diary, or assimilate the reflections in the e-portfolio, if the students didn't choose to share their reflections on-line such as in a blog or in a forum. Students were free to use the blogs in any additional way they wished, whilst adhering to the OU computing code of conduct and guidelines for working in online environments.

6.3 Research questions

Whilst there have been several studies about how blogging can support learning (e.g. Burgess 2006; Farmer 2006; Hunan et al. 2005; Williams and Jacobs 2004), there are also those that report difficulties. Problems have included haphazard contributions to blogs, minimal communication between students through their blogs and poor quality of reflection on the course materials as evidenced in blog content (Krause 2004). Homik and Melis (2006) reported that students engaged in only a minimal level of blogging which was just enough to meet the assessment requirements. Other issues from an educator's perspective have included the need for students to have developed skills in selecting appropriate material to include in their blog; the problem of plagiarising from others' blogs (e.g., Oravec 2003); and their ability to manage the tension between publishing private thoughts in a public space (Mortensen and Walker 2002).

Analysis of the various challenges has tended to focus on students' technological abilities and/or their level of compliance with activities that have been designed by their educators. It appears that little attention has been paid to exploring students preconceptions about whether blogs and blogging could support their learning, and their accounts of actual blogging experiences on their courses. Our research has been student-centred in the sense that we have primarily focused on investigating the student-experience of blogging and these research questions:[2]

> What are the functions of blogs and blogging in their learning? (Q1b)
> What are the obstacles to blogging? (Q2b)
> Which social and pedagogical factors and their inter-relationships influence blogging? (Q3b)

6.4 Data sources and data analysis

Following approval from OU's Human Participants and Materials Ethics Committee, recruitment notices were posted on the course website towards the end of the course. The notices emphasised that we had no expectations about the amount, quality and type of blog posts that students had written, and that we were interested in how they had found their blogs useful. We received 15 positive replies from 13 females and 2 males with a mean age of 47.7 years, range 29–55 years (the course as a whole consisted of 36.4% male students and 63.6% female students with most between 30–60 years of age). The participants were resident in the UK (10), Philippines (1), Canada (1), Spain (1), Cyprus (1) and the US (1).

Each student gave consent that we could access, read, analyse and use anonymised quotes from their blogs. We analysed the blogs prior to interviewing students; the blogs varied in length (from one post to around 50 posts). Analysis of the blog-content helped us to identify the themes of blog-usage (e.g., reflection, sharing photos, for catharsis, evaluating a paper) and addition blog-author-specific-questions for interviews (in addition to the generic protocol that we have developed). It was not necessary to develop a coding scheme at this stage of analysing blogs; our aim was in identifying broad types of usage as quickly and efficiently as possible. Analysis of the blogs was followed by an audio-recorded, semi-structured, telephone interview with each student. Interview questions in the generic protocols were derived from the literature and also from our research questions. The students were interviewed by two co-present researchers (the first author of the paper and a colleague) using a conference telephone; one led the interview and the second researcher had an opportunity to ask the interviewee for any additional elaborations at the end of the session.

We adopted a grounded theory approach (Glaser and Strauss 1967) for the analysis of the data. The data consisted of the blog-content, interviews-data, and course-descriptions and details of course-activities. We focused on the identification of emergent themes and hierarchy of sub-themes based on the lens (research question) that we use to analyse the data, in the same way as described in Section 4.4.

7. Evaluation of the blogging case study

The purpose of investigating the first research question (Q1b) 'What are the functions of blogs and blogging in their learning?' was to evaluate the various functions for which the students used blogs for and the pedagogical effectiveness of blogs and blogging in reflective-learning. Since the course team had been non-prescriptive of the usage of the blog (unlike the wiki case study), it was important for us to find out for what purposes students used blogs for, because students' perceptions of the blog's contribution to their learning will depend on how they used or perceived the blog and the blogging activity.

We will now present the results of our analysis of blog content and interviews with course teams, tutors, and the students to answer each of these aspects of Q1b and of the other two research questions (Q2b and Q3b).

7.1 Usage of blogs on the course

The students used blogs for a variety of purposes:

Course-related activities: The students conducted the course-related activities in the blog: For example, summarising papers — while some students presented their criticism and personal opinions on the readings, some students merely stated that they were not sure of the views being expressed by the author.

> … I would argue that his analysis hints at but does not fully recognise one of the features of the social consequences of the information revolution: the pace of change, and the quantity of unexpected but significant consequences.

> … Is his view completely justified? No doubt he thinks so… but I'm not so sure.

One student mentioned in her blog and, thereafter in the interview, how summarising papers and writing about other related resources in the blog helped her to synthesise ideas:

> … Thank you Jenni for the resources: on research skills at <URL>… on reflection and CPD at <URL>. This chimes with some of the remarks made by Perkin [an author of a paper that the students were asked to read in the course] about people's distrust of experts: that's another evening gone off topic… but beginning to pull some threads together.

TO-DO lists: Students prepared to-do lists or reminder-notes in their blogs. For example, one blog post had this list:

> … Moodle to-do; Set up user accounts for a teacher and a pupil;
> Explore Hot Potato [nickname for the e-portfolio software] quizzes and email links through CGI;

Resolutions: Some Blog-posts were for declaring resolutions or for reinforcing their near-future plans:

> … I must learn to be more reflective. [Repeated four times]

> … I'm soooooo behind with the course already (still to do my 1000 words from week 2) so after tomorrow it'll be pedal to the metal to catch up.

> … This course is relentless! ….I feel the weight of it. I don't want to lose the weak grasp I have of the course… but… slip!

Planning (what are the next steps) on the course: The course website had a week-by-week study calendar. Students wrote about their progress and which activities they were planning (based on the calendar):

> … So I am going to use the week 16 activity to create a podcast using a new desktop microphone (approx £14), the free software XXXX, some copyright free music and a free web host and aggregator.
>
> … This week I'm trying to both complete my Wk7 [week 7] assignment on portfolio products and prepare my first TMA for submission, as I've suddenly realised it's due in next Monday!!

A repository for resources: Students had collection of links related to the course or of related interests such as news items on new technologies. Some students had links to blog posts of other students often accompanied by some critique or an account of what additional insight or perspective had been obtained by looking at a fellow-student's blog-post, or whether/how the fellow-student's views were in agreement or disagreement with their views.

Self-motivation: Some students had written in the blog to self-motivate themselves if they were lagging behind in their studies or other commitments (for example, this student is also a tutor on another course at the OU):

> … Note to self: Sort out your time management issues! You can't do everything other than marking just because you like everything other than marking just that tiny bit more. Right. For the next hour I am doing nothing but mark, then I will reward myself with a cup of tea and time for bed.

Reflecting on their experiences of working through course-activities: To introduce students to podcasts and to enable them to explore their potential in their work-practices, students were asked to create a podcast and transcript, and post it on the blog. In addition to including the transcripts and the podcast on the blog, some students also give an account of their experiences:

> … The first lesson was horrible, with a lot of technical inconveniences and problems. I was too nervous and the lesson I had prepared had not been well timed. But I started to think about how to solve all of those inconveniences. So I centred in trying to see the lesson from my students' point of view.

A student reflected on the group-work:

> … I found the Group Work one of the most difficult tasks during this course due to different facts, for instance: lack of planning, coordination, effective co-operation and discussion… But I think the greatest failure was the ignorance of how important each of us is in this kind of work.

Self-Reflection: Some students 'reflected' on their own learning and activities and used these reflections for planning the next steps:

> … I think I have put some reflection into practice in my e-Portfolio and my Blog, but I need more time and practice for it to be more beneficial for my own

> development. I also realise that the more I practice writing about my own reflections, the easiest is for me to find a way to express them more clearly and briefly.

Socialisation and expressing moods and emotions via images: Most students posted photographs of self, or of family, or of family pets on the first few blog-posts. When we asked these students in the interviews about the rationale for posting these pictures (since the course team had not suggested this), the students felt that exchanging pictures was a way to introduce themselves, as an ice breaker, or to start the process of socialisation with group-members with whom they would be collaborating later on in the course on a group-activity.

Generating a community or a self-help study group: Some of the students used their blogs to share their experiences with the course materials or with the technologies on the course, or to exchange ideas/thoughts on what they were currently reading. The analysis of the blog-content revealed that if a student posted his displeasure on some aspect of the course or any technological obstacles with the tools that were provided by the CT, there were quick responses from fellow students in the form of personal experiences, thoughts or just expressing empathy. For example, when a student posted a message that she was facing usability obstacles with the e-portfolio tool, she received 9 comments on the same day. For example:

> … I am not impressed by [tool] either. I was a bit disappointed that we are not using the ePortfolio tool the OU is developing as part of Moodle [VLE environment] :-(

> … I love the way you talk crazy to yourself — it helps keep me sane! Keep up the ranting…

Another student mentioned the problem of reading online and having to print the materials to read them:

> … Well I have started reading the ePortfolio material and have confirmed my dislike of reading online so have taken to printing out chunks of material.

This student mentioned to us in her interview that this blog post (posted early on in the course) invited several comments from fellow-students and receiving comments made her aware that people were indeed reading her blog:

> … I'm with you guys on this. I find it almost impossible reading online and have already accumulated a fairly weighty folder of articles covered in notes and scribbles… I wonder when my boss will start to notice the ever decreasing supply of printer paper though…

Another student criticised the online course and its various components which she feels aren't tightly integrated and received comments supporting her views:

> … It's all too virtual. I keep having to look at my notes, the website, and rack my brains to check what this week required.
>
> It's all over the place. Have to use course website, conferences (several), wiki, blog, e-portfolio.
>
> … Quite frustrating in many ways. We haven't got the idea of using the wiki yet — seems more like conferencing.

7.2 Pedagogical effectiveness of blogs and blogging

The course materials suggest recording regular reflections on learning. We analysed the data to investigate whether students found blogging effective for reflection [to answer research question (Q1b)].

Our interviews of the tutors on the course revealed that students found it difficult to reflect on their learning: First, some students were not sure what reflection on learning meant; what it involves; how reflection is carried out; and what is its significance to their learning and the rationale for individual and group-reflection in their blogs. So instead of reflecting on their learning in the blog, they wrote about the obstacles to reflection that they were facing:

> … I find very difficult to get to grips with [reflection] no matter how hard I try. It goes so much against my learning style that I find it a chore rather than beneficial still that is part and parcel of becoming a better learner. If I do go on to become a teacher at some stage it'll be a very important practice for my students so I must get myself more warmed up to it!
>
> … Must admit I gave up a bit on the reflecting week apart from my attempt at blogging I haven't drawn up any structured ways to upload to my blog — I'd feel much happier if I did have a bit of a clue about what we should be thinking about when reflecting.
>
> … I think this my problem with it so far — I can't see the joins — the relationship between practice or action and reflection is much more interleaved for me.

The student from whose blog we have taken the last quotation (from the set of 3 quotes given above) stopped using the blog for reflection after a month in the course and started using a structured template for reflection in a word-processor and storing the files/reflections in her on-line portfolio. However, she did realise the usage of a blog beyond reflection — as she said in her blog:

> … However I do hope to add a few entries to the blog just to keep me in touch with the technology.

Analysing her blog posts it has been clear that she perceived an audience of fellow-students who read her blog and she felt committed to them (the readers). At the end of the course, she posted a farewell message:

> … Thanks for listening over the past few weeks and sorry I didn't use you all that much, but reflection and me don't mix well!

Since one of the learning outcomes of the course was that the students should be able to 'evaluate specific technologies and their uses for learning and teaching,' we asked the students whether they would be employing blogging in their teaching and learning in future. This also helped us to assess whether the students perceived the role of blogging in their professional contexts (Q1b).

Students, who were teachers, did recognise the role of blogging in their role, for sharing experiences with colleagues, and specifically as a means of communication with students who are distance-learners and integrating blogging and podcasts:

> … It is a good tool for the teacher. It is a good means of communication because sometimes you think of some teaching improvements, you can write your thoughts to communicate to other people [colleagues]…..

> … I am always thinking of new possibilities …..I can record things in the podcasts and I can write the transcripts in my blog, or pieces of news, or dialogues. There are a lot of possibilities.

Some could see the potential of blogging as a tutor or teacher but were concerned about the effort involved to maintain it.

> … I thought I'd then keep one as a tutor and put useful stuff there. But it's just too much effort.

Some school-teachers could see the potential of blogging in keeping a project-log, for sharing and providing it as a repository for students:

> … At ICT A level, particularly as there's a lot of project development work and part of that is keeping a log of how a software development project works ….. I think the sharing is important…

> … Kids could use the blog for a collection of these [web-links], maybe an image, a paragraph an idea. With comments about it; we maybe have a class[group]-blog that everyone could add to at school or from home. So other children can see it and comment. It would create a rich tank of information.

Some educators in higher-education and students on the course felt that the public nature of the blogs might be an obstacle for their student-researchers, as they might be reluctant to blog on their research ideas.

No scientist will write without a restricted readership. They may be afraid they may leak their research results in their blog. One educator was finding it hard to convince her fellow-colleagues about the potential of blogging for their students:

> ... I am trying hard to get blogs where I work but it is difficult. They're [fellow-colleagues] not really interested, probably because they just don't get what it can do. ... they are worried about plagiarism.

7.3 Obstacles to blogging

This part of the analysis in our research programme relates to our research question (Q2b). Out of the 15 students that we analysed, 4 students didn't feel positive towards the blogging experience.

Hesitation of writing in a public space: One of them didn't feel comfortable with the public nature of blogging and writing in a public space. Another felt that learning logs are personal accounts of one's learning and that the course shouldn't suggest/prescribe the activities that a student should/could carry on in a blog. She also held the view that blog-posts shouldn't be assessed:

> ... I don't think that the institution should feel like it [learning log] belongs to them and I don't think they should tell you what to write in it. I know in some courses in the XXX [where I live] the students are given credit for writing blog entries. I don't think that's the correct way to approach a blog at all. They should be independent and come from the heart.

One student posted those reflections in the blog which she felt would be of interest to readers but chose to record personal reflections (which she was hesitant to share in a public space) in the e-portfolio:

> ... I also did some reflections in my e-portfolio. I wrote a kind of reflection about the problems I found in my portfolio [software], how I was improving, what I discovered that I knew. But that kind of reflection was private it was just for me. I thought that no one was going to read it, I did it for myself. I wrote in a kind of different way in the blog because [I] thought that some people were going to read it and were going to comment. Probably they were attracted by what I as saying.

Unclear role of blogging on the course: One student couldn't see the purpose of the blog and how it fitted within the course:

> ... I couldn't actually see what use it would have or how I would use it. I couldn't picture it as a major part of the course at all.

One student felt strongly that the courses with online components should provide guidance about the usage of these technologies:

> … Providing users with realistic expectations about the technology they are using, alternatives and workarounds in case of interrupted access is I think an important part of learning online. How else do we approach building resilience in learners and teachers to technological failures?

Lack of interpretability between the tools: In this course, the students were expected to collect evidence towards the various competencies into the e-portfolio for assessment. The students were unable to link to the various blog-posts — so they had to copy and paste from the blog into the e-portfolio and some student used workarounds, but this duplicated/additional effort was time-consuming and frustrating, and also one of the reasons for student to abandon blogging and instead create and assimilate the reflective accounts within the e-portfolio itself:

> … We couldn't put a link to our blog in the eportfolio. I had to take screenshots and paste it in. It was duplication.

> … I assumed that as a blog is an ongoing living thing, I could include it in my eportfolio. I was surprised to realise that I couldn't do that. Cutting and pasting seems feeble, you lose the whole atmosphere and nature of a blog.

Realising that porting or connecting to blog from within the portfolio is not possible, some students wrote their critical reviews of papers or personal reflections in a word-processor and then posted them on to both the blog and in the e-portfolio.

> … Some weeks we had to read some documents so I copied and pasted my critical review over to my blog. So some of my blog posts are quite formal. Sometimes I didn't know what to write.

> … I wrote them originally in a word doc as I knew I would have to upload it into my eportfolio. I did it like that because blog posts needed to be converted to word to go in the eportfolio anyway.

Unclear roles of the various tools on the course: Since the course guide mentioned blog as a personal learning journal, the students viewed it as a personal-space for their own learning, thinking, planning, note-taking, reflections and opinions. Further, the course doesn't prescribe that students should visit each other's blogs. The tutor was not expected to visit the blogs of his students. If the students had any queries or wanted to discuss a course-related concept, they preferred to post a message on a course-forum or the tutor-group-forum rather than creating a blog-post. In at least one tutor-group that we are aware of, students actually stopped blogging completely and discussed in the tutor-group forum of 15–18 students, as they were assured that the tutor will intervene and guide the discussions in the forum if required, but he was not expected to visit each individual blog which would anyway have resulted in disjointed discussions spread over several blogs.

The difficulty of having several technologies on a course is that tutors as well as students can find it hard to keep track of the information, discussions, and the knowledge being constructed in various tools. The other issue is that at the end of the course, the student was keen to take-away the course-resources provided by the course team and the knowledge that was created, shared, and stored during the course's tenure. Therefore, there was a technological challenge of how these materials can be exported as pdf. files or other formats for later use by the students.

7.4 Factors that influence blogging

Analysis of the data (primarily via interviews) for the third research question (Q3b) — 'which social and pedagogical factors and their inter-relationships influence blogging?' — has shown that there are four key factors and that the combination thereof influences the blogging behaviour. The four influencing factors are:

- perceptions of, and need for, an audience, that is, who do they perceive as their readers and does the fact that somebody might read their blog matters to them;
- perceptions of, and need for, community, that is, do they want to be or perceive to be a part of the community — e.g., self-help study group or a community of practice;
- comments from other bloggers, that is, are they expecting comments on the blog-posts?;
- presentation of the blog, that is, to what extent they care for aspects such as grammar, spelling, titles of the blog posts, careful proof-reading before posting, and referring to literature sources as per a particular style.

Two students regarded their audience as a potentially valuable resource of ideas, constructive criticism, and links to further resources. They conceptualised their blogs as being a collection of resources, ideas and thoughts, and in this way their blogs portrayed their views. Community was important to these students and they aimed to be part of as large a group as possible. They sought and welcomed comments from other people and found them beneficial:

> … Sometimes they [comments] gave me new ideas or different points of view about my thoughts.

These students said that they paid attention to checking their spelling and grammar as well as making sure that their posts made sense as they wanted to make their blogs places that others would want to visit.

Three students were extremely sociable and used their blogs to reach out to other members of a small, exclusive community of other students on the course that had evolved over time. All of these students used their blogs for academic purposes but also used blogging as a source of emotional support:

> … Without the blog I don't know where I would have been. I don't think I would have completed it actually. I think quite a few other people would say something similar. It is impossible to exaggerate the importance of the blog. … When I think in my mind, where did the course happen, predominantly the location was the collective blogging space.

They said that they were not inhibited by writing in a public space and often wrote for their audience, or at least bore them in mind; they adopted an informal, warm and friendly tone and were not overly concerned about checking their posts for grammar and spelling mistakes.. All three of these students explicitly addressed their audience in a variety of ways that made their blogs engaging, such as using writing techniques to draw readers in ("it's a bit long, don't be put off", and "read on if you want to discover more of my adventure"). These blogs represented not only the students' views in comparison to others, but also their emotional and personal lives as students.

There's always a danger with an online course that you get detached and lose interest and you can get to a stage where you say 'I don't need to do this, it's not school, I could stop' whereas the blog seemed to provide an outlet for those feelings. You could write down all your rants and raves and then carry on.

Comments were very important to these students; they wanted and expected comments and read them all:

> … If you're in a classroom nine times out of ten you realise there are other perspectives and one might be the one you want to pursue, rather than the one you originally had hold of. That same thing happens with blogging. That bit of it can't come out of you reflecting on your own learning, it becomes much much more richer, it's an extra layer of reflection [on top of your own].

This group of students said that not only were the comments useful for aiding their own understanding, they were also an important source of both academic and emotional support:

> … It helped me feel as if I wasn't struggling on my own, made me feel more connected.

There were four students who engaged in self-sufficient blogging practices. They stated explicitly that their blog was mainly for themselves and that their audience was not of great importance to them.

> … When you write a study blog it's very personal and you mainly write it for yourself, and any course-mates who might look in.

> … The blog was for me and not for anybody else. I could also demonstrate to my tutor that I was alive and working.

These students' blogs were personal and they did not expect or seek comments and rarely read or responded to any comments that they received. However, they were concerned with the presentation of their posts.

> … It was a bit alarming having the tutor come in and comment because it felt like a more private space. I though, oh I should have been more careful what I wrote. It was confidence boosting when people said nice things. I felt a bit irritated when someone asked a question or made a point I couldn't follow.

We found that there were four students for whom blogging caused various degrees of anxiety as they felt that their own inexperience as learners and users of technology, and their lack of confidence and potential incompetence would be revealed to others. They all expressed discomfort and varying degrees of self-consciousness about writing in public:

> … Blogs are very public and I don't like that. I don't believe that my work is of public interest.

The content of their blogs was usually well executed and formal and none of these students explicitly addressed their audience. They said that they did not seek involvement in the course community and reported that comments were useful but unexpected. Three of these students were less concerned with style and more concerned with controlling content. The third made sure her posts were "polished".

> … Potentially, I did leave some things out, because I was worried that I had not got the right end of the stick and didn't want to look stupid

There were two students that didn't blog as they couldn't find a purpose of blogging and its role in their learning. One of them seemed happy with their traditional techniques of learning logs:

> … I highlight and write pencil comments on paper documents…blogging is not very suitable and useful for me.

However, both of these students said that they did read other blogs and left occasional comments. The evaluations of the two case studies in Sections 5 and 7 have helped to identify the factors including obstacles that influence student's learning experience. In the next section, we summarise, along with some examples from the two case studies, the pedagogical, usability, and social factors which have emerged in these two case studies. Some of these factors are in fact generic and could be applicable to technology-enabled learning environments other than wikis and blogs. These factors relate to: (a) integrating the technology within the course; (b) clarifying the role of the technology within the pedagogy of the course to the students; (c) providing guidance about the usage of the technology and related social norms; (d) ensuring usability of the technology; and (e) designing for socialisation in on-line collaborations. The research outcomes will provide guidance to course designers and educators in the choice of the technologies and for the design of the activities for integrating these technologies within the pedagogy of their courses.

8. Discussion

Several lessons have emerged from the evaluation of the two case studies in this paper. We have learned that there are key success criteria for introduction, design, and implementation of technology-enabled learning. Examples of these criteria include direct link between the learning outcomes and the activities the technology will support on the course; clarifying the role of the technology to the students; considering the requirements of tutors and students before and after the implementation in terms of staff-development and guidance/support documents; ensuring that the technology is usable by conducting user-based evaluations before the technology is deployed; and ensuring that there is a provision for early socialisation in collaborative activities.

Integrating the technology within the pedagogy of the course and justifying its role to the students: On the RE course, it was challenging to introduce collaborative activities where students had worked through the course materials on their own on other courses in the programme. However, the course team emphasised the pedagogical role of the collaboration in learning and development of communication and team-working skills, as well as the importance of wiki-based collaboration for gaining transferable skills for industrial practice. This helped the students appreciate the role of wiki on the course and the benefits of collaboration. To further emphasise the role of wiki in RE and requirements development, readings (papers from conferences/journals) on global software engineering were included in the course materials.

Consequently, the evaluations have indicated positive student learning experiences in terms of understanding the course content and the process of collaboration: Students expressed in interviews and reflective accounts that wiki-based collaboration had facilitated their learning and that they became aware of the various issues and challenges of team-working in virtual teams in real-world software engineering projects. Their reflections of the process of collaboration (in their reflective answers in the TMA) enabled them to raise issues and propose solutions for effective virtual team collaboration: For example, synchronous communication should accompany asynchronous collaboration; need for 'roles' such as a facilitator, moderator and/or editor to manage the collaborations; and 'rules' or norms are required for effective participation and collaboration.

On the e-learning course, the students were aware (from the course description) that they will be evaluating various technologies in the context of their learning and teaching. The students used blogs in various ways but their usage of the blogs didn't match with the course team's intention of blogs as being reflective personal-learning journals. However, having used the blogs on this course or being introduced to the blogging made the students aware of the technology and their personal explorations have enabled them to devise strategies on how they would use blogs in their teaching. So in a way, the learning outcome — 'evaluate specific technologies and their uses of learning and teaching' — was achieved.

Guidance and supporting documents: On the RE course, guidance related to the usage of the tool, performance of collaborative activities in the wiki environment, social norms of collaboration, and the ways in which the individual contributions and group-work will be assessed was quite prescriptive and structured. As a result, there were no queries from students on the purpose of the tool, how to use it, and so on, and they could, therefore, concentrate on the collaborative activities and on the underlying course concepts.

In contrast, on the e-learning course, guidance on key pedagogical and technology-related aspects to the students and tutors was rather open-ended, limited and non-prescriptive. For example, apart from some web-based resources on reflection, there was no advice on the interpretation of reflection, role of reflective-learning, usage of blogs in reflective learning, and how blogging can be used in conjunction with other tools such as wikis and forums. The students were introduced to the tools and given some suggestions on the possible applications. For example, the course guide stated: "you will be encouraged to use personal blog (web log) as a learning journal to record and reflect upon your course activities, professional practices and development needs as you progress through the course."

The students on the e-learning course seemed to struggle with some fundamental aspects such as how to reflect on learning and the benefits of reflection. The suggestions of reflecting in a blog and using blog as a personal journal in the course material raised further concerns for some students — especially related to the public nature of the blogs. Our interviews of tutors provided further insights of student-concerns: Although the tutors felt that the fast-pace of the course could have been one of the reasons that students didn't reflect effectively, they felt that course teams need to provide more guidance on reflection; reflection should have been tightly defined, and guidance on reflective-learning via blogging should have been given. As the tutors mentioned in the interviews to us, that samples/case-studies of reflective accounts would have further helped the students.

Reflecting in a personal diary is different from reflecting in a public space. Therefore, if the course team had intended the blogs to be reflective on-line diaries, students would have benefited from guidance on how to reflect in a public space; should they invite comments and ideas, who is their audience; are they expected to build a community or be a part of the community?; and how individual reflection in a personal journal is different from group reflection with fellow-students in a blog?

Our empirical investigations have revealed that one of the tutors on the e-learning course kept a regular watch on all the blogs of students in his tutor-group (he had book-marked all the blogs), while another tutor felt that looking at the student's blog would be like trespassing in somebody's personal space and so she never visited any of her students' blogs. Yet another tutor was unsure what her role was and, therefore, left it to her students to prompt her if they wanted her to look at her blog post. Therefore, guidance to tutors on the intended learning outcomes, how blogs should be used by the students and monitored/commented by the tutors, and the clarity in expectations from tutors would be helpful for consistent support to the entire cohort of students on the course.

Ensuring usability of the technology: As with every technology, usability is a key attribute for a positive user experience. As we have seen in the wiki case study, poor usability of an educational technology can over-shadow the pedagogy and disrupt the learner experience. Almost all the usability obstacles with the wiki tool discussed in this paper have since been addressed by the OU's VLE team.

Designing for socialisation in on-line collaborations: In both these courses, the students did not meet face-to-face. It is only through online socialisation activities that the students get to know one another. This socialisation is required to facilitate networking, group-working, peer-reviewing and peer-critiquing and commenting. Since both the courses have a short presentation period (around 5 months), there is little time to allow students to engage in essential socialisation activities. Ehrlich and Chang (2006) state that co-ordination of work in distributed teams is accomplished through spontaneous informal communication and an important precursor to informal communication is awareness of other team members: What they are doing, and when they would be available for collaborative work. Although the ice-breaker activities that we have suggested or discussed may help in developing 'awareness' of one another in both the courses that we have analysed, the duration of the two courses may not be sufficient for the development of trust and shared understanding.

Face-to-face communication can promote relationship building (Peters and Manz 2007) and can generally help expedite negotiations and decision-making. Face-to-face meetings are not feasible in these distance-education courses, so at the OU we are considering generating the sense of presence of fellow-learners in the virtual space through real-time interactions within a 3-D multi-user virtual environment (MUVE). 3-D MUVEs provide virtual worlds which have avatars (digital surrogates) that move around within the digital world and interact with others and with the objects in real-time in a virtual environment. Second Life (www.secondlife.com) is an example of 3-D MUVE which can offer realism, immersion and interaction, and a sense of presence for the 'avatars' which may facilitate relationship-building which is an antecedent for effective operation of a virtual team. The OU is planning to set up work-spaces and activities in Second Life (SL) for real-time interactions such as: Ice-breaking tasks; holding meetings in SL and making notes/keeping records of transcripts of conversations in SL (for reporting in TMAs); and attending live events in SL. Other synchronous technologies that could be considered are audio or web conferencing tools such as Lyceum (http://lyceum.open.ac.uk, last accessed 13th March 2008) and Elluminate (http://www.elluminate.com/, last accessed 13th March 2008) for real-time interaction and early socialisation in the course.

To address the problem that the students faced in scheduling time for collaborative activities, the next cohort of students have been asked to consider a simple meeting scheduler (e.g., http://www.meetomatic.com/calendar.php, last accessed 15th March, 2008), to plan a schedule for collaboration and synchronous communication.

We are continuing to monitor the students' experiences with technology-enabled learning through an iterative cycle of feedback-improvement-evaluation. The feedback is being collected through interviews, formal university end-of-course surveys and reflective accounts of students to evaluate how effective the technologies are in meeting the learning objectives and the students' expectations. We intend to present our further evaluations in future publications.

Notes

1. The Q1w, Q2w, …, refer to research questions related to the wiki case study.
2. The Q1b, Q2b, …, refer to research questions related to the blog case study.

References

Bartlett-Bragg, A. 2003. "Blogging to learn". Available online at: http://knowledgetree.flexiblelearning.net.au/edition04/html/blogging_to_learn_intro.html (last accessed 13th March, 2008).

Bruns, A. and Humphreys, S. 2005. "Wikis in teaching and assessment: The M/Cyclopedia project". Presented at WikiSym'05, ACM 1-59593-111-2/05/0010, 25–32.

Burgess, J. 2006. "Blogging to learn, learning to blog". In B. Axel, and J. Jacobs (eds), *Uses of Blogs*. New York: Peter Lang, 105–115.

Damian, D. 2007. "Stakeholders in global Requirements Engineering: Lessons learned from practice". *IEEE Software* 24(2): 21–27.

Daudelin, M.W. 1996. "Learning from experience through reflection". *Organizational Dynamics* 24(3): 36–48.

Decker, B., Ras, E., Rech, J., Jaubert, P., and Rieth, M. 2007. "Wiki-based stakeholder participation in Requirements Engineering," *IEEE Software* 3(2): 28–35.

Dougiamas, M.1998. "A journey into constructivism". Available online at: http://dougiamas.com/writing/constructivism.html#social (last accessed 13th March, 2008).

Du, H.S. and Wagner, C. 2007. "Learning with weblogs: Enhancing cognitive and social knowledge construction". *IEEE Transactions on Professional Communication* 50(1): 1–15.

Ehrlich, K. and Chang, K. 2006. "Leveraging expertise in global software teams: Going outside boundaries". *IEEE International Conference on Global Software Engineering* (ICGSE'06), 149–159.

Farmer, J. 2006. "Blogging to basics: How blogs are bringing online learning back from the brink", in B. Axel and J. Jacobs, (eds) *Uses of Blogs*. New York: Peter Lang, 91–105.

Farrell, J. 2006. "Wikis, blogs and other community tools in the enterprise". Available online at: www-128.ibm.com/developerworks/library/wa-wikiapps.html (last accessed 13th March, 2008).

Friske, M. and John, M. 2007. "Transforming ideas into requirements". Position Paper at the Second International Workshop on Multimedia Requirements Engineering (MeRE'07), Hamburg, 27th March.

Glaser, B.G. and Strauss, A.L. 1967. *The Discovery of Grounded Theory: Strategies for Qualitative Research*. New York: Aldine Publishing Company.

Homik M. and Melis E. 2006. "Using blogs for learning logs". *Proceedings of ePortfolio* (Oxford). Available online at http://www.activemath.org/pubs/HomikMelis-ep2006.pdf (last accessed 15th March, 2008).

Huann T., John O. and Yuen J. 2005. "Weblogs in education, a literature review". Availabe online at http://edublog.net/mt4/2005/09/weblogs-in-educ.html (last accessed 15th March, 2008).

Horizon Report from EDUCAUSE Connect. 2007. Available online at http://connect.educause.edu/library/abstract/2007HorizonReport/37041 (last accessed 13th March, 2008).

Krause, S.D., 2004. "When blogging goes bad: A cautionary tale about blogs, email lists, discussion, and interaction". Kairos 9(1). Available online at http://english.ttu.edu/kairos/9.1/binder.html?praxis/krause/index.html (last accessed 13th March, 2008).

Louridas, P. 2006. "Using wikis in software development". *IEEE Software* 3(2): 88–91.

Minocha, S., Schencks, M., Sclater, N., Thomas, P., and Hause, M. 2007. "Collaborative learning in a wiki environment: Case study of a requirements engineering course". *Proceedings of the European Distance and E-learning Network (EDEN) Annual Conference — on 'NEW LEARNING 2.0? Emerging digital territories, Developing continuities, New divides'*, Naples.

Available online at http://www.eden-online.org/eden.php?menuId=353&contentId=587. (last accessed 9th June, 2008).

Mortensen, T. and Walker, J. 2002. "Blogging thoughts: Personal publication as an online research tool". In A. Morrison (ed.) *Researching ICTs in Context, InterMedia Report*; Oslo, 249–279.

Nardi, B.A., Schiano, D.J., Gumbrecht, M., and Swartz, L. 2004. "Why we blog". *Communications of ACM* 47(12): 41–46.

Oravec, J.A. 2003. "Blending by blogging: Weblogs in blended learning initiatives", *Journal of Educational Media*, vol. 28, no. 2–3, 225–233.

Parker, K.R. and Chao, J.T. 2007. "Wiki as a teaching tool," *Interdisciplinary Journal of Knowledge and Learning Objects*, 3, 57–72.

Peters, L.M. and Manz, C. 2007. "Identifying antecedents of virtual team collaboration," *Team Performance Management*, vol. 13, no. 3/4,117–129.

Robertson, S. and Robertson, J. 2006. *Mastering the Requirements Process*, Massachusetts, Addison-Wesley.

Schneider, D.K., Synteta, P., Frete, C., and Girardin, S. 2003. "Conception and implementation of rich pedagogical scenarios through collaborative portal sites: Clear focus and fuzzy edges", paper presented at the International Conference on Open and Online Learning, University of Mauritius.

Williams, J. and Jacobs, J. 2004. "Exploring the use of blogs as learning spaces in the higher education sector" *Australasian Journal of Educational Technology*, vol. 20, no. 2, 232–247.

Wilson, S. 2005. "Can web service technology really help enable 'coherent diversity' in e-learning?" http://www.elearning.ac.uk/features/pedagandws (last accessed 18th March, 2008).

Software-realized inquiry support for cultivating a disciplinary stance*

Iris Tabak and Brian J. Reiser
Ben Gurion University of the Negev / Northwestern University

What role can technology play in cultivating a disciplinary stance — raising questions, planning investigations, interpreting data and constructing explanations in a way that reflects disciplinary values and principles? How can overt and tacit expert scientific knowledge be captured, represented and used to design software that enables novices to assume a disciplinary stance in their investigations? We present *The Galapagos Finches* software designed to foster a biological and evolutionary stance. Our approach, Discipline-Specific Strategic Support (DSSS), translates the main variable types, comparison types and relationships in a discipline into manipulable objects in the interface. Pre/post-tests show how DSSS helps achieve a balance between content and process goals. A contrastive-case microanalysis of high, medium and low-achieving students' inquiry shows progress toward a disciplinary stance. Our study shows how software representations carry multiple levels of meaning, and that the efficacy of learning technologies hinges on reflection at both the navigation and disciplinary-signification levels.

Keywords: computer-based learning environments, content, discipline-specific, evolution, inquiry, representation, science, socio-cultural environment, software design

1. Introduction

Increasingly, subject matter learning is becoming associated with mastering and appropriating (Wertsch 1998) ways of communicating and acting according to the norms of particular communities of practice (Palincsar 1998). Thus, it subsumes aspects that go beyond visible and explicit knowledge, such as the accumulation of facts and the honing of skills, to such tacit aspects as the values that dictate what evidence will be garnered, and which conclusions will be most valued. For example, in mathematics, there is an attempt to cultivate socio-mathematical norms

(Cobb, Perlwitz, and Underwood Gregg 1998; Lampert 1990) that distinguish between "correct" solutions by valuing some over others as "more elegant" and consquently more mathematical and desirable.

This type of knowledge is context or community dependent. For example, the *same* graph can be differentially but "correctly" interpreted by scientists in different fields. Some may attend to the minima or maxima depicted in the graph, while others may attend to the shape of the curve, depending on the knowledge goals that are valued in their respective fields, such as valuing ecological realism or valuing descriptions of stable and unstable equilibria (Bowen, Roth, and McGinn 1999). Possessing this knowledge reflects pragmatic understanding, because in communicative acts among scientists the particular course of interpretation is implicitly understood, despite an awareness of alternatives. This means that professional expertise includes such pragmatic competence, and that cultivating expertise among novices should include instruction that fosters this understanding.

In this paper, we are concerned with the question of how to cultivate this understanding among young science learners. In particular, we are interested in exploring the role of learning technologies in this process. Research in language socialization suggests that through repeated use of language in practice children develop pragmatic understanding (Garrett and Baquedano-Lopez 2002; Geer, Tulviste, Mizera, and Tryggvason 2002; Schieffelin and Ochs 1986). Similarly, working side by side with experts, novices develop the pragmatic understanding of their profession (Goodwin 1994; Hobbs 2004). Here we ask: What role can technology play in enculturating initiates into a community of practice? Can learning technologies be designed to fulfill some of the roles traditionally assumed by more established members of the community in fostering pragmatic understanding through joint practice?

Thus, we asked how can overt and tacit expert scientific knowledge be represented and used to design software tools. These tools would need to accomplish many goals. They would need to provide an environment in which authentic scientific investigations could be pursued, and they would need to help novices manage the complexity involved in real-world investigations. Moreover, in line with our goals of fostering pragmatic understanding, they would need to help novices assume what we call a *disciplinary stance*: An understanding of the type of explanations that prevail in a discipline, and an ability to incorporate these disciplinary considerations in studying and explaining natural phenomena.

We present a design approach, *Discipline-Specific Strategic Support*[1] *(DSSS)* (Tabak 1999; Tabak, Smith, Sandoval, and Reiser 1996) aimed at fostering a disciplinary stance. We also present a computer-based inquiry environment, *The Galapagos Finches* (Tabak, Reiser, Sandoval, Leone, and Steinmuller 2001), which was developed using this approach, and is intended to help students develop a biological and evolutionary stance. We open our discussion with the theoretical underpinnings for cultivating a disciplinary stance. Next, we describe the DSSS approach and the Galapagos Finches software. We present findings from two years of classroom studies that illustrate the role that such software can play in cultivating a disciplinary stance, and discuss the implications for the design of learning technologies.

2. A Disciplinary Stance

2.1 Disciplinary stance: An example

Suppose you were investigating a decline in a population of finches on a Galapagos island, and you conjectured that the finches were dying due to an increase in predation. You could compare observations of the number of owls on the island before the finch decline and during the finch decline. You could conduct a pellet analysis on the owls' pellets, and you could compare the number of lizards (the owls' other prey) before and during the finch decline. Assume your data showed that the number of owls increased, that the number of lizards remained about the same, and that there were lizard and finch bones in the owls' pellets.

Would you have a convincing case? If you were speaking to an audience of biologists, it seems that you would have a convincing case. You showed that there is an inverse relationship between the number of finches and the number of owls, and you showed a possible causal relationship between the decrease in the finch population and the increase in the owl population. You also refuted alternatives by showing that something that could account for the number of owls increasing without affecting the number of finches did not hold (i.e., showing that there was not a decrease in the number of lizards).

In order to successfully negotiate this problem it was necessary to focus on a number of variables and relationships out of the myriad of possibilities. However, in order to produce an explanation that was not just sensible, but was sensible to a particular audience, it was important to know what types of explanations are valued in that community. In the example above, we employed the general strategy of *making comparisons to look for changes and relationships*, but we used the biology-specific form of the strategy by *making comparisons across time in the predator of the organism of focus*. The decision to make this particular comparison out of the many possible comparisons would be an obvious choice to an audience of biologists, as would be the implied knowledge claims. It is the knowledge of the role that time and predator-prey relationships play in the mechanism of natural selection, and the ability to subsume this knowledge into the application of general investigation strategies, such as comparisons, that constitutes a disciplinary stance.

2.2 Sociocultural and cognitive warrants for the notion of disciplinary stance

A disciplinary stance characterizes the performance of established members of a community of practice. It reflects the unwritten rules of a discipline. Its existence is more discernabile when comparing the practice of different fields than when observing scientists within a single field. For example, Knorr-Cetina (1996) claims that different scientific fields, such as high energy physics or molecular biology, are distinguished on many levels, in their orientation toward the use of signs, their framing of questions and their criteria for knowledge claims.

Similarly, in a study of oceanographers, Goodwin (1995) noted that he, as an outsider to the community of oceanographers, could not detect features of interest to the oceanographers. He notes that in order to attend to these features one must be equipped with the "interpretive structures that locate particular phenomena as relevant and interesting," which are derived from, and honed through membership in a community of practitioners. He calls this type of "insider" knowledge *Professional Vision* (Goodwin 1994), an idea very similar to what we refer to here as a disciplinary stance.

From a cognitive perspective, a disciplinary stance can be viewed as the intersection between investigation strategies and disciplinary knowledge. In an investigation, the choice of variables and types of observations influences the conclusions that can be derived from these observations (Schauble, Glaser, Raghavan, and Reiner 1991). At the same time, knowledge of a topic or setting influences the choice of variables, observations and data interpretations (Klahr and Dunbar 1988). Therefore, disciplinary knowledge can help to identify the variables and observations that are most valued in a particular discipline, and consequently lead to the generation of more disciplinary knowledge.

In his interpretation of studies of expert physicists (i.e., Chi, Feltovich, and Glaser 1981; Larkin 1983), Greeno (1983) argues that expert problem solving includes the availability of domain-dependent conceptual entities as arguments for general methods of reasoning. In a study conducted by Schauble and colleagues (1991), students who had more knowledge of electric circuitry, *as well as* more sophisticated investigation strategies, were better able to uncover rules governing the performance of electrical circuits. Studies of both experts and successful novices (Klahr, Fay, and Dunbar 1993; Schauble 1990, 1996) provide converging evidence that effective inquiry is characterized by an integration of disciplinary knowledge and investigation skills.

We see that both cognitive and sociocultural perspectives point to the notion of a disciplinary stance — a shared propensity to focus on particular questions, attend to particular concerns and utilize particular ways of reasoning — as a characterizing feature of established members of scientific communities of practice.

Further, they suggest that developing competence in a discipline involves the appropriation of such a stance.

3. Discipline-specific strategic support (DSSS): Technological support for cultivating a disciplinary stance

As we have noted, our aim was to develop learning technologies that help young science learners develop a disciplinary stance as well as scientific knowledge and skills. Learning technologies play an increasing role in science teaching. Yet, their role in helping students negotiate scientific data is better understood than their role in scientific socialization.

Learning technologies are key in presenting students with rich problems and engaging them in critical data analysis and synthesis (Bell, Davis, and Linn 1995; Jackson, Stratford, Krajcik, and Soloway 1994; Snir, Smith, and Grosslight 1995; White and Frederiksen 1995). Learning technologies can import into the classroom inquiry-contexts, which otherwise would not be available to students. For example, they can provide real time dynamic data (e.g., Gomez, Fishman, and Pea 1998; Songer 1996), provide observations of data from distant sites (e.g., Bell et al. 1995; Tabak et al. 1996), or make normally invisible processes visible (e.g., White 1993). Learning technologies can engage students in scientific analyses that might otherwise be too difficult for them, by providing simplified versions of scientific tools (e.g., Edelson, Gordin, and Pea 1997; Jackson et al. 1994). Technological tools can offer a means for viewing, filtering, organizing, and labeling information so that they create a balance between furnishing students with a sophisticated dataset and helping them manage this complexity (Blumenfeld et al. 1991; Loh 1997; Tabak and Reiser 1997). In addition, software prompts can encourage students to take actions that they are not inclined to take spontaneously, such as reflecting on how a collection of data can warrant a specific argument (Davis 1996; Loh et al. 1997; Sandoval 2003, 2004).

Studies that consider learning technologies in terms of scientific socialization tend to discuss technological tools as focal points in transformative conversations (Pea 1992; Roth 1995), or as venues for discussion (O'Neill 2001). Less research has focused on learning technologies as purveyors of cultural knowledge. In this study, we developed an approach we call *Discipline-specific strategic support (DSSS)* that is intended to explicitly represent cultural knowledge.

In developing DSSS we consult with subject matter experts, develop pseudo task analyses based on scientific reports, and synthesize studies of students' conceptions in order to derive an *investigation model* (Tabak et al. 1996). An investigation model makes a field's disciplinary stance explicit by noting some of the implicit strategies used by experts in the domain. The components of the model propose ways to recognize and interpret patterns that are privileged in the discipline. It includes the core concepts and assumptions of a discipline, and the set of strategies available to investigate phenomena of interest within that discipline.

Designing DSSS involves using the investigation model to design interfaces that focus students on key variables and relationships in the discipline. Both overt and tacit expert investigation strategies are rendered visible and accessibe to students by making them into objects students can manipulate in the software. For example, "compare variation in physical characteristics between survivors and casualties", which is a helpful strategy in studying natural selection in the wild, would be an action students could perform by making a menu selection or other interface manipulation. In this way, DSSS is a form of software-realized scaffolding (Guzdial 1994), that is, software supports that enable a novice to accomplish tasks that he or she would not be able to accomplish independently.

In the next section we describe software we developed to support investigations of natural selection in the wild, which incorporates discipline-specific strategic support. We describe the investigation model we developed for this type of investigation, and how this model is reified in the design of the analytical tools and software scaffolds.

4. The Galapagos Finches software: Instantiating DSSS in the context of natural selection in the wild

4.1 Evolution — a test case

The topic of evolution provided an interesting test case for our approach. Evolution is a central component of scientific literacy goals (AAAS 1993; NRC 1996; NSTA 1996), and a driving theory in contemporary biology (Dobzhansky 1973). Yet, many students persist in maintaining alternative conceptions, even after instruction (Bishop and Anderson 1990; Clough and Wood-Robinson 1985; Pedersen and Hallden 1994; Settlage 1994). Choosing to have students learn a conceptually difficult topic through inquiry provided fertile ground in which to explore the role of learning technologies in cultivating a disciplinary stance. The pervasive discrepancy between students' ideas and scientific ideas concerning evolution suggest that students' attempts at inquiry will not resemble those of practicing scientists. We were interested in finding out whether our approach encouraged students to broach their investigations in a way that brought the concerns of evolutionary biologists to bear on the particular episode they were investigating.

4.2 The Galapagos Finches problem context

In this problem scenario students investigate microevolution on a Galapagos island. It is based on a longitudinal study of finches on the island Daphne Major (Grant 1986). This study and the scientists' work is documented and richly described in a trade book, *The Beak of the Finch* (Weiner 1994). In the problem scenario, students are asked to explain why a population of finches are suffering a severe decline in population, and why the finches that survive are able to survive. Although this is not presented to the students, the currently accepted scientific explanation states that due to a drought the finches' normal food resources, which consist of soft seeds and fruits, were depleted. The remaining resource were seeds encased in a large thorny shell. Finches with a slightly larger (deeper) beak were better able to crack this shell open and obtain the seeds, and therefore were more likely to survive.

Our goal was to design a software environment that would provide students access to some of the primary data that would have been available had they conducted the field study themselves. In determining the scope of data we relied on pilot studies in which we presented students with the top level problem, and noted the range of hypotheses they raised and the inquiry paths they suggested. The analytical tools used to gather, analyze and synthesize these primary data sources are structured according to the investigation model we developed for investigating natural selection in the wild. These are described following the presentation of the investigation model below.

4.3 An investigation model for natural selection in the wild

Constructing a natural selection explanation involves identifying pressures exerted on an organism, evaluating the variability of traits in terms of the ability to withstand these pressures, and examining the changing proportions of these traits in the population (Bloom 1988; Endler 1986; Grant 1986; Weiner 1994).

Biologists make use of comparisons (Clutton-Brock and Harvey 1984) to examine these issues. They compare observations across time, individuals and populations, noting changes and trends. Constructing an explanation involves moving from a description of temporal changes to articulating causal relationships, most prominently, structure-function relationships, and pressure to adaptive trait relationships.

These relationships combine to tell a causal story of how a trait enables a behavior that is effective in withstanding a particular pressure. These conceptual tasks that evolutionary biologists undertake in order to explain an episode of natural selection in the wild are delineated as a set of observational actions, comparison actions, relate actions and explanation actions, as described in Table 1.

Table 1. Investigation model for natural selection in the wild

General strategy	How it is employed from a disciplinary stance
Observe	– Look for structural or behavioral variation between/within species and for environmental dependencies that could lead to a selection pressure.
Compare	– Compare environmental conditions across time to identify selective pressures. – Compare behavior of individuals across time to identify changes that could indicate that they are under stress. – Compare variation in structural characteristics between animals that die and animals that survive to identify advantageous traits. – Compare variation in behavioral characteristics between animals that die and animals that survive to identify advantageous traits. – Compare distribution of structural traits across time to see if there are changes in the distribution of a particular trait in the population.
Relate	– Relate structure to function to identify why/how particular traits might be advantageous or disadvantageous.
Explain	– Explain the adaptive value of characteristics in terms of selection pressures and genetic fitness.

Table 1 shows how general strategies (column 1) are instantiated within the stance of a particular discipline, in this case natural selection in the wild (column 2).

4.4 Enabling novices to investigate from a disciplinary stance: Reflecting the investigation model in software tools and prompts

The investigation model specified the types of actions which students needed to perform: Observation, comparison and relationship construction.[2] In addition, it delineated the parameters on which these actions operate: Physical characteristics and behavior as variables, and individuals, populations and time as dimensions along which these variables are to be compared. The next two sub-sections describe how we translated this into software tools and interface representations.

4.4.1 *Observe and compare: Constructing questions that reflect a disciplinary stance*

The software tools that enable students to generate and analyze data are designed to draw their attention to the central comparisons noted in the investigation model. Data requests are made through a question-based interface, where students construct questions by first selecting a question header from a list of options, and then selecting a question stem from another list of options. The question headers are a list of comparison categories, and the question stems are a list of variable categories (see Figure 1).

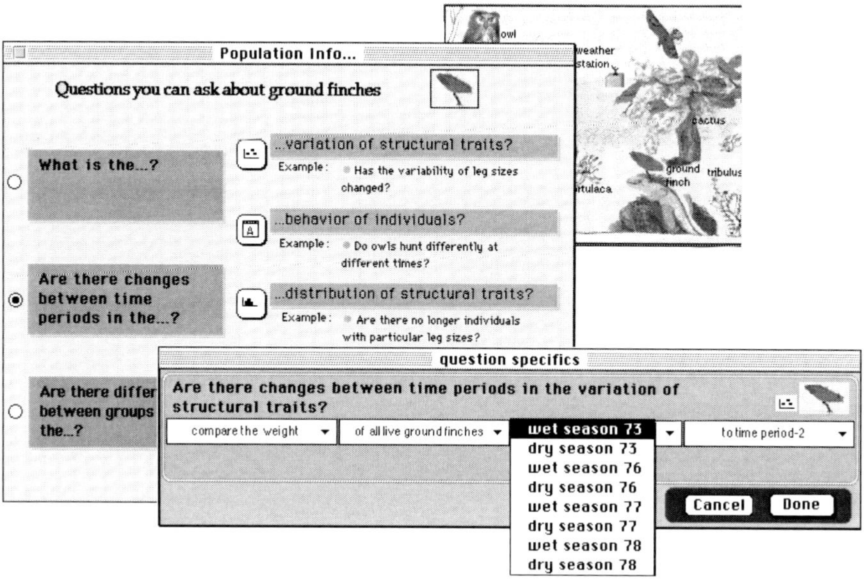

Figure 1. Discipline-specific question-based data query

The larger boxes in the left hand side of the window titled "Population Info..." in Figure 1 list the comparison types: Comparison across time and comparison between groups (e.g., survivors and casualties) which are key comparisons in identifying relationships that explain natural selection processes. The boxes in the right hand side of this same window list the variable types: Variation of structural characteristics, behavior of individuals, distribution of structural traits, and relationship between structural traits (obscured in Figure 1).

An example completed question is "Are there changes between time periods in the variation of structural traits?". Once a question has been constructed a dialogue appears displaying the general form of the question, and prompting students to specify particular parameters (the window titled "question specifics" in Figure 1). For example, students can specify that they want to examine the particular trait of weight, of all the live finches between the dry season of 1976 and the dry season of 1977.

As a result of this example query a graph appears displaying individual weight values of each of the live finches for each of the two specified time periods, dry season of 1976 and dry season of 1977 (see Figure 2). Students can make comparisons of the aggregate data, such as the population mean, depicted in this view, and directly access profiles for individual birds through graphs generated from this comparison. Profiles are cross-referenced to field notes showing behavioral descriptions of finches, such as descriptions of finches' foraging and mating behaviors (see Figure 2).

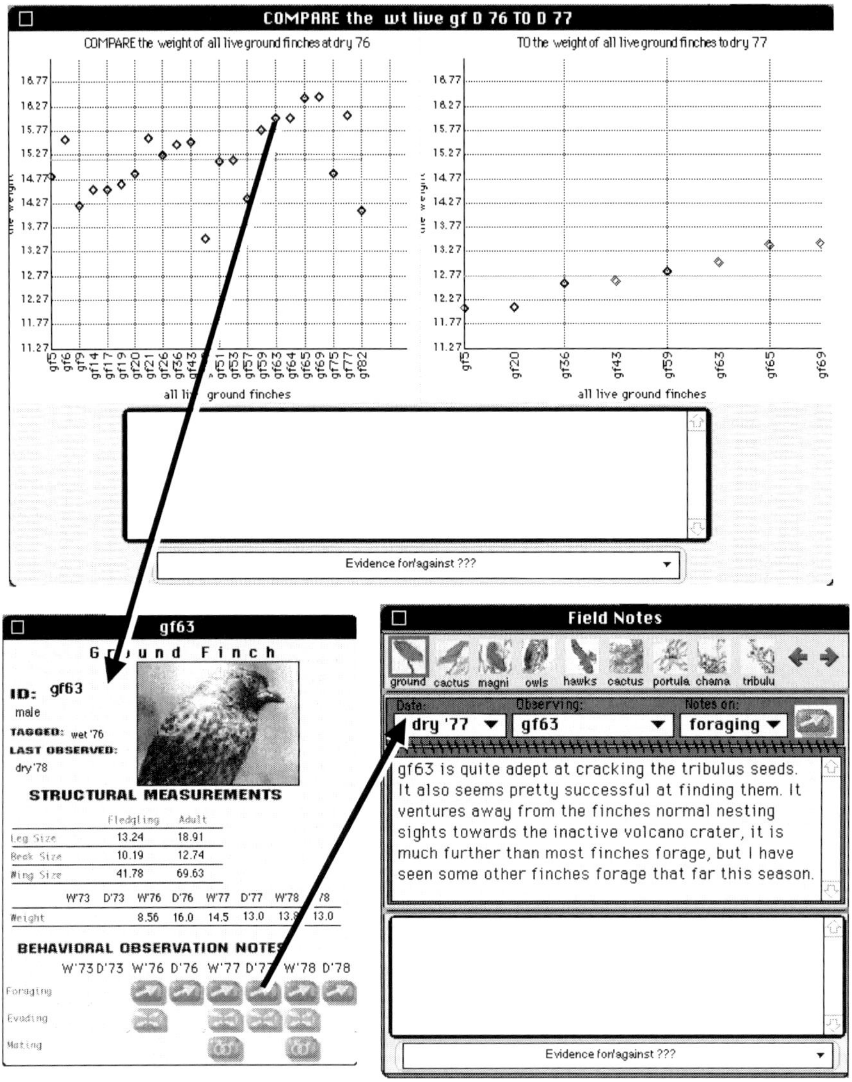

Figure 2. Multiple sources and levels of data: Aggregate and individual, physical and behavioral

This type of design helps students to focus on how they can use the data to explore hypotheses, rather than on the type of data display (e.g., scatter plot or histogram), which is often the focus of generic analysis tools. Thus, in discipline-specific strategic support different inquiry goals are represented as different actions in the system, which can help students learn to connect particular comparisons with particular inquiry goals.

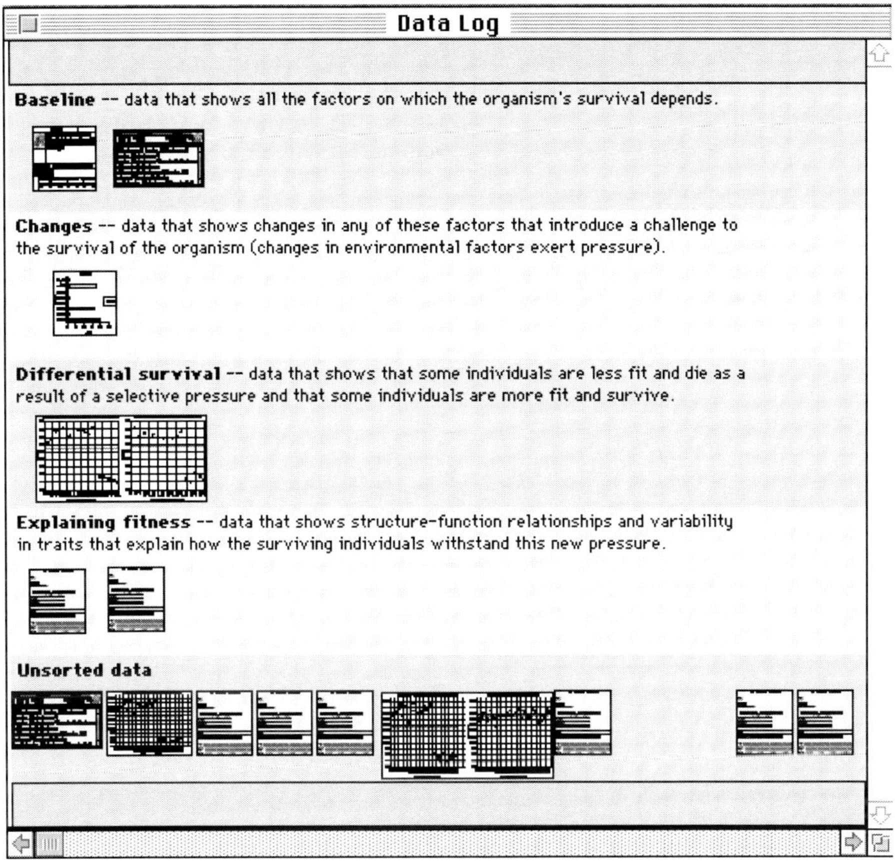

Figure 3. The data log: Sorting evidence by discipline-specific categories

4.4.2 *Reflect and relate: Categorizing evidence from a disciplinary stance*

The Galapagos Finches Software includes a Data Log (see Figure 3) that helps students manage the complexity of the investigation by organizing the data they collect according to evidence categories, which are provided by the system, and are derived from the investigation model for investigating natural selection in the wild. Any observation students make is automatically stored in the data log under the "unsorted" category (last row in the data log window in Figure 3). Students can categorize a piece of data either in the data log directly by dragging the thumbnail of the data into the desired slot (row), or when viewing the data by using a pull down menu listing these categories. Deciding how to categorize a particular piece of evidence encourages students to reflect on the relationship of individual data to the overall goal of the investigation. In particular, it focuses students on the argumentative goals of investigating natural selection.

4.5 DSSS: Software as an agent in enculturation processes

We have described how The Galapagos Finches software presents students with a set of tools for analyzing and synthesizing primary data in a way that connotes a disciplary stance — the tacit and overt concerns and perspectives of evolutionary field biologists. As students work with the Galapagos Finches software and consider what observations they would like to make they are continually confronted with concepts such as "comparisons across time", "comparisons between survivors and casualties", "variation of structural traits", and "differences in behavior". These types of concerns and perspectives are what one would expect to permeate the interactions of newcomers and oldtimers as they engage, side-by-side, in the day-to-day practices of the community (Lave and Wenger 1991). In the Galapagos Finches, as the students make conjectures and query data, the structure of the environment fashions these actions and sense-making to conform with the mold of the disciplinary framework, creating a dynamic similar to the ways in which pragmatic knowledge is gained through language socialization (Schieffelin and Ochs 1986).

4.6 DSSS against the backdrop of the challenges of inquiry-based science learning

Traditional curricula that break skills down to discrete components and that rely on rote learning have been criticized for producing inert knowledge where learners are unable to apply their knowledge outside of instructional settings (e.g., Bransford, Brown, and Cocking 2000). In addition, such curricula typically do not foster an appreciation for the norms, values and habits of mind that characterize a discipline. Therefore, contemporary research calls for creating learning environments in which students grapple with real-world complex problems that reflect authentic professional practice (Bransford et al. 2000; Chinn and Malhotra 2002; NRC 2000). Paradoxically, the knowledge and skills necessary for negotiating such problems are precisely the knowledge and skills that these problems are intended to foster. This creates the challenge of creating learning environments that are complex enough to offer these types of veridical experiences, yet provide sufficient scaffolding so that students do not flounder unproductively.

Conducting investigations in ways that are consistent with scientific methods is not a simple or intuitive feat. Studies examining novices' and students' self directed experimentation processes show that they have trouble monitoring their progress, and relating findings to hypotheses (Klahr, Dunbar, and Fay 1990; Kuhn, Schauble, and Garcia-Mila 1992; Schauble et al. 1991; Shute and Glaser 1991). Students do not make extensive use of comparisons and find it difficult to setup comparisons that will yield informative results (Krajcik et al. 1998; Schauble and Glaser

1990; Schauble, Glaser, Duschl, Shulze, and John 1995; Schauble et al. 1991). So, the challenge of creating appropriate scaffolding is to provide cues and structure that will compensate for novices' limited knowledge and skills without depriving them of control and autonomy.

Inquiry-based science learning also poses a challenge for content learning. Inquiry-based learning is similar to case-based or problem-based learning where students learn a topic by examining specific, real-world cases. Such an approach can contribute to more integrated understanding of principles, and a deeper appreciation for the ways in which theoretical principles apply to reality (Kolodner 1997; Williams 1992). However, there are also some barriers to learning associated with this approach. One limitation is that the set of principles that are manifest in any one natural episode are usually only a subset of the set of principles called for in national and state learning standards (Marx et al. 1994). Another limitation is that students may be so immersed in the particulars of the episode they investigate that they do not reflect on the implications and connections to the underlying principles of the discipline. In fact, one of the main critiques of inquiry-based learning is that process learning comes at the expense of content learning (Von Secker and Lissitz 1999).

5. The present study: The role of software-realized scaffolding in cultivating a disciplinary stance in science classrooms

In this paper, we examine whether software tools can be used to reify norms and practices of experts in order to help learners adopt a disciplinary stance. We report on two years of classroom studies in 9th grade biology classes conducted as part of the broader Biology Guided Inquiry Learning Environments (BGuILE) project (e.g., Reiser et al. 2001). Our research design strategy included a multi-faceted analysis of one, archetypical classroom, and a comparison of this archetype to two other classrooms where a narrower analysis was conducted. We wanted to understand how a myriad of verbal, material and technological supports in a typical classroom cotribute to content and process learning. We also wanted to understand the range of interactions and learning trajectories that are possible by exploring the enacted curriculum in an honors, regular and low-track class.

One of our central assumptions concerning the nature of learning is that it is a gradual process cultivated through cognitive, social and material tools (Collins, Brown, and Newman 1989; Tabak 1999; Wertsch 1998). We posit that it is important that software environments, like the one we presented here, be seamlessly integrated within a synergistic system of supports (Tabak 2004). Limiting our present discussion to the software is for analytical clarity.

We present findings from two sources of evidence that help us understand the role that DSSS plays in cultivating a disciplinary stance. The first, is a pre/post-test that provides an index for the aggregate changes in the archetypical students' ability to recognize normative explanations of evolutionary phenomena, and to recognize the significance of particular observation types for studying animal survival. The second is a contrastive-case microanalysis of the inquiry processes of a focus group from each participating classroom: A group of high, medium, and low achieving students.

6. Methods

This study was conducted in three 9th grade introductory biology classrooms in three different schools, referred to as North '97, City '97 and West '98. Each class participated in a five week unit on evolution which we designed. The unit consisted of novel activities designed by our research group as well as published activities commonly used by our participating teachers. Table 2 shows each of the unit activities.

Table 2. Summary of activities in the Galapagos Finches evolution unit

Activity	Time[a]	Principles	Type of Activity
Intro	1–2	learning goals, overview of theory of natural selection	
Variation Lab	1	variability in traits exists in a population	principle-focused
Structure-Function Lab	1	structural traits enable advantageous functions	principle-focused
Galapagos Iguanas	6	variability, structure-function relationships	investigation, teacher directed/modeled
Selection Simulation	2	selective pressure results in differential success of individuals	principle-focused
Galapagos Finches	6	variability, structure-function relationships, environmental selection factors	investigation, student-directed
Salamander Migration	1	speciation — variation, migration, isolation, differential environments	principle-focused
Florida Panthers	6	genetic variation, selection factors, speciation, use of science in policy	investigation, student-directed
Culmination	1	summary and review	

[a]Number of 45 minute class periods

6.1 The schools

6.1.1 *North '97*

North High School[3] is a public high school in an affluent suburb of a large Midwestern city. It ranks in the top 5% of state standardized tests on both reading and mathematics achievement. The student population is fairly homogenous (e.g., 85.6% White, 1.0% Black, 2.3% Hispanic, 11.0% Asian or Pacific Islander, 0.1% Native American). The participating class from this school, referred to as North '97, was a required introductory honors biology class. Students were admitted into this class based on reading and writing achievement, and did not necessarily have exceptional science achievement or interests. This class was taught by Mr. Goodson.

6.1.2 *City '97*

City High School is a public high school in a large Midwestern City. It ranks about average relative to state standardized tests on reading and mathematics achievement. It has a diverse student population (e.g., 30% White, 27% Black and 23% Hispanic, 20% other). The participating class from this school was a required regular level introductory biology class taught by Ms. Patrick.

6.1.3 *West '98*

West High School is a public high school in a suburb of a large Midwestern City. It ranks average to slightly below average on state standardized tests on reading and mathematics achievement. The school is not very ethnically diverse (e.g., 86.3% White, 0% Black, 12.1% Hispanic, 1.6% other). Although, the particular class with which we worked had a large number of students who were recent immigrants whose first language was not English (many from Eastern European countries). This class was an ABC Science Class (9th grade), which was the third and lowest ranking class among the three possible ranks of the required introductory biology and science classes at West High School (honors, regular, and ABC science).

6.2 Groups of focus for the contrastive-case analysis

The groups of focus for this paper were chosen to reflect a gamut of academic acheivement, subject-matter knowledge and inquiry experience based on class track (e.g., honor or regular). The three contrastive case groups are: Dana, Eileen and Gill (DEG), from the honors class at North High School (North '97); BK, Tanya and Cathy (BTC), from a regular level class at City High School (City '97); and Paul, Bea, and Maggie (PBM), from the ABC Science class (lower than average ranked class) at West High School (West '98). These groups were chosen based on the teacher's recommendation of a representative group from a list of candidate groups in which one of the members of the group was interviewed by the researchers (an aspect of the study not reported in this paper). Pre-test scores also support the teacher's recommendation. At least two of the three members of each group scored within one standard deviation of the mean of the pre-test. This further indicates, that these groups do not stand out as particularly high or low achieving within their respective classrooms.

6.3 Data collection and analysis

The first author conducted observations in each participating classroom, during every class period of the unit. Data sources included: Written tests, structured interviews, log files (automated transcripts of students' actions using the software: See Appendix D for an example excerpt of a logfile tracking students' interactions with the software), student artifacts (final written explanations and reflective journals), and classroom observations (field notes, recordings and transcripts). The groups of focus were either videotaped or audiotaped during their investigation sessions. The set of video/audio recordings of the case groups' investigation sessions were fully transcribed. All of these sessions were also observed (listened to) to gain a sense of the tone, gestures and mood behind the written text. A close examination of the written transcripts enabled a fine grained analysis of the students' actions and speech, and made it easier to cross reference the students' dialogue with the data observations that they made in the software.

6.3.1 *Pre/post-test*

The pre/post-test targeted both content – conceptual understanding of natural selection and evolution — and process knowledge — knowledge of the utility of particular observation and comparison types. Where possible, items were adapted from published instruments (e.g., Jensen and Finley 1996).

The test had two versions (with isomorphic questions that targeted the same principles, but differed in surface features, such as the animal or trait in question). The test was administered using counterbalanced procedures, and was scored using double-blind procedures. Appendix A includes the full text of one version of the test, and Appendix B includes the full text of the second, isomorphic version of the test.

Pre to post scores were compared using a repeated measures ANOVA. There was no significant difference between the test order conditions, nor significant interactions between test and version. This makes us confident that the counterbalanced versions were isomorphic.

The test included three sets of questions targeting conceptual knowledge: Evolutionary Questions I, II, and III; and three sets of questions targeting process or inquiry knowledge: Investigation Questions I, II, and III. Evolutionary Questions

I presented an evolutionary phenomenon and three forced choice questions about this phenomenon, where students need to evaluate the accuracy of two competing accounts (i.e., scientific and common misconception). Evolutionary Questions II included three forced choice questions where students identify the response that most accurately describes part of the mechanism of natural selection. Evolutionary Questions III asks students to note how a biologist might explain how a species with a current unique ability could have evovled from ancestors having a different ability. Investigation Questions I present a problem phenomenon and three Likert questions, where students are asked to rate how important it is to make a particular type of observation when investigating the problem phenomenon. Investigation Questions II ask students to reason from data by asking them to evaluate competing explanations in light of a set of data graphs. Investigation Questions III asks students to generate an inquiry plan specific to investigating evolutionary phenomenon.

All questions included a free-text response section where students were asked to justify their responses. Free-text responses were coded to identify scientific and alternative conceptions of evolution, and for recognizing the type of information and relationships that can be gleaned from particular observation types. Appendix C shows the coding scheme used. Few students chose to include free-text responses. There were too few free-text responses to conduct statistical tests, therefore, we only report the results from the forced choice questions.

6.3.2 *Micro-analysis of contrastive-case groups*

We constructed an investigation path narrative for each group. We segmented the investigation sessions into episodes marking critical junctures, such as moving to a different type of data (e.g., from morphology to behavior), or articulating an intermediate hypothesis. Within each episode we noted the points in which students had insights that took their discovery process forward. We distilled this list of insights to the most critical in formulating their final explanations and constructed the inquiry path narratives. In addition, the computer log files were used to identify which interface selections the students made, and frequncy counts were made of the different selections (types of observations and comparisons).

7. Findings

7.1 Pre/post-test findings: Aggregate changes in disciplinary knowledge and skill

The pre/post-test was designed to answer two main questions: (1) Are students better able to explain natural selection events in ways that conform to current scientific conceptions? (2) Are students better able to consider biological factors in designing investigations to study animal survival? Overall, the results show statistically significant changes on both.

Recall that the set of questions called Evolutionary Questions I presented a brief description of an evolutionary phenomenon (such as ducks evolving webbed feet) followed by three forced choice questions that ask students to evaluate competing explanations (scientific and typical misconception) concerning implications of this phenomenon (such as what would happen to the ducks if they were forced to live in non-aquatic regions). More students favored the scientific explanations over the competing explanation on the post-test (42%) than on the pre-test (16%), The mean score increased from 2.0 (SD = 0.7) to 2.6 (SD = 0.65), $F(1,16) = 6.47$ $p < 0.05$.

In Evolutionary Questions II, students were given three multiple choice questions that ask students to identify the response choice that most accurately describes part of the mechanism of natural selection (for example, explaining mosquito resistance to DDT). The mean score on these questions improved from pre-test M = 0.75 (SD = 0.72) to post-test M = 1.2 (SD = 0.89), $F(1,18) = 4.86$ $p < 0.05$. Although we could not test for statisticaly significant differences in students' free-text justifications, there was a drop in the number of alternative conceptions expressed from the pre-test (31) to the post-test (19).

There was a similar improvement in the ability to subsume biological disciplinary knowledge in inquiry skills. Although a written test cannot assess process skills directly, a set of questions on the test evaluated whether students had developed an appreciation for the utility of particular observation types to investigating animal survival. Students were presented with a problem investigation similar to the ones they had encountered in their investigations during the unit, and were asked to rate (1–10, Likert) the importance of different observation types and explain how the observation would inform the study. Specifically, we tried to ascertain whether students recognize that it is important to consider physical characteristics when studying animal survival, and whether they understand that comparing physical characteristics between surviving and non-surviving individuals can help to identify advantageous traits. There was a significant increase in students' rating of the importance of this observation type from pre-test to post-test. Mean rating of significance increased from M = 5.7 (SD = 2.6) to M = 7.4 (SD = 2.4), $F(1,11) = 6.56$ $p < 0.05$.

Students that provided free text justifications for their rating seemed to include more references to form-function relationships. This would suggest a deep understanding of the significance of this observation type, rather than surface recognition, but there were too few responses to test for significance. Students tended to rate observations of behavior (differences between survivors and casualties) and environmental factors (changes over time) highly on the pre-test and there were no significant changes between pre-test and post-test.

The pre/post-test results suggest that the software scaffolds as part of the overall instructional scheme were effective in fostering a disciplinary stance. In particular, we see changes in both content and process knowledge. Interestingly, students who on the post-test tended to rate the relevance of physical characteristics to investigating survival as high also tended to score higher on the post-test questions examining evolutionary understanding (Pearson $r = 0.54$ $p < 0.05$). This correlation was not present on the pre-test ($r = 0.39$, $p > 0.05$).

7.2 Contrastive-case analysis: Exploring differences in DSSS-supported interactions

Productive inquiry that reflects a disciplinary stance involves making purposeful queries that will enable the articulation of normative explanations. In software environments, inquiry decisions translate into deciding which interface selection to make. The different representations in the software represent different aspects or types of observations. Limiting the range of observations to only some types of data limits the strength of the argument.

Students' understanding of the type of information they can expect to find from an observation and how that information might inform the current line of inquiry will influence the extent to which their decisions are purposeful or simply a matter of manipulating the interface. Students' remarks as they make selections help to reveal these understanings. For example, "Do you want to look at individual profiles, see if these are like bad or anything? The average is like totally changed...," suggests that these students understand the utility of coordinating observations at the aggregate and individual levels of analysis. In contrast, "click on some individuals," is ambigous as to whether students have an understanding that goes deeper than rote recognition of interface labels.

We open with an overview of each group's investigation processes. We then present differences between the three case groups in terms of the range of observations they explored, and in how meaningful they found the software representations.

7.2.1 *Overview of investigations*

DEG. Dana, Eileen and Gill (DEG) are three girls in Mr. Goodson's honors introductory biology class at North High School. The three get along very well. All three were very expressive and communicative throughout the project, occasionally interspersing social discussions with substantive discussions. They devote considerable attention to understanding the task and planning their next actions. They reflect on each piece of data they observe, try to form connections between their observations, and use the evidence categorization facilities in the software. They challenge each other on the validity of their claims, and raise alternative hypotheses to explain observed data patterns at various junctures in the investigation. The teacher was not observed approaching the group or interacting with them at any point throughout the project. There were a few instances when the group engaged in discussion with a researcher, but these discussions focused on clarifications concerning software functionality.

BTC. BK, Tanya and Cathy (BTC) are a boy and two girls in Ms. Patrick's class, a regular level introductory biology class at City high school. They get along well, and all three are actively engaged in the investigation, although Tanya and Cathy are the predominant speakers. The three are engaged in the task throughout the project, but they often transition abruptly between on-task and off-task discussions. Over the course of their investigation the students verbalize summaries of the data they observe, relationships between observations, and hypotheses they generate along the way. In particular, this group tends to articulate their explanation by entering it in data annotation fields, reporting it to each other or to the teacher. Occasionally, one student would question the interpretations or conclusions the other student made. Ms. Patrick interacted with this group a great deal (as she did with the other groups in the class). She would join the group and collaborate with them as a fellow team member.

PBM. Paul, Bea and Maggie (PBM) are a boy and two girls in Ms. Quill's ABC Science class. Students in this class are considered under qualified for the required regular level introductory biology class. The history of PBM's investigation is more difficult to reconstruct. After only brief investigation sessions, Paul had Saturday detention during which he decided to work on the finch investigation (Ms. Quill happened to be the Saturday detention teacher as well), during this two hour Saturday session Paul made a number of discoveries which he imported back to the group setting. Unfortunately, there are no log files, recordings or observations of Paul's session. This group of students was able to respond to most of the teacher's questions when she worked with the group, but they made little progress when they were working independently.

PBM often had difficulty getting along and would occasionally make disparaging comments to each other. This rift existed in particular between Paul and the two girls, Bea and Maggie. The group rarely worked as a threesome. At times, one student would be disengaged from the group preferring to focus on social or other activities.

7.2.2 *Differences in range of observations*

The three groups all seem to explore a range of observation types (see Table 3). BTC do not examine changes or differences in the distribution of traits in the population which is an important observation to make in constructing a natural selection argument. PBM do not make observations of the number of individuals.

Another aspect of the range of observations is the extent to which the students employ different types of comparisons. Extensive use of comparisons is more likely to yield elaborate explanations, since comparisons are key to identifying causal factors. The percentages of explicit comparisons made (i.e., selecting "compare across time" or selecting "compare between groups"), displayed in Table 4, are a little disappointing.

However, in judging the frequency of comparisons it is important to consider the following two points. First, non-comparative observations include observations that are also key in the inquiry process such as information about particular vegetation available on the island as food resources, or individual-level information about the birds that are investigated. For example, nearly half of the observations made during DEG's second investigation session were of birds' individual profiles — recall, that shifting between reasoning at the aggregate and at the individual level is an important component of evolutionary reasoning. Second, at times, students made implicit comparisons by making consecutive observations rather than using the comparison menu. For example, during their first investigation session the DEG group observed in sequence the number of live finches during 5 different time periods, which can be considered a longitudinal comparison of the variable number of finches. Interestingly, during their second session they

Table 3. Percentage of observations made of each variable type

	DEG	BTC	PBM
Individual Profiles	18	36	8
Variation of Physical Traits	4	25	38
Behavior	43	19	29
Number of Individuals	17	15	None
Distribution of Physical Traits	12	None	4
Environmental Information	6	5	21

Table 4. Percentage of comparisons made of each comparison type

	DEG	BTC	PBM
Longitudinal	21	4	21
Cross Sectional	3	2	21
Non-comparative Observations	76	94	58

used the comparison menu, so it may have taken them time to become familiar with the interface, especially since the menu for single observations is listed first in the menu pallete, so that it holds a position of primacy — this is perhaps a flaw in the layout that should be examined and changed in future versions.

7.2.3 *Differences in perceiving the meaning and significance of representations*

The three groups differed considerably in their perception of the meaning and significance of the software representations. These differences, as would be expected, seem to relate to the differences in the students' prior biological knowledge. DEG exhibit a good alignment between their spontaneous problem solving and the software representations, while BTC and PBM seem to pursue weak or generic methods that are loosely tied to the discipline-specific representations. What is noteworthy, is that one of the groups, BTC, experiences micro-longitudinal changes in these perceptions and progresses from a naïve to an informed perspective.

DEG think in terms of interdependency among animals, of differences between time periods and differences between survivors and non-survivors. They raise questions framed in these terms and are fairly easily able to choose software queries that match their questions.

In the example below, DEG raise a hypothesis that some of the finches might be dying, because they have a harder time avoiding their predators. They scan the choices available in the interface and decide to make observations of behavior:

> **Eileen**: About the predator prey, why some are preyed
> **Dana**: So what could be a reason why some might prey on others?
> **Eileen**: Because it's easier to get them, like you know
> **Dana**: Behavior? you want to check out behavior?
> **Eileen**: Yeah
> [**The three in unison**]: Evading [read out together, when see it as an option under behavior]
>
> [DEG first investigation session]

DEG's practices become even more aligned with disciplinary practices as the project progresses. Towards the end of the project they take up the software representatons and phrase their questions using the same language as the software scaffolds:

> **Dana**: …Are there differences between groups in the predator prey relationship? Can we do that?
>
> [DEG fifth investigation session]

Dana is interested in exploring predator prey relationships and phrases her question using the stem "are there differences between groups in the…" This is the stem associated with choosing a "compare between groups" comparison in the interface. This is also more formal scientific language.

DEG shift back and forth between having a particular inquiry goal in mind and trying to find a way to achieve it in the software, and between using the software choices as triggers for inquiry goals. So, at times the software serves as a ready-to-hand (Roth, Woszczyna, and Smith 1996) tool that provides the right tool at the right time to implement the girls' inquiry goal, and at times, it serves as a mindtool (Jonassen 2000) extending and complementing the girls' thinking.

In contrast, for BTC there is less of an alignment between their understanding and the software representations. In the early stages of the investigation, the navigational aspects of the interface rather than their inquiry or biological significance are more prominent in the students' interactions:

> **BK**: Alive, pick ones that were alive in 77 [students made a selection for behavior notes, and now are trying to choose individuals to observe]
> **Tanya**: 69 and 5 there you go, 69 and 5 I remember they were alive, 69 and 5 remember that
> **Cathy**: 69 and what
> **Tanya**: Are there changes between the time periods, this is that wrong one, cancel
> **BK**: Yeah, try at the bottom, the bottom left
> **Tanya**: That was this one — right?
> **BK**: Yeah
>
> [BTC first investigation session]

In this example, we see that the software representations are viewed as gateways to a particular type of graph they observed earlier. They are regarded as objects that will or will not retrieve a desired graph–"this is that wrong one"–, and are indexed by their location on the screen–"try at the bottom, the bottom left"–rather than viewed, regarded and manipulated as conceptual entities aligned with their understanding of the pertinent causal factors involved in natural selection and in their inquiry plan.

However, as their investigation progresses, BTC start to form a deeper understanding of the software representations. Consequently they make more purposeful queries that are aligned with the norms and concerns of the discipline. In the excerpt below, we see an example of a transition from initially regarding an interface representation as a mere label, to delving more deeply and considering how the factor represented in that software label might play a role in the investigated biological phenomenon:

> **Tanya**: What is the variation of leg size, do you think it has anything to do between their leg and their weight and stuff? Like, because remember with the gripping strength [refers to the conclusions reached in an earlier investigation]?

Cathy: But, any, it depends on where they get their food though. If they get it like in a place where they have to work hard.
Tanya: Want to try?
Cathy: Yeah
Tanya: What is the um
Cathy: Leg length? beak length? check the leg length?
BK: How about uh
Tanya: Wing length?
Cathy: Yeah wing
BK: Wouldn't
Tanya: They're ground finches, remember
BK: Yeah, how about leg length?
Cathy: They don't fly? do they fly?
Tanya: Variation of leg length of all live ground finches at dry 77, all live ground finches, their leg length

[BTC, second investigation session]

In the example above, Tanya is scanning the interface, reading off the list of possible queries. When she reaches the query focusing on observing variation in structure she asks her partners whether they think this might be a relevant observation to make, given that claw size (related to gripping strength) played a role in an earlier investigation. At this point their process transitions from exploration of the interface to discussing biological significance and implications. Cindy focuses their discussion by pointing out that a particular physical trait, such as leg size, would only be relevant if it plays a role in their survival, for example, if it influences their ability to access food resources. BTC's subsequent interactions vary between purposeful and exploratory interactions. They exhibit progress toward purposeful biological expert-like interactions, but not to the degree exhibited by DEG, the honor's group.

Similar to BTC and unlike DEG, PBM do not have a well formulated model of the domain and of the task, and they do not recognize the significance and utility of the observation types which are represented as software selection options. In this class, after the first brief investigation session, the teacher, Ms. Quill, felt that her students were overwhelmed by the complexity of the problem. She thought that they would not be able to direct their own investigations supported only through the software scaffolds and her visits with the groups. She created a worksheet with some subquestions to the driving question of the problem (why are the finches dying and what enables the surviving finches to survive). PBM's inquiry process was driven by this worksheet. However, they had a difficult time mapping between the inquiry goal set by the questions on the worksheet, such as "what are the behaviors of the living finches," and appropriate interface selections. For example:

Bea: What are the behaviors of the living finches [reads question from worksheet]?
[brief exchange about the fact that this is a day when school lets out early]
Bea: How are we supposed to find this one?
Paul: About behavior? We have to read all these ones [points to field notes window] see what they're doing
Bea: OK, well then [starts reading the first field note. Maggie is controlling the mouse, she asks what field note to turn to next, and Paul tells her to follow the list of live finches which they wrote the other day, Maggie pages to the next field note]
Bea: That one's eating like, so they're eating like all the time. Are we doing foraging or what?
Maggie: I don't know.

[PBM third investigation session, first full period devoted to investigation]

In this example, we see that Bea and Maggie do not know how to find information about behavior in the system. Despite the fact that at least one vehicle for retrieving information about behavior is quite visible. Unlike the students in the BTC, Bea and Maggie are reluctant to explore the options that are available in the software. As a result, although both groups started out with little, if any, knowledge of the biological significance of the different observation types, BTC are able, through their exploration, to extend this understandig and to make more progress.

7.2.4 *Differences in the construction of final explanations*

Each group's final explanation as it appeared in the software tool, Explanation Constructor (Sandoval 2004), designed to support the construction of discipline-specific explanations, is depicted in Figures 4 through 6, respectively. Not surprisingly, these explanations vary in quality in ways that are similar to the differences in investigative processes. DEG provide a parsimonious explanation, well articulated with casual statements supported by some evidence and describe differential survival in terms of structure-function relationships and environmental constraints. BTC provide causal statements supported by some evidence, and include biological ways of explaining, such as structure function relationships. However, BTC also include leanly supported claims and their explanation lacks parsimony. PBM provide a less sophisticated explanation. They rarely use causal language, and do not explain the advantage of the selected trait in terms of structure-function relationships and environmental constraints. Further, they provide only minimal data to support their claims.

DEG's explanation is most consistent with the scientific account, noting that the birds that survived are the ones with the advantageous beak that enabled them to consume the larger seeds that were the remaining food after the drought. Interestingly, PBM's explanation is more consistent with the canonical explanation than BTC's. This is likely a result of the extensive assistance that PBM received,

Template: Selective pressure
Status: Believable, but no supporting data
Environmental pressure:
The factor in the environment exerting a pressure was the drought that started in 1976 and ended in 1977.
  Evidence: rainfall info
Environmental effect:
This puts pressure on the finches because their normal food source (Portulaca, Chamae) died. They were forced to rely on Tribulus which is not easily accessible.
  Evidence: Portulaca info; Chamae info; Tribulus info;
Selective advantage:
The trait selected by this pressure is the beak of the finch. This is because the finches with bigger beaks are able to crack open the seeds of the Tribulus, and the ones that have shorter beaks cannot. These finches died during the drought because of their lack of food.
  Evidence: compare distribution of beak length of live finches between wet '73 and dry '77

* This explanation was reconstructed from log files due to a missing file. Status setting may not be accurate. May be missing some supporting evidence.

Figure 4. DEG final explanation

Template: Selective pressure
Status: Very confident, lots of supporting data
Environmental pressure:
Rainfall. Due to less rainfall, and in some seasons none at all, this has lead to a pressure in the environment. This has caused some finches to die.
  Evidence: rainfall info
Environmental effect:
It puts pressure on the finches that eat seeds and fruits, because the rain helps seeds & fruits grow, and the finches eat them. As a result, they die or lose weight when there is less rain.
  Evidence: gf20 foraging dry '77; variation of weight dead finches dry '73
Selective advantage:
Legs and beak. The leg length determines who lives and dies. From what we researched, they eat three things. Bugs (spiders, Ex), nuts (Tribulus, Ex) and Fruits (Portulaca, Ex). So for the finches that eat seeds they need longer legs to compete for food. The longer the legs, the faster they run, the more food they eat. For those who eat spiders, they have to have long legs in order to kick the dust to find spiders, and for the finches that eat fruits since the weather was bad.
  Evidence: compare foraging of gf5 and gf69 dry '77; gf1 foraging wet '73

Figure 5. BTC final explanation

rather than a reflection of the quality of their investigation. BTC's explanation diverges from the canonical explanation in that it cites large legs as well as large beaks as the advantageous traits. This probably reflects unfamiliarity with the scientific values of parsimony rather than a flaw in their reasoning.

Template: Selective pressure
Status: Believable, but no supporting data*
Environmental pressure:
Portulaca, Chamae, Tribulus the number of seeds declined.
Evidence: Portulaca info; Chamae info; Cactus info, Tribulus info
Environmental effect:
This pressure on the birds with the smaller beaks because Tribulus and Chamae were the only seeds left. The shell volume of the Tribulus is 12mm and the shell rigidity is hard.
Evidence: Chamae info; Tribulus info;
Selective advantage:
The trait selected for, is a bigger beak.
Evidence: compare the variation in beak length between live and dead finches in wet '77

* Also the default setting.

Figure 6. PBM final explanation

Supporting claims with evidence and parsimony are critical aspects of scientific discourse, but they are not aspects this particular implementation of DSSS is designed to support. Here support focused on disciplinary queries of data. Given our focus, we are interested in the ways in which discipline-specific inquiry strategies permeate students' investigation processes and final explanations, and are less concerned with whether students identify the same trait identified by scientists. To this end, DEG and BTC are successful examples of learning through DSSS, because their investigations and explanations revolved around structure-function relationships and selective advantage, while PBM are not a successful example, because these themes did not permeate their interactions.

8. Discussion

Our goal in this paper was to explore whether learning technologies could help initiates develop some of the pragmatic knowledge that is typically garnered through joint participation with experts in a community of practice. We called this knowledge a disciplinary stance, and it refers to the ways in which disciplinary principles, values and norms are subsumed in inquiry actions. We presented a software environment, the Galapagos Finches (Tabak et al. 2001), in which the choice of menus through which data is gathered, analyzed and synthesized, were overt manipulable representations of this tacit disciplinary stance. We examined aggregate data from a written pre/post-test that targeted conceptual understanding of evolution and understanding of the goals and utility of discipline-specific inquiry actions, as well as microanalyses of the inquiry processes of contrastive case groups — an honors group, a "regular" group, and a low-track group.

Taken together our findings demonstrate that students working with the Galapagos Finches software were able to develop some proficiency in the use of some of the conceptual tools that typify expert practice in evolutionary biology. Their investigations included comparisons of physical characteristics of live and dead finches across time, and their final explanations noted the role of structure-function relationships in survival. At the conclusion of the instructional unit, students were better able to recognize the significance of comparing physical characteristics between survivors and non-survivors to studying natural selection in the wild. They were also better able to recognize explanations of evolutionary phenomena that are consistent with scientific theories.

Before we delve into a discussion of our findings and their implications, we want to emphasize that, as we noted earlier, we focus on the software for analytical clarity, but we take a non-reductive stance toward learning. We recognize that any learning outcomes are always the product of a cumulation of factors and interactions (multiple activities, discussions, teachers, peers) that students encounter over the course of instruction. (Tabak 2004).

8.1 DSSS as a means for balancing content and process learning goals

The pre/post-test results suggest that the pedagogical approach we propose of discipline-specific strategic support is effective in helping students acquire normative knowledge, and reduces some of the tension between process and content learning goals. There was a statistically significant increase in the number of students who were able to correctly identify scientific explanations for evolutionary phenomena. We profer that this result has to do with the tight coupling of conceptual entities with inquiry actions in the software design. DSSS focuses students on key variables and relationships as they query data in the investigation environment. Such a focus favors actions that are more likely to yield knowledge that is consistent with extant theories (e.g., thinking in terms of differential survival based on advantageous traits), and thus an individual's knowledge of the domain also increases.

The literature on students' alterantive conceptions of evolution (Bishop and Anderson 1990; Clough and Wood-Robinson 1985; Pedersen and Hallden 1994; Settlage 1994) shows that one pervasive belief is that individual organisms change in response to a need. If students consider behavior to be a primary factor in survival, and physcial characteristics to be secondary or irrelevant, they may be more likely to adopt this alternative view. According to both scientific and lay views, behavior, unlike physical characteristics (excepting tanning, hair loss, and the like), is more readily subject to change in response to the environment. However, if students come to recognize the importance of physical characteristics to survival they may be more likely to recognize an incogruence between the inability to change physical characteristics and their views of natural selection as a change in response to a need.

The post-test results show that students developed a greater appreciation for the role of differences in physical characteristics to differential survival, and that this greater appreciation was correlated with stronger conceptions of evolution, a correlation that did not exist on the pre-test. Students' use of comparisons of physical characteristics of live and dead finches across time and their mention of the role of physical characteristics in survival in their final explanations, may partly explain how these understandings developed. In addtion, students may recognize this incongruence, because they have an opportunity to examine concrete features of individual organisms and not just aggregate or abstract representations. Interleaving reasoning at the aggregate and individual levels, is one aspect of the disciplinary stance that the software aimed to cultivate. The microanalysis of interaction shows that students used this functionality and made observations at both levels. Recognizing such incongruencies can lead to conceptual change (Posner, Strike, Hewson, and Gertzog 1982), which can explain the improvement in students' understanding of evolution.

Our aggregate results concerning students' ability to identify scientific explanations of natural selection are promising. Recall that students' alternative conceptions of evolution are very persistent (Bishop and Anderson 1990; Demastes, Settlage, and Good 1995; Greene 1990). Moreover, the test questions pose a departure from most of the examples encountered during the instructional unit. Classroom examples tended to focus on events that occurred on smaller time scales, of two or three generations, compared to thousands or millions of generations depicted in the test questions. Our post-test results concerning students ability to generate scientific explanations and subsume disciplinary considerations into inquiry plans are not as strong. These aspects of learning were elicited through free-text questions, but free-text responses were too scant for statistical analysis. So while differences in raw percentages of scientific statements suggest movement in desired directions, these results are inconclusive. Nonetheless, the challenges of learning general principles through the investigation of particular telling cases, and of maintaining content learning goals despite an emphasis on inquiry, seem to have been met.

8.2 DSSS and free exploration: From rudimentary exploration to disciplinary intent

The microanalysis of interaction provides us with a purview to the nuances of investigation processes that are not apparent in aggregate pre/post-tests. The contrastive case analysis further points to differences that students of varying academic achievement experience in their interactions with the software and with scientific inquiry. This has implications for future design and enactment.

Contrary to prevalent attitudes that contend that first-hand scientific investigations are only appropriate for high achieving students (e.g., Zohar, Degani, and Vaaknin 2001), this study contributes to a growing body of literature (e.g., Yerrick 2000) that shows that such activities, with the right scaffolding, are also suitable and desirable for lower achieving students. The emphasis on discipline-specificity in structuring students' data queries helped students of different academic levels to not only negotiate primary data to construct knowledge, but to generate knowledge claims consistent with disciplinary (evoutionary) argument patterns. For example, even students who entered the unit with little knowledge of evolution, as represented by the BTC group, considered structure-function relationships in their investigation, and pointed to these relationships in their final explanation.

One conclusion we can draw is that supports that enable students to setup comparisons by exploiting system-provided options that reflect domain principles offer a good middle ground between autonomous work in realistic environments and guidance or scaffolding. The Galapagos Finches has been deemed epistemologically well aligned with scientific practice (Chinn and Malhotra 2002), but it still provides enough structure for learners to gain competency in productive strategies. The repertoire of variable-categories and comparison-types available in the system compensate for students' lack of prior knowledge, and serve as specific suggestions for inquiry directions that would otherwise require prior process and content knowledge. These supports do not however undermine students' control and intellectual automony. Students must still exercise scientific judgment in deciding which comparisons to construct, and how well these comparisons fit with current inquiry paths and conjectures. In fact, the problem was complex enough so that a high end group, DEG, still found it compelling and engaging.

The contrastive-case analysis points to the ways in which students with different academic backgrounds will attend differently to the software prompts, and consequently vary in their learning potential. The implications extend beyond the obvious distinctions in performance between honors, regular, and low-track students. If students' performance was only a function of their academic track we would expect the differences to revolve mostly around the depth and accuracy of their interpretations, their ability to synthesize data, and to draw conclusions. Yet, we found differences in the extent to which students engaged in free exploration of the software. Both the honors, DEG, group and the regular level, BTC, group engaged in exploration (though the DEG group was quite purposeful from the start), and they both showed micro-longitudinal changes in the extent to which they took-on an evolutionary stance in their inquiry.

We posit that there are two key points that can explain why the regular level BTC group was able to undergo changes and growth that the low track PBM group did not experience. One point is the difference between BTC's and PBM's propensity to explore the sotware representations. The second point is the additional support provided by BTC's teacher. Of course, we cannot deny additional factors, such as the social dischord among the PBM members.

Initially, the investigative processes of BTC and PBM appear quite similar. Both experienced considerable confusion and frustration. However, as the investigation continued, BTC freely explored the interface options. Early in the investigation the software representations were opaque, they did not hold much navigational or biological meaning for the students. Despite this opacity, because the students were inclined to "cick around" they serendipitously encountered information. This enabled them to make some intermediate inferences and conclusions, which in turn reduced their confusion and increased their confidence in their ability to contend with the investigation. As they continued to work, the scope of their inferences and intermediate explanations increased, as did the extent to which their navigation became intentional and biologically driven. By the end of the investigation they also appeared to appropriate the representations, as exhibited in their use of structure-function relationships.

In contrast, PBM's interactions with the software were more constrained. PBM's teacher, concerned that the problem was too complex for her students, distributed a worksheet with a list of questions that the students needed to answer by finding information in the software environment. This worksheet dictated PBM's interactions with the software, and they seemed entirely focused on completing the worksheet, rather than on delving into the problem phenomenon. We believe that this stood in the way of their making meaningful intermediate inferences and explanations, and of appropriating the software representations. So, paradoxically, in her effort to reduce complexity and assist the students, she actually undermined their inquiry and learning.

The BTC group were not only more inclined and encouraged to engage in free exploration of the software, they also benefitted from extensive and constructive teacher support. We did not include analyses of the teacher-student interactions in this paper, because our focus was on the software support and representations. We discuss these in detail elsewhere (Tabak 2004; Tabak and Baumgartner 2004;

Tabak and Reiser 1997). We should note though that some students will not be able to make productive progress without additional mediation beyond the software scaffolds. This is an idea that we have previously presented (Tabak 2004), and is consonant with the idea that effective adoption of technological innovation must occur through seamless integration with the social fabric of the adoption context (Suchman, Blomberg, Orr, and Trigg 1999).

8.3 Learning technology representations: From navigation to signification

One of the broader implications of this study is that representations in learning technologies can hold multiple levels of meaning and that recognizing and reflecting on these different levels is key to learning. BTC and DEG considered the interface labels as projecting disciplinary knowledge and not just as a way of distinguishing one interface option (menu or button) from another. This helped them attend to and appropriate the knowledge structures that the interface was designed to reflect. One anecdote from the honors group exemplifies this process: One of the group members mentioned to the others that she expected physical characteristics to be important because they appear so often in the interface.

In addition, for software prompts to be effective in communicating the tacit, pragmatic, cultural knowledge of a domain, learners must work at two levels: (1) the navigational level, using the interface options to access information and actions; and (2) the signifier level, reflecting on the disciplinary meaning of the interface labels and structure. Some students seem to work at both levels spontaneously, while others may need to be explicitly directed to do so. With software representations, just like with classroom instruction, we cannot rely on the simple or direct transmission of knowledge. These two levels of interaction can also be a subject of class discussion as part of additional processes of mediation.

9. Conclusion

In this paper, we explored how our understanding of cognitive processes in inquiry and of the pragmatic knowledge of practicing scientists can be used to design learning technologies to support young learners' inquiry-based science learning. We proposed that a central part of science learning involves developing a disciplinary stance — developing the propensity to focus on particular questions, attend to particular concerns and utilize particular ways of reasoning, which are shared by members of a disciplinary community.

We examined whether technological tools could fulfill some of the roles assumed by established members of a community of practice in initiating new members and helping them develop such a stance. In particular, we examined how expert scientific knowledge in a particular discipline, evolutionary field biology, could be captured and represented in inquiry support tools. Our approach, Domain-Specific Strategic Support (DSSS), identifies investigation strategies that reflect disciplinary concerns and realizes them as objects students can manipulate in the software in order to make these strategies visible and accessible to students.

We have found that the DSSS approach, embedded in a curriculum and classroom environment consistent with this approach, can help students in their transition toward a disciplinary stance. The emphasis on discipline-specificity in structuring students' data queries helped high achieving as well as lower achieving students to not only negotiate primary data to construct knowledge, but to generate knowledge claims that are consistent with argument patterns typical to the discipline. In this way, computer-based learning environments can serve as purveyors of cultural knowledge and as agents in enculturation processes.

Notes

* This work was supported, in part, by Grant 97-57 from the James S. McDonnell Foundation to Brian J. Reiser and by a Spencer Dissertation Fellowship and a Rashi–Guastalla Fellowship for the Advancement of Science Education to Iris Tabak. The findings and opinions expressed here are the authors' and do not necessarily represent the views of these foundations. We thank and gratefully acknowledge the contributions of our collaborators on the BGuILE project, in particular William A. Sandoval, and our biology consultants, including Jeff Hoyer and Hans Landel, and Tammy Porter Massey. Our deepest appreciation goes to the teachers and students who welcomed us into their classrooms and made this research possible.

1. Appears elsewhere also as "Domain-Specific Strategic Support".

2. The investigation environment The Galapagos Finches ran in conjunction with another tool, Explanation Constructor (Sandoval 2004), which encapsulated the discipline-specific scaffolding of the "explain" component of the investigation model.

3. All names of participating schools, teachers and students listed in this paper are pseudonyms.

References

Bell, P., Davis, E.A., and Linn, M.C. 1995. "The knowledge integration environment: Theory and design". In J.L. Schnase and E.L. Cunnius (eds), *Proceedings of CSCL '95: The First International Conference on Computer Support for Collaborative Learning*. Bloomington, IN: Erlbaum, 15–21.

Bishop, B.A. and Anderson, C.W.1990. "Student conceptions of natural selection and its role in evolution". *Journal of Research in Science Teaching* 27: 415–427.
Bloom, J.W. 1988. "A case study of evolutionary biologists: Implications for secondary biology curriculum and teacher training". *Paper presented at the 1988 Annual Meeting of the American Educational Research Association*, New Orleans, LA.
Blumenfeld, P.C., Soloway, E., Marx, R.W., Krajcik, J.S., Guzdial, M., and Palincsar, A.S. 1991. "Motivating project-based learning: Sustaining the doing, supporting the learning". *Educational Psychologist* 26(3–4): 369–398.
Bowen, G.M., Roth, W.M., and McGinn, M.K. 1999. "Interpretations of graphs by university biology students and practicing scientists: Toward a social practice view of scientific representation practices". *Journal of Research in Science Teaching*, 36(9): 1020–1043.
Bransford, J., Brown, A., and Cocking, R.R. (eds). 2000. *How People Learn: Brain, Mind, Experience and Schools*. Washington, D.C.: National Academy Press.
Chi, M.T.H., Feltovich, P., and Glaser, R. 1981. "Categorization and representation of physics problems by experts and novices". *Cognitive Science* 5: 121–152.
Chinn, C.A., and Malhotra, B.A. 2002. "Epistemologically authentic inquiry in schools: A theoretical framework for evaluating inquiry tasks". *Science Education* 86(2): 175–218.
Clutton-Brock, T.H. and Harvey, P.H. 1984. "Comparative approaches to investigating adaptation". In J.R. Krebs and N.P. Davies (eds), *Behavioral Ecology: An Evolutionary Approach*, 2nd ed. Sunderland, MA: Sinauer Associates, 7–29.
Cobb, P., Perlwitz, M., and Underwood Gregg, D. 1998. "Individual construction, mathematical acculturation, and the classroom community". In M. Larochelle and N. Bednarz (eds), *Constructivism and Education*. New York: Cambridge University Press, 63–80.
Collins, A., Brown, J.S., and Newman, S.E. 1989. "Cognitive apprenticeship: Teaching the crafts of reading, writing, and mathematics". In L.B. Resnick (ed), *Knowing, Learning, and Instruction: Essays in Honor of Robert Glaser*. Hillsdale, NJ: Erlbaum, 453–494.
Davis, E. 1996. "Metacognitive scaffolding to foster scientific explanations". *Paper presented at the Annual Meeting of the American Educational Research Association*, New York.
Demastes, S.S., Settlage, J., and Good, R. 1995. "Students' conceptions of natural selection and its role in evolution: Cases of replication and comparison". *Journal of Research in Science Teaching* 32: 535–550.
Edelson, D.C., Gordin, D.N., and Pea, R.D. 1997. "Creating science learning tools from experts' investigation tools: A design framework". *Paper presented at the 1997 Annual Meeting of the National Association for Research in Science Teaching*, Oak Brook, IL.
Endler, J.A. 1986. *Natural Selection in the Wild*. Princeton, NJ: Princeton University Press.
Garrett, P.B., and Baquedano-Lopez, P. 2002. "Language socialization: Reproduction and continuity, transformation and change". *Annual Review of Anthropology* 31: 339–361.
Geer, B.D., Tulviste, T., Mizera, L., and Tryggvason, M.-T. 2002. "Socialization in communication: Pragmatic socialization during dinnertime in Estonian, Finnish and Swedish families". *Journal of Pragmatics* 34(12): 1757–1786.
Gomez, L.M., Fishman, B.J., and Pea, R.D. 1998. "The CoVis project: Building a large scale science education testbed". *Interactive Learning Environments* 6(1–2): 59–92.
Goodwin, C. 1994. "Professional Vision". *American Anthropologist* 96(3): 606–633.
Goodwin, C. 1995. "Seeing in Depth". *Social Studies of Science* 25(2): 237–274.
Grant, P.R. 1986. *Ecology and Evolution of Darwin's Finches*. Princeton, NJ: Princeton University Press.

Greene, E.D. 1990. "The logic of university students' misunderstanding of natural selection". *Journal of Research in Science Teaching* 27(9): 875–885.
Greeno, J.G. 1983. "Conceptual entities". In D. Gentner and A.L. Stevens (eds), *Mental Models*. Hillsdale, NJ: Erlbaum, 227–253.
Guzdial, M. 1994. "Software-realized scaffolding to facilitate programming for science learning". *Interactive Learning Environments* 4: 1–44.
Hobbs, P. 2004. "The role of progress notes in the professional socialization of medical residents". *Journal of Pragmatics* 36: 1579–1607.
Jackson, S.L., Stratford, S.J., Krajcik, J., and Soloway, E. 1994. "Making dynamic modeling accessible to precollege science students". *Interactive Learning Environments* 4: 233–257.
Jonassen, D.H. 2000. *Computers as Mindtools in Schools: Engaging Critical Thinking*. Columbus, OH: Merril/Prentice-Hall.
Klahr, D. and Dunbar, K. 1988. "Dual space search during scientific reasoning". *Cognitive Science* 12: 1–48.
Klahr, D., Dunbar, K., and Fay, A.L. 1990. "Designing good experiments to test bad hypotheses". In J. Shrager and P. Langley (eds), *Computational Models of Scientific Discovery and Theory Formation*. Palo Alto, CA: Morgan Kaufmann Publishers, 355–402.
Klahr, D., Fay, A.L., and Dunbar, K. 1993. "Heuristics for scientific experimentation: A developmental study". *Cognitive Psychology* 25: 111–146.
Knorr-Cetina, K. 1996. "The care of the self and blind variation: The disunity of two leading sciences". In P. Galison and D.J. Stump (eds), *The Disunity of Science: Boundaries, Contexts, and Power*. Stanford, CA: Stanford University Press, 287–310.
Kolodner, J. 1997. "Educational implications of analogy: A view from case-based reasoning". *American Psychologist* 52(1): 57–66.
Krajcik, J., Blumenfeld, P.C., Marx, R.W., Bass, K.M., Fredericks, J., and Soloway, E. 1998. "Inquiry in project-based science classrooms: Initial attempts by middle school students". *The Journal of the Learning Sciences* 7(3–4): 313–350.
Kuhn, D., Schauble, L., and Garcia-Mila, M. 1992. "Cross-domain development of scientific reasoning". *Cognition and Instruction* 9: 285–327.
Lampert, M. 1990. "When the problem is not the question and the solution is not the answer: Mathematical knowing and teaching". *American Educational Research Journal* 27: 29–63.
Larkin, J.H. 1983. "The role of problem representation in physics". In D. Gentner and A. L. Stevens (eds), *Mental Models*. Hillsdale, NJ: Erlbaum, 75–99.
Lave, J., and Wenger, E. 1991. *Situated Learning: Legitimate Peripheral Participation*. New York, NY: Cambridge University Press.
Loh, B., Radinsky, J., Reiser, B.J., Gomez, L.M., Edelson, D.C., and Russell, E. 1997. "The progress portfolio: Promoting reflective inquiry in complex investigation environments". In R. Hall, N. Miyake, and N. Enyedy (eds), *Proceedings of Computer Supported Collaborative Learning '97*, Toronto, 169–178.
NRC. 2000. *Inquiry and the National Science Education Standards: A Guide for Teaching and Learning*. Washington, DC: National Academy Press.
O'Neill, D.K. 2001. "Knowing when you've brought them in: Scientific genre knowledge and communities of practice". *The Journal of the Learning Sciences* 10(3): 223–264.
Palincsar, A.S. 1998. "Social constructivist perspectives on teaching and learning". *Annual Review of Psychology* 49: 345–375.

Pea, R.D. 1992. "Augmenting the discourse of learning with computer-based learning environments". In E. d. Corte, M. Linn, and L. Verschaffel (eds), *Computer-Based Learning environments and Problem-Solving* (Vol. F84 NATO Series, subseries F: Computer and System Sciences). New York: Springer, 313–343.

Posner, G.J., Strike, K.A., Hewson, P.W., and Gertzog, W.A. 1982. "Accommodation of a scientific conception: Toward a theory of conceptual change". *Science Education* 66: 211–227.

Reiser, B.J., Tabak, I., Sandoval, W.A., Smith, B.K., Steinmuller, F., and Leone, T.J. 2001. "BGuILE: Strategic and conceptual scaffolds for scientific inquiry in biology classrooms.". In S.M. Carver and D. Klahr (eds), *Cognition and Instruction: 25 Years of Progress*. Mahwah, NJ: Lawrence Erlbaum Associates, 263–306.

Roth, W.M. 1995. "Affordances of computers in teacher-student interactions: The case of interactive physics". *Journal of Research in Science Teaching* 32: 329–347.

Roth, W.M., Woszczyna, C., and Smith, G. 1996. "Affordances & constraints of computers in science education". *Journal of Research in Science Teaching* 33(9): 995–1017.

Sandoval, W.A. 2003. "Conceptual and epistemic aspects of students' scientific explanations". *The Journal of the Learning Sciences* 12(1): 5–52.

Sandoval, W.A. 2004. "Explanation-driven inquiry: Integrating conceptual and epistemic scaffolds for scientific inquiry". *Science Education* 88: 345–372.

Schauble, L. 1990. "Belief revision in children: The role of prior knowledge and strategies for generating evidence". *Journal of Experimental Child Psychology* 49: 31–57.

Schauble, L. 1996. "The development of scientific reasoning in knowledge-rich contexts". *Developmental Psychology* 32(1): 102–119.

Schauble, L., and Glaser, R. 1990. "Scientific thinking in children and adults". In D. Kuhn (ed), *Developmental Perspectives on Teaching and Learning Thinking Skills*, Vol. 21 London: Karger, 9–27.

Schauble, L., Glaser, R., Duschl, R.A., Shulze, S., and John, J. 1995. "Students' understanding of the objectives and procedures of experimentation in the science classroom". *The Journal of the Learning Sciences* 4(2): 131–166.

Schauble, L., Glaser, R., Raghavan, K., and Reiner, M. 1991. "Causal models and experimentation strategies in scientific reasoning". *The Journal of the Learning Sciences* 1: 201–238.

Schieffelin, B.B., and Ochs, E. 1986. "Language socialization". *Annual Review of Anthropology* 15: 163–191.

von Secker, C.E. and Lissitz, R.W. 1999. "Estimating the impact of instructional practices on student achievement in science". *Journal of Research in Science Teaching* 36(10): 1110–1126.

Shute, V., and Glaser, R. 1991. "An intelligent tutoring system for exploring principles of economics". In R.E. Snow and D.E. Wiley (eds), *Improving Inquiry into Social Science: A Volume in Honor of Lee J. Cronbach*. Hillsdale, NJ: Lawrence Erlbaum Associates, 333–366.

Snir, J., Smith, C., and Grosslight, L. 1995. "Conceptually enhanced simulations: A computer tool for science teaching". In D.N. Perkins, J.L. Schwartz, M.M. West, and M.S. Wiske (eds), *Software Goes to School: Teaching for Understanding with New Technologies*. New York: Oxford University Press, 106–129.

Songer, N.B. 1996. "Exploring learning opportunities in coordinated network-enhanced classrooms: A case of kids as global scientists". *The Journal of the Learning Sciences* 5: 297–327.

Suchman, L., Blomberg, J., Orr, J.E., and Trigg, R. 1999. "Reconstructing technologies as social practice". *American Behavioral Scientist* 43(3): 392–408.

Tabak, I. 1999. *Unraveling the Development of Scientific Literacy: Domain-Specific Inquiry Support in a System of Cognitive and Social Interactions.* Unpublished Doctoral Dissertation, Northwestern University, Evanston, IL.

Tabak, I. 2004. "Synergy: A complement to emerging patterns of distributed scaffolding". *The Journal of the Learning Sciences* 13(3): 305–335.

Tabak, I., and Baumgartner, E. 2004. "The teacher as partner: Exploring participant structures, symmetry and identity work in scaffolding". *Cognition and Instruction* 22(4): 393–429.

Tabak, I., and Reiser, B.J. 1997. "Complementary roles of software-based scaffolding and teacher-student interactions in inquiry learning". In R. Hall, N. Miyake, and N. Enyedy (eds), *Proceedings of CSCL '97: The Second International Conference on Computer Support for Collaborative Learning.* Mahwah, NJ: Lawrence Erlbaum and Associates, 289–298.

Tabak, I., Reiser, B.J., Sandoval, W.A., Leone, T.J., and Steinmuller, F. 2001. "BGuILE: The Galapagos Finches — The struggle for survival [Computer software]". In J.R. Jungck (ed), *The BioQuest Library VI.* San Diego, CA: Harcourt Academic Press.

Tabak, I., Smith, B.K., Sandoval, W.A., and Reiser, B.J. 1996. "Combining general and domain-specific strategic support for biological inquiry". In C. Frasson, G. Gauthier and A. Lesgold (eds), *Intelligent Tutoring Systems: Third International Conference, ITS '96.* Berlin: Springer, 288–296.

Weiner, J. 1994. *The Beak of the Finch: A Story of Evolution in Our Time.* New York: Alfred A. Knopf.

Wertsch, J. V. 1998. *Mind as Action.* New York: Oxford University Press.

White, B.Y. 1993. "Intermediate causal models: A missing link for science education?". In R. Glaser (ed), *Advances in Instructional Psychology*, vol. 4. Hillsdale, NJ: Erlbaum, 177–252.

White, B.Y., and Frederiksen, J.R. 1995. *An Overview of the ThinkerTools Inquiry Project* (Causal Models Report No. 95–04). Berkeley: University of California.

Williams, S.M. 1992. "Putting case-based instruction into context: Examples from legal and medical education". *The Journal of the Learning Sciences* 2: 367–427.

Yerrick, R. 2000. "Lower track science students' argumentation and open inquiry instruction". *Journal of Research in Science Teaching* 37(8): 807–838.

Zohar, A., Degani, A., and Vaaknin, E. 2001. "Teachers' beliefs about low-achieving students and higher order thinking". *Teaching and Teacher Education* 17(4): 469–485.

Appendix A: Biology Pre/Post-test Isomorphic Version A

Filling out this survey will have no effect on your grade. We ask that you work alone and answer the questions thoroughly and to the best of your ability. Your participation in this survey is very helpful to our research — thank you!

Name: ______________________________

1) Suppose you were doing a field study examining a herd of giraffes in a region of Africa, as part of your investigation you caught as many **adult** giraffes in the herd as you could and measured their neck length and drew a graph to show the measurements.

Draw a bar graph below to illustrate the measurements you expect to find. (Assume that the average neck length is 10ft).

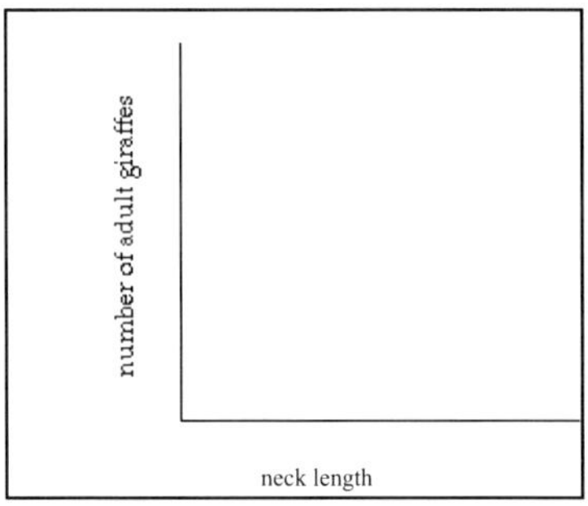

<u>Explain what your graph shows:</u>

2) Cheetahs (large African cats) are able to run faster than 60 miles per hour when chasing prey. How would a biologist explain how the ability to run fast evolved in cheetahs, assuming their ancestors could only run 20 miles per hour?

3) Cave salamanders are blind (they have eyes which are not functional). How would a biologist explain how blind cave salamanders evolved from sighted ancestors?

For questions 4 through 6

Suppose you were investigating a population of black bears where many black bears were suddenly dying, and you wanted to explain why so many black bears were dying, and what enabled the surviving black bears to survive.

Below are a number of observations you could make. For each one, rate on a scale from 1 to 10 (where 1 is the least useful and 10 is the most useful), how useful this test or observation would be for your investigation. Then answer the question that follows.

4) How useful would it be to compare the environment (for example, weather or number of predators) now to the environment a year ago?

1 2 3 4 5 6 7 8 9 10

comparing the environment now to a year ago **is not** very useful	comparing the environment now to a year ago **is** very useful

How could this information help to explain why so many black bears are dying, and why others are able to survive?

5) How useful would it be to compare measurements (such as leg length) of surviving black bears to measurements of black bears that died?

1 2 3 4 5 6 7 8 9 10

comparing measurements of black bears that survived with black bears that did not survive **is not** very useful	comparing measurements of black bears that survived with black bears that did not survive **is** very useful

How could this information help to explain why so many black bears are dying, and why others are able to survive?

6) How useful would it be to compare the behavior (such as how they hunt or shelter themselves) of surviving black bears to the behavior of black bears that died (from observations made before they died).

1 2 3 4 5 6 7 8 9 10

comparing behavior of black bears that survived with black bears that did not survive **is not** very useful	comparing behavior of black bears that survived with black bears that did not survive **is** very useful

How could this information help to explain why so many black bears are dying, and why others are able to survive?

7) Scientists studied a population of lizards on an island from 1945 to 1965. In 1950 the scientists started sighting hawks flying over the island and hunting the lizards. This surprised the scientists, since there were rarely any hawks sighted on the island before that time. Over the next 15 years hawk sightings remained high and many lizards were hunted by the hawks. At first, the scientists feared that the lizards would be killed off and become extinct on that island, but although many lizards died, some survived.

Here are some of the scientists' observations:

	1950	1955	1965
Total lizard population	1000	500	550

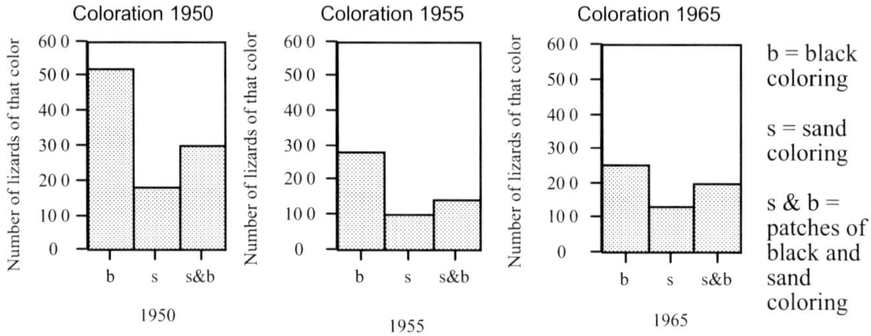

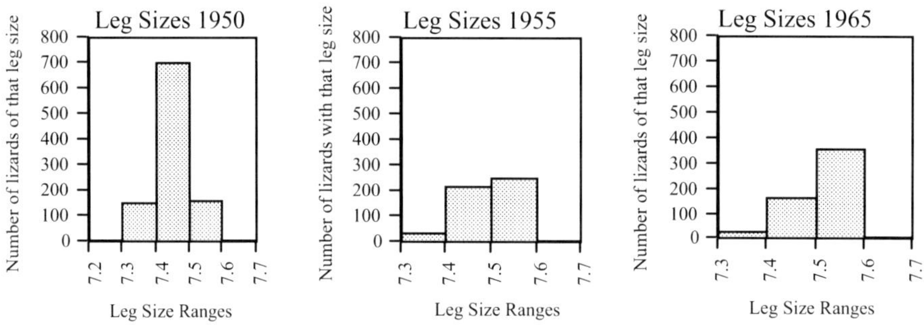

Here are some possible explanations for what enables the surviving lizards to survive. Which one is best supported by the observations above?

___ (a) Lizards with large leg sizes are better able to escape the hawks.

___ (b) Lizards that live survive by chance.

___ (c) Lizards that are sand colored are better able to avoid being eaten.

___ (d) None of the above explanations (a-c) are supported by the data.

Why did you choose this answer (**Be sure to describe how you used the graphs**)?

non-webbed feet webbed feet

Ducks are aquatic birds. Their feet are webbed and this trait makes them fast swimmers.

8) **While ducks were evolving webbed feet:**

a) all ducks were equally likely to survived and reproduced, regardless of the quantity of webbing on their feet.

b) those ducks without any webbing were less likely to survive and reproduce than those with some webbing.

Check the response that best describes what you think about statements (a) & (b) above
____ (a) is the **only** correct statement
____ (b) is the **only** correct statement
____ (a) is **more** correct than (b)
____ (b) is **more** correct than (a)
____ **both** (a) and (b) are **equally** correct
____ **neither** (a) nor (b) are correct

Why did you choose this answer:

9) Suppose you could go back in time to the generations when ducks were evolving webbed feet, and that you could make any tests, measurements, observations or comparisons that you liked.

What tests, measurements or observations would you take to find out whether all ducks survive and reproduce at the same rate regardless of the quantity of webbing on their feet?

Explain why you would make each of these tests, measurements or observations:

10) Now that webbed feet are present in ducks :

a) there still exists considerable variation in the quantity of webbing in ducks' feet.

b) there exists no variation in the quantity of webbing in ducks' feet.

Check the response that best describes what you think about statements (a) & (b) above
____ (a) is the **only** correct statement
____ (b) is the **only** correct statement
____ (a) is **more** correct than (b)
____ (b) is **more** correct than (a)
____ **both** (a) and (b) are **equally** correct
____ **neither** (a) nor (b) are correct

Why did you choose this answer:

11) If a population of ducks were forced to live in a habitat where water was not present:

a) many ducks would die because their feet were poorly adapted to this environment.

b) each generation of ducks would have a little less webbing until eventually, for example, 50 or 60 generations, most all the webbing would be gone.

Check the response that best describes what you think about statements (a) & (b) above
____ (a) is the **only** correct statement
____ (b) is the **only** correct statement
____ (a) is **more** correct than (b)
____ (b) is **more** correct than (a)
____ **both** (a) and (b) are **equally** correct
____ **neither** (a) nor (b) are correct

Why did you choose this answer:

12) A number of mosquito populations are today resistant to DDT (a chemical used to kill insects), even though those species were not resistant to DDT when it was first introduced. Biologists believe that DDT resistance evolved in mosquitoes because:

Choose the <u>best</u> answer:
a) individual mosquitoes built up a resistance to DDT after being exposed to it. This resistance was then passed on to their offspring.
b) mosquitoes needed to be resistant to DDT in order to survive.
c) a few mosquitoes were probably resistant to DDT before it was ever used.
d) mosquitoes learned to adapt to their environment.

<u>Why did you choose this answer</u>:

13) Which of the following provides the best example of the process of evolutionary adaptation.

Choose the <u>best</u> answer:

A. Fifty wild dogs successfully switch from hunting rabbits to mice because the rabbit population has become extinct. All 50 dogs survive the transition from rabbits to mice.

B. A large population (100) of dogs are able to produce heavy fur coats in a winter with severe cold and thus all are able to survive. All of these dogs' offspring have slightly heavier coats than their parents.

C. Due to extreme cold, half of a large dog population (100) dies. The other half survives and reproduces because their fur coats were heavier and better able to protect them from the weather.

D. A dog is moved to a warmer climate and responds by shedding large quantities of fur to help remain cool. The dog's offspring is born with a very heavy coat of fur, but is also able to shed the unneeded fur.

<u>Why did you choose this answer</u>:

14) If a population of wild dogs are in an environment that drastically changes (for example, a change in temperature of 20 degrees Celsius for 100 days and their regular food source is driven to extinction) which of the following events will most likely occur?

A. It is likely the population will become extinct.

B. The individuals within the population will learn to adapt to the changes.

C. Some individuals would die, but the total population would remain constant.

D. Individuals able to cope with the changes would pass on traits which help the next generation.

E. Individuals would modify their physical characteristics in order to maintain the balance of nature.

<u>Why did you choose this answer</u>:

Appendix B: Biology Pre/Post-test Isomorphic Version B

Filling out this survey will have no effect on your grade. We ask that you work alone and answer the questions thoroughly and to the best of your ability. Your participation in this survey is very helpful to our research — thank you!

Name: ___________________________

1) Suppose you were doing a field study examining a population of baboons in a region of Africa, as part of your investigation you caught as many **adult** baboons in the population as you could and measured the length of their canine teeth (long sharp teeth toward the front of the mouth), and drew a graph to show the measurements.

Draw a bar graph below to illustrate the measurements you expect to find. (Assume that the average canine length is 30mm).

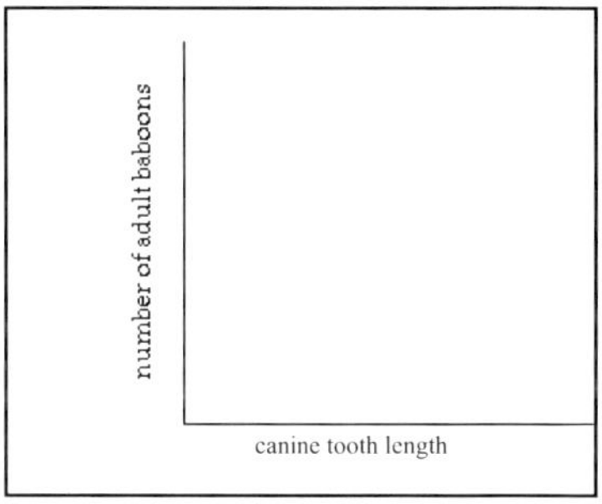

Explain what your graph shows:

2) Peregrine falcons (large predatory birds) are able to dive onto prey at speeds of up to 200 miles an hour, faster than any other birds of prey. How would a biologist explain how the ability to dive fast onto prey evolved in Peregrine falcons, assuming their ancestors could only dive onto prey at 70 miles an hour?

3) Ostriches are big flightless birds (they have wings but they are non-functional, they can't use them to fly). How would a biologist explain how flightless ostriches evolved from ancestors that could see?

For questions 4 through 6
Suppose you were investigating a population of black bears where many black bears were suddenly dying, and you wanted to explain why so many black bears were dying, and what enabled the surviving black bears to survive.

Below are a number of observations you could make. For each one, rate on a scale from 1 to 10 (where 1 is the least useful and 10 is the most useful), how useful this test or observation would be for your investigation. Then answer the question that follows.

4) How useful would it be to compare the environment (for example, weather or number of predators) now to the environment a year ago?

1 2 3 4 5 6 7 8 9 10

comparing the environment now to a year ago **is not** very useful — comparing the environment now to a year ago **is** very useful

How could this information help to explain why so many black bears are dying, and why others are able to survive?

5) How useful would it be to compare measurements (such as leg length) of surviving black bears to measurements of black bears that died?

1 2 3 4 5 6 7 8 9 10

comparing measurements of black bears that survived with black bears that did not survive **is not** very useful — comparing measurements of black bears that survived with black bears that did not survive **is** very useful

How could this information help to explain why so many black bears are dying, and why others are able to survive?

6) How useful would it be to compare the behavior (such as how they hunt or shelter themselves) of surviving black bears to the behavior of black bears that died (from observations made before they died).

1 2 3 4 5 6 7 8 9 10

comparing behavior of black bears that survived with black bears that did not survive **is not** very useful — comparing behavior of black bears that survived with black bears that did not survive **is** very useful

How could this information help to explain why so many black bears are dying, and why others are able to survive?

7) Scientists studied a population of mice on an island from 1955 to 1975. In 1960 merchant or tourist ships accidentally introduced some foxes to the island. The scientists started sighting the foxes hunting the mice. Over the next 15 years fox sightings remained high and many mice were hunted by the foxes. At first, the scientists feared that the mice would be killed off and become extinct on that island, but although many mice died, some survived.

Here are some of the scientists' observations:

	1960	**1965**	**1975**
Total mouse population	1000	500	550

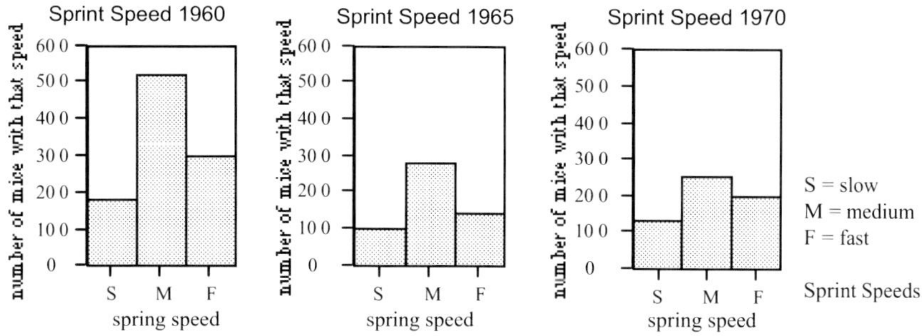

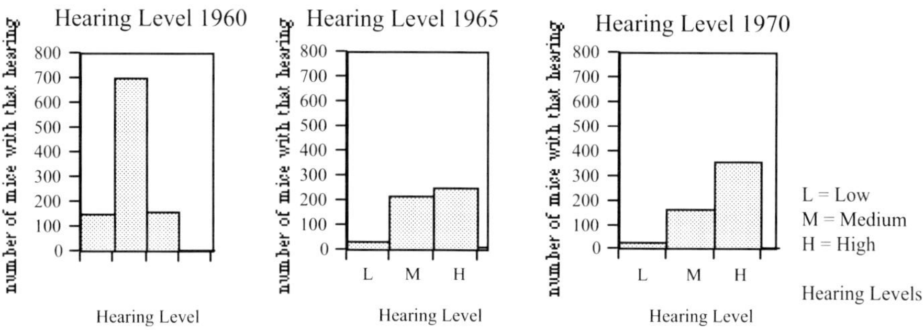

Here are some possible explanations for what enabled the surviving mice to survive. Which one is <u>best</u> supported by the observations above?

___ (a) Mice with higher hearing levels are better able to avoid being eaten.
___ (b) Mice that live survive by chance.
___ (c) Mice that have a faster sprint speed are better able to avoid being eaten.
___ (d) None of the above explanations (a–c) are supported by the data.

<u>Why did you choose this answer (**Be sure to describe how you used the graphs**)?</u>

Elephants are tall, heavy four legged land animals. They have a long trunk. This trait enables them to reach water to drink, and collect food, while standing and supporting their weight with all four feet.

8) **While elephants were evolving long trunks**

a) all elephants were equally likely to survive and reproduce, regardless of the length of their trunk.

b) those elephants without a trunk were less likely to survive and reproduce than those with some length of trunk .

Check the response that best describes what you think about statements (a) & (b) above

____ (a) is the **only** correct statement
____ (b) is the **only** correct statement
____ (a) is **more** correct than (b)
____ (b) is **more** correct than (a)
____ **both** (a) and (b) are **equally** correct
____ **neither** (a) nor (b) are correct

Why did you choose this answer:

9) Suppose you could go back in time to the generations when elephants were evolving long trunks, and that you could make any tests, measurements, observations or comparisons that you liked.

What tests, measurements or observations would you take to find out whether all elephants survive and reproduce at the same rate regardless of the length of their trunk?

Explain why you would make each of these tests, measurements or observations:

10) Now that trunks are present in elephants :

a) there still exists considerable variation in the trunk length of elephants.

b) there exists no variation in the trunk length of elephants.

Check the response that best describes what you think about statements (a) & (b) above
____ (a) is the **only** correct statement
____ (b) is the **only** correct statement
____ (a) is **more** correct than (b)
____ (b) is **more** correct than (a)
____ **both** (a) and (b) are **equally** correct
____ **neither** (a) nor (b) are correct

Why did you choose this answer:

11) If a population of elephants were forced to move from their current habitat where vegetation is abundant to a habitat where vegetation is sparse and the elephants have to walk great distances to reach food:

a) many elephants would die because they were poorly adapted to this environment because their long trunks interfered with walking great distances.	b) each generation of elephants would have slightly shorter trunks until eventually, for example, 50 or 60 generations, most all the long trunks would be gone.

Check the response that best describes what you think about statements (a) & (b) above
____ (a) is the **only** correct statement
____ (b) is the **only** correct statement
____ (a) is **more** correct than (b)
____ (b) is **more** correct than (a)
____ **both** (a) and (b) are **equally** correct
____ **neither** (a) nor (b) are correct

Why did you choose this answer:

12) A number of bacteria populations are today resistant to certain antibiotics (a chemical used to kill bacteria), even though those species were not resistant to this anitbiotic when it was first introduced. Biologists believe that antibiotic resistance evolved in bacteria because:

Choose the best answer:

a) individual bacteria built up a resistance to an antibiotic after being exposed to it. This resistance was then passed on to their offspring.
b) bacteria needed to be resistant to antibiotics in order to survive.
c) a few bacteria were probably resistant to this antibiotic before it was ever used.
d) bacteria learned to adapt to their environment.

Why did you choose this answer:

13) Which of the following provides the best example of the process of evolutionary adaptation.

Choose the best answer:

A. Sixty snakes successfully switch from hunting mice to baby birds because the mouse population has become extinct. All 60 snakes survive the transition from mice to baby birds.

B A large population (100) of dogs are able to produce heavy fur coats in a winter with severe cold and thus all are able to survive. All of these dogs' offspring have slightly heavier coats than their parents.

C. Due to extreme cold, half of a large dog population (100) dies. The other half survives and reproduces because their fur coats were heavier and better able to protect them from the weather.

D. A dog is moved to a warmer climate and responds by shedding large quantities of fur to help remain cool. The dog's offspring is born with a very heavy coat of fur, but is also able to shed the unneeded fur.

Why did you choose this answer:

14) If a population of wild dogs are in an environment that drastically changes (for example, a change in temperature of 20 degrees Celsius for 100 days and their regular food source is driven to extinction) which of the following events will most likely occur?

A. It is likely the population will become extinct.

B. The individuals within the population will learn to adapt to the changes.

C. Some individuals would die, but the total population would remain constant.

D. Individuals able to cope with the changes would pass on traits which help the next generation.

E. Individuals would modify their physical characteristics in order to maintain the balance of nature.

Why did you choose this answer:

Appendix C: Coding Scheme for Observations Rating Justifications

Scoring was "all or none," responses that met the criteria described in the table below received a point, and responses that did not meet the criteria did not receive a point. There were three observation types, so the highest possible justification score was 3.

Observation Type	Code For	Example
Comparison of physical characteristics between survivors and non-survivors	Note that these types of observations can yield information regarding relationships between structure, function and survival.	"This information is helpful because some of the length of the black bears probably are inable [sic] to reach such high points for certain food and died of starvation."
Comparison of behavioral characteristics between survivors and non-survivors	Note that these types of observations can yield information regarding relationships between behavior and survival.	"Maybe that would explain why the bear are dying, because they can't hunt well or hide from the climate."
Observations of environmental factors across time	Note that these types of observations can yield information regarding changes that can introduce a pressure.	"Maybe last year's weather was something the bears were use to and this year it got too cold for them. Maybe this year, they are being hunted more."

Appendix D: Sample Log File Excerpt (DEG group second session)

10:25:09 AM	Selected Population Info for: ground finches
10:25:37 AM	Asked data question: differences variation structure of ground finches
10:29:00 AM	View graph: COMPARE variation wing live ground finches dry 76…
10:29:38 AM	Annotation of grc 21 from wd COMPARE variation wing live ground finches dry 76… COMPARE variation wing live ground finches dry 76…
10:29:55 AM	Request individual view: gf5 from compare graph hot spots: COMPARE variation wing live ground finches dry 76…
10:29:57 AM	View individual: gf5
10:29:57 AM	View ind: gf5
10:30:43 AM	Request individual view: gf1 from compare graph hot spots: COMPARE variation wing live ground finches dry 76…
10:30:45 AM	View individual: gf1
10:30:45 AM	View ind: gf1
10:31:33 AM	Request individual view: gf5 from compare graph hot spots: COMPARE variation wing live ground finches dry 76…
10:31:33 AM	View ind: gf5 already viewed before.
10:31:35 AM	View
10:31:44 AM	Request individual view: gf7 from compare graph hot spots: COMPARE variation wing live ground finches dry 76…
10:31:47 AM	View individual: gf7
10:31:47 AM	View ind: gf7
10:31:59 AM	Request individual view: gf7 from compare graph hot spots: COMPARE variation wing live ground finches dry 76…
10:31:59 AM	View ind: gf7 already viewed before.
10:32:01 AM	View
10:32:05 AM	Request individual view: gf2 from compare graph hot spots: COMPARE variation wing live ground finches dry 76…
10:32:05 AM	View ind: gf2 already viewed before.
10:32:07 AM	View
10:32:21 AM	Request individual view: gf9 from compare graph hot spots: COMPARE variation wing live ground finches dry 76…
10:32:24 AM	View individual: gf9
10:32:24 AM	View ind: gf9
10:32:37 AM	Request individual view: gf34 from compare graph hot spots: COMPARE variation wing live ground finches dry 76…
10:32:38 AM	No data avail: gf34
10:32:40 AM	Request individual view: gf29 from compare graph hot spots: COMPARE variation wing live ground finches dry 76…
10:32:41 AM	No data avail: gf29
10:32:43 AM	Request individual view: gf16 from compare graph hot spots: COMPARE variation wing live ground finches dry 76…

Perceptual learning and the technology of expertise

Studies in fraction learning and algebra*

Philip J. Kellman[a], Christine Massey[b], Zipora Roth[b], Timothy Burke[a], Joel Zucker[a], Amanda Saw[a], Katherine E. Aguero[b], and Joseph A. Wise[c]
[a]University of California, Los Angeles / [b]University of Pennsylvania / [c]New Roads School

Learning in educational settings most often emphasizes declarative and procedural knowledge. Studies of expertise, however, point to other, equally important components of learning, especially improvements produced by experience in the extraction of information: *Perceptual learning*. Here we describe research that combines principles of perceptual learning with computer technology to address persistent difficulties in mathematics learning. We report three experiments in which we developed and tested *perceptual learning modules* (PLMs) to address issues of structure extraction and fluency in relation to algebra and fractions. PLMs focus students' learning on recognizing and discriminating, or mapping key structures across different representations or transformations. Results showed significant and persisting learning gains for students using PLMs. PLM technology offers promise for addressing neglected components of learning: Pattern recognition, structural intuition, and fluency. Using PLMs as a complement to other modes of instruction may allow students to overcome chronic problems in learning.

Keywords: algebra, fluency, fractions, learning technology, mathematics instruction, mathematics learning, pattern recognition, perception, perceptual learning, perceptual learning module (PLM)

1. Introduction

What does it mean to learn? To understand? To have expertise in some domain? Although approaches to mathematics teaching and learning vary widely, virtually all current approaches emphasize some combination of declarative knowledge — facts, concepts, and lines of reasoning that can be explicitly verbalized — and procedural knowledge — sequences of specified steps that can be enacted. Verbalizable knowledge may include memorized facts or co-constructed explanations, and procedures may be invented by learners or taught by direct instruction. Regardless of the pedagogical approach used to acquire them, these kinds of learning still fit within the typology of declarative and procedural knowledge.

A primary goal of this paper is to introduce a different dimension of learning that we believe has been neglected in most instructional settings. In contrast to declarative and procedural learning, we focus on *perceptual learning*, which refers to experience-based improvements in the learner's ability to extract structural patterns and relationships from inputs in the environment.[1] Rapid, automatic pick-up of important patterns and relationships –including relations that are quite abstract — characterizes experts in many domains of human expertise. Experts tend to see at a glance what is relevant to a problem and to ignore what is not. They tend to pick up relations that are invisible to novices and to extract information with low attentional load. From the standpoint of conventional instruction, the expert's fluency is mysterious — attainable only by long experience or "seasoning". Yet the passage of time is not a satisfactory explanatory mechanism for cognitive change.

We believe that persistent problems in mathematics learning, including difficulties in retention, failure to transfer, lack of fluency, and poor understanding of the conditions of application of knowledge, might be improved by systematically introducing perceptual learning interventions. In this article we consider the hypotheses that (1) some perennial difficulties in learning and instruction derive from an incomplete model of learning, specifically a neglect of *perceptual learning*, and (2) perceptual learning can be directly engaged, and accelerated, through appropriate instructional technology.

1.1 Perceptual learning

Perceptual learning (Gibson 1969) refers to experience-induced improvements in the pick-up of information. Unlike most computer-based sensor systems, which pick up information using unchanging routines,[2] humans have an astonishing ability to change their information extraction to optimize particular tasks. Although seldom mentioned in discussions of instruction or learning technology, perceptual learning underlies many, if not most, of the profound differences between experts and novices in any domain — differences such as rapid selection of task-relevant information, pick-up of higher-order relations and invariance, and effective classification.

Perceptual learning (PL) actually involves several kinds of improvements in information processing (Gibson 1969; Goldstone 1998). Kellman (2002) has argued that these may be broadly categorized in terms of *discovery* effects and *fluency* effects. Table 1 shows some of these effects and categorizes them according to this dichotomy. Discovery effects refer to learners finding the information that is most relevant to a task. One well-known discovery effect is increased attentional selectivity. With practice on a given task, learners come to pick up the relevant information for classifications while ignoring irrelevant variation (Gibson 1969; Petrov, Dosher, and Lu 2005). Practice also leads learners to discover invariant or characteristic relations that are not initially evident (cf. Chase and Simon 1973) and to form and process higher level units (Goldstone 2000; for reviews, see Gibson 1969; Goldstone 1998; Kellman 2002). These discovery processes, while seldom addressed explicitly in school learning, are pervasive, natural forms of learning. When a child learns what a dog, toy, or truck is, this kind of learning is at work. From a number of instances, the child extracts relevant features and relations. These allow later recognition of previously seen instances, but more important, even a very young child quickly becomes able to categorize *new* instances. Such success implies that the learner has discovered the relevant characteristics or relations that determine the classification. As each new instance will differ from previous ones, learning also includes the ignoring of irrelevant differences.

Fluency effects refer to changes in the efficiency of information extraction rather than discovery of the relevant information. Practice in classifying leads to

Table 1. Some characteristics of Expert and Novice information extraction. *Discovery* effects involve learning and selectively extracting features or relations that are relevant to a task or classification. *Fluency* effects involve learning to extract relevant information faster and with lower attentional load. (See text.)

	Novice	Expert
Discovery effects		
Selectivity:	Attention to irrelevant and relevant information	Selective pickup of relevant information / Filtering
Units:	Simple features	"Chunks" / Higher-order relations
Fluency effects		
Search type:	Serial processing	More parallel processing
Attentional load:	High	Low
Speed:	Slow	Fast

fluent and ultimately automatic processing (Schneider and Shiffrin 1977), where automaticity in PL is defined as the ability to pick up information with little or no sensitivity to attentional load. As a consequence, perceptual expertise may lead to more parallel processing and faster pickup of information.

The distinction between discovery and fluency effects is not razor sharp. For example, becoming selective in the use of information (a discovery effect) surely increases efficiency and improves speed (fluency effects). Nonetheless, clear cases of each category are evident. Experimentally, one might expect to see effects of discovery in pure accuracy measures (without time constraints), whereas fluency changes may be more evident in speed (or speed/accuracy relations when time constraints are present).

PL should not be considered a detached aspect of learning. Rather, it is intertwined with, in fact *presupposed by,* declarative and procedural knowledge. To be useful, both facts and procedures need to be deployed in relevant situations. Relevance depends on classifying the situation. In a geometry problem, one might recall the theorem specifying that a triangle having two equal sides must also have two equal angles. Whether this recollection is immediately useful or merely distracting, however, depends entirely on classifying the situation at hand. Classifying depends on picking up information about the structure of a problem or situation. The abilities to classify, discriminate, recognize patterns, and notice invariance in new instances are exactly the abilities that improve in task-specific fashion via PL (Gibson 1969; Kellman 2002). Applying procedures also depends on pattern recognition. For example, some leading approaches to computer-based learning (e.g., Anderson et al. 1992; Anderson, Corbett, Koedinger, and Pelletier 1995) have emphasized the analysis of learning content into sets of particular procedures ("productions," in a production-system approach). Instruction then consists of teaching these productions that make up the "cognitive model" for the task. Implicit in these approaches is the need for the learner to come to *recognize* the situations in which particular procedures apply. This task is not directly instructed in most applications, yet it is a crucial complement to the learning of procedures. When concrete instances reoccur, classifying or recognizing can be merely a matter of specific memory, but in real-world tasks, this is seldom the case. More commonly, problem-solving situations vary in many particulars but possess underlying structures that determine which procedures can be fruitfully applied. For the learner, extraction of this relevant underlying structure across variable examples is crucial. This is the role of PL, and evidence suggests such abilities change dramatically with practice and form a crucial foundation of expertise.

The PL effects listed in Table 1 are very general. They suggest that methods for addressing PL in instruction would have applications to almost any learning domain. As these characteristics of expertise are well-known, we might wonder why conventional instructional methods rarely address PL directly. Likewise, computer-based and web-based instructions mostly incorporate the traditional emphases on declarative and procedural knowledge. Substantial work has gone into making tutorial formats more realistic in computer-based learning (e.g., by incorporating realistic facial expressions in an animated tutor on screen), but technology to address PL has been missing.

In our view, the lack of focus on PL derives both from inadequate appreciation of certain dimensions of learning and from a lack of suitable techniques. We can teach, or at least present, facts and procedures, but how do we teach pattern recognition or structural intuition? Whereas some PL no doubt occurs during the consideration of examples in a lecture or in the working of homework problems, these activities are not strong methods for targeting perceptual learning.

In most learning domains, the answer for the student has been to learn the facts and procedures and then to spend time immersed in that domain. This advice applies to the student pilot who cannot judge the proper glide slope on approach to landing, the radiology resident who cannot spot the pathology in the image, the chess novice who cannot see the imminent checkmate, and the algebra student who cannot see that an expression can be simplified by using the distributive property in reverse (e.g., $(2x^2 - x + 2x - 1)$ can become $(2x - 1)(x + 1)$). The expert's magical ability to see these patterns at a glance has various names: Judgment, insight, intuition, perspicacity, and brilliance. These originate from vague sources: Experience, practice, seasoning. None of these are methods of instruction; rather, they point enigmatically to the passage of time, a range of experiences, or to an innate ability.

A special issue in teaching information extraction skills is that these often involve unconscious processing. The skilled expert who intuitively classifies a problem or grasps a complex relationship often cannot verbalize the process or content of these accomplishments. Even when the process or content can be stated, hearing the description does not give a student the expert's vision or fluency.

These limitations of instruction need not be fatal. We believe there are systematic approaches for engaging PL in instructional settings. These can be realized through a combination of PL principles and digital technology.

1.2 Research in perceptual learning

Although issues of PL have been considered off and on for more than a century (e.g., James 1890; Gibson and Gibson 1955; E. Gibson 1969), not many educational applications have flowed from this work. Since the late 1980s, there has been a resurgence of basic research in PL. Overwhelmingly, however, the contemporary focus has been on low-level, sensory aspects of information extraction (for a review, see Fahle and Poggio 2002; for a critique, see Garrigan and Kellman 2008). The reason for this focus is that sensory change can provide an important window into plasticity in the brain (e.g., Recanzone, Schreiner, and Merzenich 1993). In the most recent wave of research, there has been little effort to connect PL with issues of higher-order structure (as the Gibsons emphasized earlier) and not much integration with issues of learning and thinking in cognitive psychology.

Some efforts have been made in recent years to apply PL methods in real-world learning environments. Success has been reported in adapting auditory discrimination paradigms to address speech and language difficulties (Merzenich et al. 1996; Tallal, Merzenich, Miller, and Jenkins 1998). Tallal et al. showed that auditory discrimination training in language-learning-impaired children, using specially enhanced and extended speech signals, improved not only auditory discrimination performance but speech and language comprehension as well. Similar methods have also been applied to complex visual tasks. Kellman and Kaiser (1994) designed PL methods to study pilots' classification of aircraft attitude (e.g., climbing, turning) from primary flight displays (used by pilots to fly in instrument conditions). They found that an hour of training allowed novices to process configurations as quickly and accurately as civil aviators averaging 1000 hours of flight time. Experienced pilots also showed substantial gains, paring 60% off their response times. More recently, PL technology has begun to be applied to the learning of structure in mathematics and science domains, such as the mapping between graphs and equations, or apprehending molecular structure in chemistry (Silva and Kellman 1999; Wise et al. 2000). However, applications to middle school mathematics that we report here, specifically investigating PLMs for fraction learning and algebra, have not previously been attempted.

1.3 Elements of PLMs

The critical learning activity for PL involves classification episodes. In applications to structure in mathematics and mathematical representations, the learner may be asked to recognize or discriminate a relational structure or asked to map related structures across different representations (e.g., graphic versus numeric representations) or across transformations (e.g., algebraic transformations). In designing learning interventions based on principles of PL, we engage the learner in *large numbers of brief classification episodes* — not just one or two examples. This approach departs from common practice in mathematics classrooms in two notable ways. First, learners see many more instances of the target structures and relationships and in more contexts than would normally occur in classroom settings. There, most often, a teacher works one or two problems with the whole class, students explore a rich example in small groups, or a textbook presents a small number of worked examples in each chapter section, and students may then go on to solve problems that are similar to the model in fairly obvious ways. Often it is assumed that clear statement of relevant aspects of a problem type or procedure should be sufficient for good students to learn it. Yet, this assumption is suspect and, even when correct, refers to the declarative or procedural content with little consideration of pattern recognition skills. This is related to the second characteristic of PLMs: When PL is the instructional goal, students' time and effort is devoted to *problem recognition and classification*, rather than completing calculations and procedures to solve problems. Learning trials go quickly: A student might complete a dozen or more classification trials in the time it would take to work a problem.

Another critical feature of PL is that the learning instances must incorporate *systematic variation* across classification episodes. To allow the learner to extract invariant structure, it must appear in a variety of contexts. Irrelevant aspects of problems need to vary, so that the learner does not mistakenly correlate incidental features with the structure to be learned. The failure of conventional instruction to fulfill this requirement is responsible for many limitations in math learning, such as the familiar observation that students solve algebra problems more easily when "X" naturally ends up on the left side of the equation.

When the learning task involves discriminating among a set of target structures, particularly ones that may initially be confused with each other, learning trials should incorporate direct contrasts. Learning to discriminate among a set of items that at first look alike is a frustrating learning problem commonly faced by novices. What is more, this learning problem is often underestimated by experts who have already automatized the discriminations, without necessarily being able to articulate how they make them. Because the goal of PL is learning to pick up invariant structure across varying contexts, the learning set should include novel and varied instances. In this respect, PL differs from "drill" characterized by rote repetition. In rote repetition, the same learning items repeat over and over. In PL, particular instances ideally *never* repeat. PL thus gives the learner the ability to intuit relevant structure and relations in novel contexts, whereas rote learning does not. Motivationally, the situation also differs from rote learning. Properly arranged, the seeing of increasingly discernible structure in each new instance is exciting to the learner, as it is in natural learning situations, such as when a novice birdwatcher becomes able to recognize a new bird.

Computer-based learning technology provides a natural environment for PL interventions. It can allow learners to interact in systematic ways with large sets of examples that have the desired kinds of variability. It also allows continuous tracking of the performance of each individual learner (e.g., collecting accuracy and response time data on each trial), to evaluate progress toward mastery, and to customize the learning experience so time and effort are spent where they are most needed. These same features also make learning technology a powerful tool for conducting research on PL. Elements such as feedback, task format, learning sets, and problem sequencing can be naturally and systematically manipulated, and detailed performance data automatically collected for each user provide useful dependent measures for tracking and assessing learning.

1.4 Applying perceptual learning to high-level, symbolic, explicit tasks

We anticipate at this point a natural concern. How can PL apply to high-level, symbolic, and explicit domains such as mathematics? Perceptual aspects may be thought to apply only to low level or relatively incidental aspects of mathematics, such as the use of specific visual representations (e.g., pie slices used to teach fractions). Higher-level relations and structure are often considered non-perceptual. Moreover, mathematics is symbolic in that the relation between its representations and their meanings is often arbitrary (e.g., use of the character "4" to represent the number four). Arbitrary meanings, arguably, cannot be discovered from the pickup of information available in scenes, objects, or events — i.e., they are non-perceptual. Finally, mathematics is largely an explicit discipline. Not only is understanding important, but it is important to give reasons and proofs. If structural intuitions gotten from PL are not consciously accessible, they cannot be sufficient for mathematics.

Although these concerns are plausible, we find them to be ultimately ill-founded. With regard to the scope of perception, it is not uncommon to encounter the view that "perceptual" attributes are things like color, but relations and higher-order structure are cognitive constructs. Such ideas represent in part the long shadow of traditional empiricist theories of perception and in part a confusion of sensory properties with perceptual ones (for discussion, see J. Gibson 1966; Kellman and Arterberry 1998). We share with a number of modern theorists of perception (such as James and Eleanor Gibson, David Marr, Albert Michotte, and Gunnar Johansson) the idea that perception is not primarily about low-level sensory properties, such as color; it involves extracting information about the meaningful structures of objects, arrangements, and events. This extraction uses stimulus relations of considerable complexity. Michotte, for example, offered compelling evidence and arguments that we *perceive* causality and that perception often has an "amodal" character — i.e., it is not tied to simple, local, sensory stimulation (Michotte 1962; Michotte, Thines, and Crabbe 1964). J. Gibson (1966, 1979) was most programmatic in arguing that perception involves extraction of higher-order invariance in the service of acquiring functionally relevant information about objects, relations, and events.

Applied to mathematics, what this means is that mathematical ideas, as given in the representations we use to communicate them, have structure, and efficient processing of this structure is a crucial component of learning. There is structure in equations, for example, and also in graphs. Even fraction notation or the superscripting of a number to indicate exponentiation are structural features important to doing mathematics. If the novice fails to notice some important marking or relation, fails to select the aspects relevant to a problem, fails to map a structural feature to the correct concept, expends cognitive resources too heavily, or simply processes structure too slowly, advancement in math will be impaired.

One virtue of a higher-order, ecological view of perception is that it leads naturally to the idea that structural representations furnished by perception form the foundations of other cognitive processes (Barsalou 1999; Kellman and Arterberry 1998). Real-world learning and thinking tasks partake of both perceptual extraction of structure and symbolic thinking in seamless and cooperative fashion. Being involved with only one of these or the other may be a property of research communities but not of cognitive activities in complex tasks.

1.5 Perceptual learning and cognitive load

Some of the issues we raise regarding fluency and structure learning have been examined in the context of research on cognitive load effects in learning. Considerable evidence indicates that cognitive load is an important determinant of learning and performance in various domains (Chandler and Sweller 1991), including mathematics learning. In problem solving contexts, manipulations as straightforward as combining, rather than separating, textual information and diagrams can make an appreciable difference in outcomes (Sweller, Chandler, Tierney, and Cooper 1990). Presumably, such effects indicate that the demands of extracting information or processing relations in a learning or problem solving situation may exceed limits in attentional or working memory capacity.

Most efforts to ameliorate cognitive load limits in instruction have focused on altering instructional materials. In learning or problem solving, performance may be improved by combining graphics and text (Chandler and Sweller 1991), using visual and auditory channels in ways that expand capacity (Mayer and Moreno

1998), or presenting passively viewed worked examples (Paas and van Merrienboer 1994; Sweller, Chandler, Tierney, and Cooper 1990). The value of such interventions has been clearly demonstrated. Our approach, however, suggests another avenue for escaping cognitive load limits: Changing the learner. It has long been known that practice in information extraction leads to faster grasp of structure (Chase and Simon 1974) with lower cognitive load (Shiffrin and Schneider 1977), freeing up attentional capacity to organize the parts of a task or to allow attention to higher-order structure (Bryan and Harter 1899). PL technology has the potential to allow learners to overcome load limits and access higher level structure.

1.6 Experimental objectives

In the experiments below, we report initial attempts to apply PL concepts directly to mathematics learning in the middle and early high school years. We chose domains that are known to present difficult hurdles for many students: Reasoning and problem solving with fractional quantities, and algebra. These domains make plausible points of entry for at least two reasons. First, we suspect that a substantial part of students' learning difficulties in these areas involve structure extraction, pattern recognition, and fluency issues potentially addressable by PL interventions. Moreover, these areas are both central to the mathematics curriculum, and both form important foundations of later mathematics.

2. Experiment 1: Perceptual learning in fractions

Learning in the domain of rational numbers is complicated (e.g., Behr, Harel, Post, and Lesh 1992; Lamon 2001; Post, Behr, and Lesh 1986), and we did not take on its full scope, but rather focused on several important ideas. We selected issues that are known to be problematic for many learners and that may reveal the value of PL technology in improving learning.

Specifically, we targeted students' abilities to recognize and discriminate among structures that underlie the kinds of fraction problems commonly encountered in the upper elementary and middle school curriculum. We also addressed students' ability to map these structures across different representational formats, including word problems, fraction strips, and number sentences. In designing the instructional interventions for this study (both classroom lessons and learning software), we drew heavily on detailed analyses of the conceptual progressions involved in the development of fraction concepts and problem solving that have appeared in the research literature in recent years (e.g., Hackenberg 2007; Olive 1999, 2001;

Olive and Steffe 2002; Olive and Vomvoridi 2006; Steffe 2002; Thompson 1995; Thompson and Saldanha 2003; Tzur 1999).

Consider the following two problems:

(1) 10 alley cats caught 5/7 of the mice in a neighborhood. If they caught 70 mice, how many mice were in the neighborhood?

(2) A school principal ordered computers for 10 classrooms. 5/7 of the computers came with blue mice. How many mice were blue, if there were 70 mice in all?

Both of these word problems use the same object quantities (70 mice), fraction (5/7), irrelevant number information (10), and the same order of presentation of the numeric quantities (10, 5/7, and 70). Despite these superficial similarities, the two problems have contrasting underlying structures. The first problem could be restated in a simplified way as "70 mice is 5/7 of how many mice?" while the second problem could be restated as "How many mice is 5/7 of 70 mice?" Problem (1) is what we term a "find-the-whole" problem — we know that 70 mice is 5/7 of a whole quantity and we need to use that information to figure out what that whole quantity is. Problem (2) is a "find-the-part" problem — we know that the whole quantity of mice is 70 and we need to use that information to figure out how many mice would comprise 5/7 of that whole. The structural distinction between these two problems is not transparent in the structure of the word problem, and many upper elementary and middle school students do not seem to be able reliably to extract the underlying structure and carry out a corresponding solution strategy. (Indeed, we have repeatedly observed that when students encounter a find-the-part and find-the-whole problem with similar "cover stories" in a test or classroom assignment, they will frequently complain that the teacher made an error and gave them the same problem twice.)

In Experiment 1 we targeted these issues using PL technology. A central goal of the study was to help students become fluent in recognizing and discriminating find-the-whole and find-the-part fraction problems. A second, related goal was to enable them to identify and map these abstract structures across a series of different but mathematically relevant representations. That is, whether presented with a full word problem, a simplified question, a fraction strip representation, or a set of number sentences, they should be able to identify which kind of structure it represents and connect it to the corresponding structure in the other representational formats. Our hypothesis was that fluency in structure recognition and mapping is a critical component in problem solving, and that training that focuses on achieving it will transfer to significant improvements in open-ended problem solving.

The design of this study also provided an opportunity to explore another issue related to incorporating PL approaches into the learning interventions. As described above, a critical feature in PL is exposure to a widely varying set of examples that embody the relevant structures. Naturally occurring PL situations, such as children learning categories like dog or toy or machine, indicate that PL proceeds perfectly well in complex natural environments that have not been deliberately decomposed in any particular way to facilitate the child's learning. This observation is somewhat at odds with common approaches to the design of instruction in classroom settings, in which knowledge domains are often deliberately broken down and sequenced, with simpler concepts being introduced first and then used as building blocks for more complex concepts and relationships. Also, some experimental research on PL suggests that introduction of easy cases first may facilitate learning (e.g., Ahissar and Hochstein 1997).

In research on memory and motor learning, the related issue of blocked vs. randomized learning trials has received significant attention, with findings that might seem surprising in the K-12 classroom. Schmidt and Bjork (1992), for instance, argue from a review of a number of training studies that mixing item types to be learned produces better long-term learning, as well as better ability to apply learning appropriately in a variety of circumstances. Paradoxically, mixing may actually depress performance levels during (and immediately at the end of) training, but it leads to better performance in the long run.

In this context, we considered the specific question of whether to introduce first *unit fraction* examples and problems (i.e., those involving fractions with a numerator of 1) as a simple case and then build to the more complex cases of non-unit fractions. Alternatively, unit and non-unit fractions could be introduced at the same time, so students might notice relations between them from the beginning.

With these contrasting ideas in mind — a progression from simple to complex versus mixed complexity and task variability throughout the learning period — we developed two different forms of the learning software. For one group, unit fractions were introduced first, in a series of classroom lessons and then in training sessions with PLM software that involved only unit fraction problems. Subsequently, the students in this group participated in another round of classroom instruction that introduced non-unit fractions and then worked with PLM software that intermixed unit and non-unit fractions. In a contrasting condition, students participated in classroom instruction that introduced both unit and non-unit fractions and then worked with a version of the PLM software in which both types were intermixed from the beginning.

This study also included a control group that, like the two PLM groups, participated in a full 16-lesson instructional sequence on fractions and problem solving with fractions but did not work with the PLM technology. Both the software and classroom lessons were designed with an explicit focus on structural aspects of problems involving fractions and on relating and mapping fraction concepts across different representations. The control group allowed us to ask whether deliberately introducing and developing fraction concepts and problem solving strategies from a structural point of view in teacher-led instruction is (a) effective at all in promoting learning and problem solving with fractions, (b) sufficient in itself, or (c) able to be further complemented by additional PLM training. Comparing PLM and No-PLM conditions provided an assessment of the value of the PL intervention. A pre-test, immediate post-test, and delayed post-test design allowed us to us to compare these conditions in both immediate learning gains (at the end of instruction) and also in terms of durability of learning over time.

2.1 Methods

2.1.1 *Participants*

Participants were 76 students (44 female, 32 male) who were enrolled in the 7th grade in an urban public school serving a predominantly minority low-income neighborhood. Details of their demographic profile and related information may be found in Supplementary Materials at http://www.kellmanlab.psych.ucla.edu.

2.1.2 *Design*

All students were pre-tested on a custom-designed pencil and paper assessment and then randomly assigned to conditions with the constraint that the groups have approximately equal pre-test scores. Students in all three conditions participated in a series of classroom lessons. Students in the Unit First PLM condition and the Mixed PLM condition spent a number of sessions working individually with the software. Students in the No-PLM Control group had no further learning intervention after the classroom lessons. Following the learning phase, students were given an immediate post-test. A delayed post-test was given approximately 9 weeks later. No research-related learning activities occurred between the immediate post-test and the delayed post-test.

2.1.3 *Materials*

Classroom lessons. The classroom instruction involved a series of 16 interactive lessons, each about 40 minutes long, designed and conducted by one of the authors (ZR, an experienced middle school mathematics teacher and curriculum specialist). These lessons presented a foundational introduction to fractions, with a focus on structural relationships that underlie fraction concepts. In direct instruction

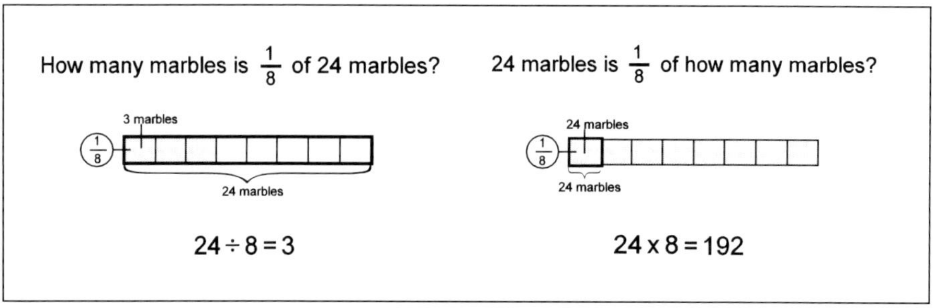

Figure 1. Examples of simple question, fraction strip, and number sentence representations for contrasting "Find-the-Part" (left) and "Find-the-Whole" (right) fraction problems. These representations were used in both the classroom instruction and PLM software in Experiment 1.

and in small group activities, four different representations were used to help students develop useful intuitions about and to reason quantitatively with numeric quantities involving fractions. The same representations were also used in the PLM software, so the classroom instruction also served as an orientation to the software.

After instruction on fraction concepts and representations, these were connected to problem solving situations with "find-the-whole" and "find-the-part" problems (as described above). Four kinds of representations were introduced, which were also used in the PLM software. These four representation types were termed Word Problems (WP), Simple Questions (SQ), Number Sentences (NS), and Fraction Strips (FS). Figure 1 gives an example of three of these representations for the two contrasting problem types.

The Simple Questions were open-ended questions stated in a direct, canonical form. Fraction strips were representations that summarized the information that was known in relation to the overall problem structure. The fraction strip was a continuous strip segmented according to the number of units in the fraction denominator. In the Find-the-part problem, the known quantity was the total, indicated by a labeled bracket underneath the fraction strip. In the corresponding Find-the-whole problem, the known quantity was the fractional part, indicated by a labeled bracket. Green highlighting indicated the quantity the student was trying to find. Fraction strips also included a marker that pointed to the unit fraction. The Number Sentences represented a solution strategy that could be used to find the unknown quantity.

In addition to working with the Simple Question, Fraction Strip, and Number Sentence representations, students worked on solving open-ended find-the-whole and find-the-part Word Problems, extracting a Simple Question from a Word Problem and representing the Word Problem in a Fraction Strip. Over the course of these lessons, students worked on solving a total of 10 open-ended fraction problems. The final activity in the sequence of classroom lessons involved matching all four representations to each other for both kinds of problem types. This concluding lesson also served as an orientation to the learning tasks for students in the two PLM conditions.

It is important to note that both the instructor-led classroom lessons and the learning software were created using design principles drawn from PL research: Specifically, they focused on (1) developing clear concepts of the structural relationships and patterns involved in quantities expressed as fractions, (2) the relationship between fractions and the operations of multiplication and division, and (3) recognition and mapping of target structures and patterns across representational formats. The critical differences between the classroom instruction and the PLM software were that the PLMs engaged students with a much larger and more varied set of examples, and the software-based learning experiences were designed to help students extract the target relationships on their own by interacting with them in a structured way, rather than having the learning guided and explained by a teacher. Our hypothesis was that both the classroom instruction and PLM software would advance students' learning; however, we predicted that the PLMs would enhance students' learning of structure and improve the *fluency* and *durability* of students' ability to recognize and reason with the targeted concepts.

2.1.4 *PLM software*

The PLM software presented learners with many short learning trials on which their task was to map a target structure given in one representational format to the corresponding structure in a different representational format. Learners selected from among several choices, which typically included distractor items that corresponded to common errors. Learners did not have to perform calculations or solve problems — instead the focus was on recognizing, discriminating, and mapping target structures. Figure 2 illustrates a typical learning trial.

Requiring learners to find a common structure across different representation types on each trial promotes the extraction of an abstract relational structure that cuts across superficial similarity. The choices, which were always of the same representation type, resembled each other much more than any one of them resembled the target. Thus the learner had to discriminate among stimuli with similar appearances (the choices) while mapping an abstract structure across stimuli with very different appearances (the target and its corresponding choice). The software drew on a large set of learning items so that unique items were presented on each learning trial, and memorization of the particulars of a correct answer on any given trial was not likely to help on other trials. Users received feedback on each trial as to whether they were correct or incorrect; if they were incorrect, the cor-

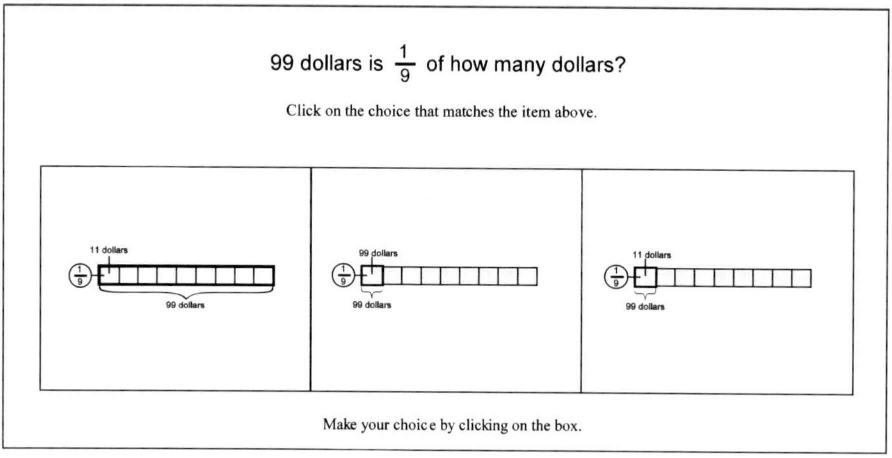

Figure 2. Sample learning trial from fractions PLM software. Learners match a target in one representational format (e.g., simple question) to the corresponding structure in another format (e.g., fraction strip). In this case, the correct choice is in the center.

rect response was illustrated with a short interactive feedback sequence (described further below).

The learning set consisted of 6 categories of items, representing bidirectional pairings of each of the four representation types with each other. Learning trials contained one target representation and three choices, except for trials in which Word Problems were presented in the choice position, in which case only two choices were presented. This was done to reduce the cognitive load for learners with weaker reading skills. The program drew from a set of 112 problem families (i.e., sets of representations using the same fractions, quantities, and objects), each containing 8 potential target items and all of the related choice sets. This created a large pool of problem combinations.

The Simple Questions, because they were stated in a canonical form, had a sentence structure such that the fraction always appeared before the whole number in find-the-part problems (e.g., How many dollars is 1/5 of 20 dollars?) and vice versa for find-the-whole problems (e.g., 20 dollars is 1/5 of how many dollars?). This rigid structure may invite learners to form a rule based on the order in which the numbers appear that could guide their choice of a matching representation. To prevent such superficial rules from being useful, the Word Problems introduced the fractions and the quantities in varying orders in the same kind of problem. In addition, Word Problems included irrelevant numbers to discourage "number grabbing" strategies. These irrelevant numbers were used as distractors in corresponding incorrect choices.

Additional considerations related to constructing distractors included the use of common student errors, particularly in confusing structural relationships

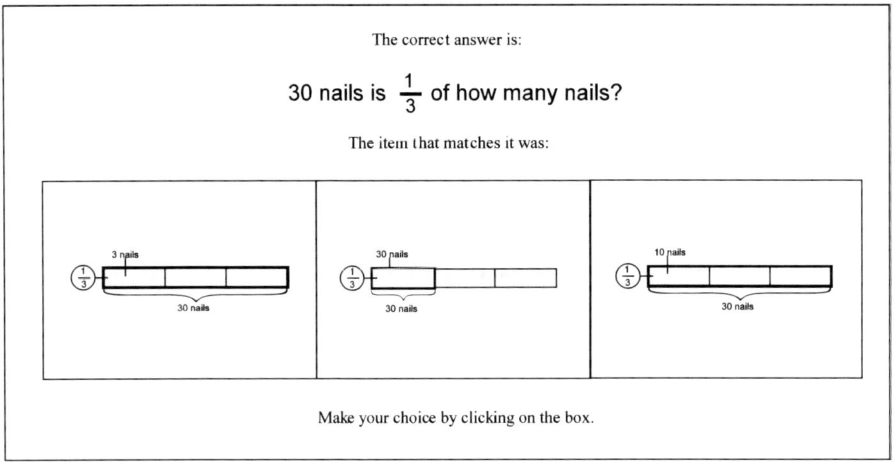

Figure 3. Active feedback screen following an incorrect response. Note that the correct response becomes the target in the active feedback on an incorrect response and the learner must match it to the original problem.

involved in find-the-part and find-the-whole problems. In all cases the number sentences were mathematically correct, and all fractions were fully reduced except for fractions with 100 as the denominator, which served as a bridge to thinking about percents.

The PLM software automatically created a time-stamped record of the problem presented on each trial, the student's responses, and reaction time. It also tracked the student's performance level within each category according to a set of pre-determined mastery criteria. A given category was considered to be mastered, and retired from the learning set, when the student answered 10 of the last 12 items correctly and met certain response time criteria. Time criteria were less than 90 sec per item for problems containing Word Problems and 20 seconds per item for others. As students mastered various categories, their learning effort was automatically concentrated on categories they had not yet mastered.

Feedback. The PLM provided students feedback on their performance in three ways: immediate feedback on accuracy, active feedback on incorrect responses, and block feedback on every twelve problems. Active feedback (see Figure 3) followed mistakes and presented the student with the correct answer again. The student was then asked to select the *question* that matches it. If the user was encoding the feedback, this selection was simple, because it had just been shown on the preceding screen. If an error occurred, the correct answer was highlighted. This active feedback was designed so that the student would have to attend to feedback information before moving on and could also gain practice on matching the representations in the opposite direction. Bi-directional practice may enhance discovery of relevant structures. Block feedback (every 12 problems) provided information on the student's accuracy and average reaction time. It also displayed a horizontal "mastery" bar that indicated (as a percentage) how close to completion the student was on the PLM. Thus, the student was able to see his or her cumulative progress.

2.1.5 *Pre-test/post-test fraction assessment*

To test for learning gains and their durability over an extended period of time, equivalent versions of a 27-item pencil-and-paper learning assessment were administered to students as a pre-test at the beginning of the study, after students had completed the learning activities for their condition, and after a delay of about two months. Items on the assessment were divided into six subscales related to different aspects of fraction knowledge and fraction problem solving. The assessment was comprised primarily of problems that did not directly resemble the kinds of problems that students worked on in either the classroom instruction or in the PLM training and thus emphasized transfer of learning. No problem on the test was identical in structure to the learning trials included in the training. However, some — particularly the open-ended Simple Questions — were fairly close. Although students never had to solve such problems during their PLM training, they did gain considerable experience in mapping them to Number Sentences. Other problems on the assessment were less directly related to the PLM training and focused more on knowledge such as understanding unit fractions in relation to non-unit fractions and interpreting numerators and denominators in fractions. The assessment also required students to solve open-ended word problems that mixed other types of fraction problems in with find-the-whole and find-the-part problems. The subscales comprising the assessment are described in detail in the Supplementary Materials.

2.1.6 *Apparatus*

Students completed the PLM sessions on laptop PCs using the Windows operating system. The laptops were arranged on separate desks in an empty classroom at the students' school. Monitors were 13–15" in diagonal measurement.

2.1.7 *Procedure*

Classroom Instruction. Following the pre-test, students in all three conditions participated in the first round of classroom instruction involving unit fractions, which was the same for all conditions, in their regular math classes. The first round of instruction included nine lessons on unit fractions, followed by seven lessons on non-unit fractions. One of the researchers, an experienced middle school math teacher who was familiar to most of the students, designed and led the instruction with assistance from several research assistants who were available to help students as they worked on their own or in small groups. Following the first set of unit fraction lessons, students in the Unit First condition started the Unit First PLM. Simultaneously, students in the Mixed PLM and No-PLM Control conditions continued with classroom instruction that incorporated non-unit fractions. When they had completed this set of lessons, students in the Mixed PLM condition began PLM training on a version of the PLM software that intermixed unit fraction and non-unit fraction problems from the start. Students in the Unit First PLM condition completed the first phase of PLM training working only with unit fraction problems, then returned for the remaining seven classroom lessons incorporating non-unit fraction problems. They then returned to PLM training using the Mixed PLM.

PLM Sessions. Students in the Mixed and Unit-First groups were taken out of their regular classrooms for 30–40 minute sessions with the PLM software. A mini-computer lab was created using eleven laptops in an empty classroom. Students were given calculators and scrap paper but were not required to use them.

In addition to the category retirement criteria described above, the Unit First group had a group criterion in which all students had to either reach criterion within each category or complete at least 400 learning trials before all students in this group moved to Phase II. In Phase II students worked on the PLM until they either reached criterion or were stopped by the researcher due to time constraints. Students in both PLM conditions thus completed a varying number of PLM sessions, depending on their level of performance. Number of sessions ranged between 2 and 6 in Phase 1 of the Unit First PLM, 2 and 9 in Phase 2, and 2 and 13 for the Mixed PLM.

Immediate and delayed post-test administration. After reaching criterion or concluding their use of the PLM, each participant completed an immediate post-test. Students in the No-PLM Control group received their post-test following completion of instruction on non-unit fractions. Delayed post-tests were administered to all participants nine weeks later. At each administration, participants were allowed to use scrap paper and a calculator. There was no time limit, although most students completed each part of the assessment in less than thirty minutes.

2.2 Results

2.2.1 *Overall results*

The main results of Experiment 1 are shown in Figure 4. All three groups improved from pre-test to immediate post-test and delayed post-test. In the immediate post-test, the two PLM groups showed similar performance, with both outperforming the No-PLM Control Group. In the delayed post-test, however, the Mixed PLM

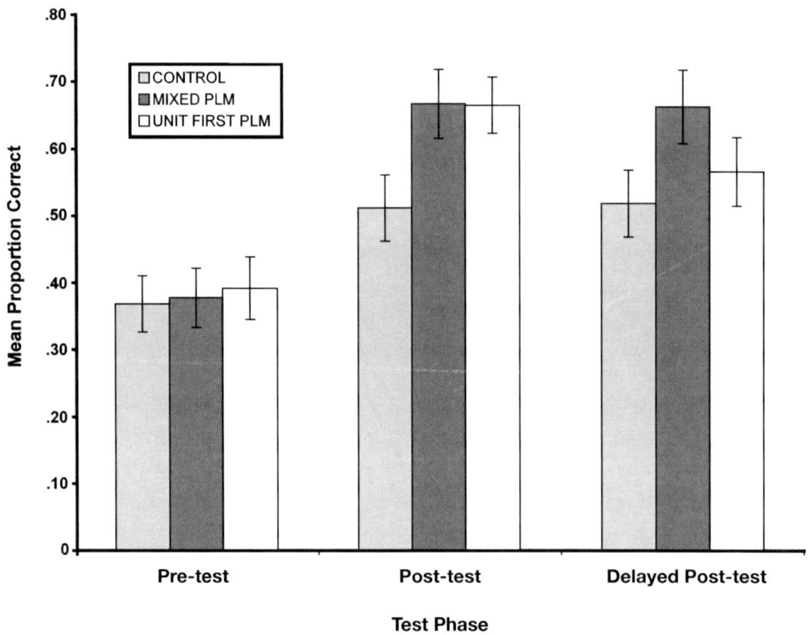

Figure 4. Mean accuracy by condition and time of test on the fraction assessment. Error bars indicate ±1 standard error of the mean.

group showed best performance, maintaining its learning gains over the 9-week interval. The No-PLM Control Group maintained its smaller learning gain after the delay. The Unit First PLM group's mean score dropped in the delayed post-test to a level lower than that of the Mixed PLM but higher than that of the control group.

These observations were confirmed by the statistical analyses. A two-way repeated measures ANOVA with Test Phase (Pre-test, Immediate Post-test, Delayed Post-test) as a within subjects factor and Condition (Unit First PLM, Mixed PLM, No-PLM Control) as a between subjects factor was performed on students' proportion correct scores on the fractions learning assessment. There was a main effect of Test Phase, $F(2,138)=89.66$, $p<0.001$. There was no reliable main effect of Condition, but there was a significant Condition by Test Phase interaction, $F(4,138)=5.396$, $p<0.001$, indicating different learning effects across conditions.

Planned comparisons (two-tailed t-tests) were carried out to examine the condition differences in more detail. The improvement between pre-test and immediate post-test was greater in the Unit First PLM Group than in the Control Group, $t(51)=2.60$, $p<.02$, and improvement was also greater in the Mixed PLM than in the Control Group, $t(47)=3.07$, $p<.01$. Improvement from pre-test to immediate post-test did not differ between the Unit First PLM Group and the Mixed PLM Group, $t(48)=0.34$, n.s.

Table 2. Performance on assessment subscales by condition. Pre-test columns show average proportion correct. Other columns show change from pre-test to post-test for immediate and delayed post-tests.

	Pre-test proportion correct			Change from pre-test to immediate post-test			Change from pre-test to delayed post-test		
Subscale Type	Unit First PLM	Mixed PLM	No PLM Control	Unit First PLM	Mixed PLM	No PLM Control	Unit First PLM	Mixed PLM	No PLM Control
Open-ended Word Problems	.30	.28	.26	+.27	+.29	+.18	+.18	+.29	+.20
Simple Find-the-part and Find-the whole Problems	.35	.33	.30	+.35	+.36	+.17	+.15	+.30	+.15
Fraction Comparisons	.64	.64	.76	+.09	+.16	−0.08	+.03	+.23	−0.07
Unit Fractions	.44	.44	.42	+.30	+.29	+.16	+.23	+.26	+.16
Find-the-Whole	.24	.32	.30	+.34	+.30	+.14	+.25	+.23	+.14
Find-the-Part	.33	.26	.24	+.28	+.34	+.15	+.12	+.33	+.21

Learning gains between the pre-test and delayed post-test did not differ reliably between the Unit First PLM and the Control groups ($t(48) = -0.528$, n.s.). However, the Mixed PLM Group showed greater improvement from pre-test to delayed post-test than both the Control Group, $t(43) = 2.86$, $p < .01$, and the Unit First PLM Group, $t(47) = 2.15$, $p < .04$.

2.2.2 *Results by subscale*

The subscales that comprise the fraction assessment provided a profile of different aspects of students' understanding. Table 2 summarizes the changes in average scores for each subscale from the pre-test to the immediate post-test and from the pre-test to the delayed post-test by condition.

Students in each condition showed substantive learning gains on all of the subscales. The largest and most durable learning gains generally favored the Mixed PLM condition, which also had the highest average scores in every subscale on the delayed post-test (as can be seen by adding their change score to their pre-test score). Statistical tests showed that most of these gains were highly reliable, including 5 of 6 subscales showing robust main effects of Test Phase ($p < .001$) and 4 of 6 subscales showing a reliable interaction of Condition by Test Phase. (See Supplementary Materials.)

2.3 Discussion

On both overall assessments and individual subscales from pre-test through delayed post-test, all conditions showed significant learning gains. The Mixed PLM intervention, however, was most effective in yielding substantial learning gains (on the order of 80%) that were fully maintained more than two months later. These primary assessments were not tests of improvement in the PLM tasks but measured transfer to fundamental learning tasks, such as solving problems involving fractions and comparing fractional quantities.

These results provide clear empirical support for our motivating hypotheses. First, instruction that focuses on identifying structural patterns related to fractions, as opposed to focusing on computing solutions, is effective in leading to gains in students' ability to solve fraction problems. Although the PLM interventions required students to practice recognizing and differentiating structures, the assessments required them to solve open-ended problems. These problems were in formats differing from what students saw during the learning phase.

Second, supplementing the classroom instruction with PLM training substantially increased both overall levels of performance and the durability of learning over a two-month period. Although students in the No-PLM condition showed significant learning gains following the series of 16 classroom lessons, they did not, on average, achieve the same levels of performance as students in the PLM conditions. This suggests that classroom instruction in mathematics may aptly address some aspects of learning but not others. Declarative and procedural components need to be supplemented by learning activities in which learners practice extraction of structure and reach some level of fluency with the structures and classifications in a given domain. It suggests, further, that PLM instructional resources may be a cost-effective way to help students to attain the relevant information extraction skills and fluency. Our data indicate that students varied widely in the amount of practice needed to achieve mastery criteria. The technology introduced here constitutes an efficient way to provide varying amounts of practice to different students, as well as to monitor and certify their individual progress.

A third important finding from this experiment was that the Mixed PLM condition produced stronger learning gains than either the Unit First PLM or the No-PLM Control conditions. The Mixed PLM condition was distinctive in yielding both high levels of performance following the instructional intervention *and* long-term durability of learning. There was virtually no decrement in performance after a delay exceeding two months. The finding is noteworthy, given that the two PLM conditions were similar in many respects: Both groups experienced the same classroom lessons, and the software used by the Unit First group in Phase 2 was identical to that used by the Mixed PLM group throughout. The critical difference was that students in the Mixed PLM group saw unit and non-unit fraction problems intermixed from the beginning of their PLM training.

Why should this manipulation make such a difference? The result is consistent with earlier research indicating the value of mixed rather than blocked practice (e.g., Schmidt and Bjork 1992). In this domain, we suggest that presenting the more complete and complex learning set from the beginning allows learners to compare and contrast elements, so that their understanding of concepts such as unit and non-unit fractions and their relationship to a whole quantity is constructed in a more comprehensive and relational way from the outset. Breaking the learning apart in a simple-to-complex progression may give the learner an incomplete understanding of the elements and relationships, which must then be revised when more complexity is introduced.

3. Perceptual learning in algebra: Experiment 2

A major function of ordinary perception is to register the shapes and arrangements of objects and spatial layout in the world. Equally crucial is perceiving change, the structure of *events,* and the potential for transformation (J. Gibson 1966, 1979; Shipley and Zacks 2008). These abilities are not static: PL leads to improvements, often vast, in picking up structure, selecting relevant aspects, and becoming aware of potential for action and change (E. Gibson 1969; Goldstone 1998; Kellman 2002).

If knowledgeable scholars were asked to name specific contexts to which these descriptions of perception and PL apply, it would be a shock if any mentioned *algebra.* The idea that these concepts apply not only to ordinary perception but to higher mathematics is admittedly a novel one. Indeed, we assume we are among few if any investigators ever to suggest such a thing (but see Landy and Goldstone, 2007).

On reflection, however, the idea may not be preposterous. Algebraic equations and expressions have structure, and the doing of algebra is related to the seeing of this structure. Selectivity is important: Some characteristics of algebraic representations, such as the shapes of characters, their order and arrangements, are crucial to comprehending algebra, but others, such as the size of the characters or their colors, are not. The chunking of groups of characters into meaningful entities is important in working with equations, as it is in other domains demanding perceptual expertise (e.g., Chase and Simon 1973). Efficient detection of important relations in novel exemplars — relations invisible to novices — is also key. And becoming aware of the potential for transforming equations or expressions is the bread and butter of symbolic manipulation in algebra — in simplifying an expression, classifying structure, or solving an equation.

If these aspects of learning in algebra are important, it is a matter of consequence that conventional instructional methods do little to address them directly. As in a number of complex PL domains, the expert's intuitive grasp of structure may not be available to conscious access (Chase and Simon 1973; Gibson 1969; Hoffman and Murphy 2006; Kellman 2002; Mettler and Kellman 2006). If so, the relevant pattern recognition is unlikely to be conveyed by lectures or tutorials. Even if relevant structural relations can be described, hearing the description does not turn the learner into an expert pattern recognizer. Working problems contributes to the relevant learning but perhaps not in the most systematic and efficient manner.

In two experiments, we applied PL technology to algebra learning. We were motivated by two linked hypotheses. One is that there is a learning gap in conventional instruction, such that students learn the factual and procedural aspects of algebra in their first algebra course, but are relatively impaired in terms of the seeing aspects, as might be evidenced in the speed and fluency of problem solving. The other is that PLMs providing practice in seeing structure and mapping across transformations of equations might rapidly improve these missing dimensions of instruction.

It is important to emphasize that we believe the declarative and procedural components of mathematics learning are important. Our aim is not to replace these components, but to address complementary, and neglected, learning issues, specifically those related to structure extraction and fluency. In light of this goal, in both studies we worked with students who were past mid-year in their first algebra course (Algebra I), expecting that these students would have reasonable knowledge of the facts and goals of algebra and the procedures for solving equations in one variable. We hypothesized that they might nevertheless have poor recognition skills and fluency. We predicted that a relatively short intervention, consisting of two to three days' use of a PLM with 40–45 minutes per day, might make a large and lasting difference in fluency and possibly accuracy of pattern recognition and problem solving in algebra.

Experiment 2 tested the primary hypotheses, along with tests relating the generality of problem types seen in learning to transfer. Experiment 3 was designed especially to examine endurance of learning gains, as tested after a 3-week delay, in a larger sample. Secondarily, Experiment 3 also made a first attempt to look at novel category sequencing algorithms that adapt to the individual learner.

The primary goal of Experiment 2 was to test whether principles of PL embodied in PLMs could noticeably impact algebra pattern recognition and fluency. The PLM was designed to provide practice in seeing the structure of equations and mapping across algebraic transformations. On each trial a target equation was presented, along with 4 equations shown below, labeled A through D. The participant's task was to select which of the choices could be obtained by a legal algebraic transformation of the target equation. Accuracy and speed were measured, and feedback was given.

We hypothesized that, despite offering learners no new explicit declarative or procedural information, they would show improvement from pre-test to post-test in their speed and accuracy of processing algebraic transformation problems. We also hypothesized that PLM experience might show its influence on a transfer task: Algebra problem solving. Given that solving of equations in one variable had already been taught to students, we expected that they would come to the experiment with some level of proficiency in obtaining correct answers. However, we predicted that PLM training would have a large impact on fluency, as revealed by students' speed in solving equations. A secondary objective of Experiment 2 was to look at variations in structure mapping experience. Specifically we varied the number of operations involved and direction of transformations.

3.1 Methods

3.1.1 *Participants*

Participants were 13 9th grade students and 17 8th grade students at an independent philanthropic school system in Santa Monica, California, all taking Algebra I.

3.1.2 *Apparatus*

The learning modules were tested on standard PCs using the Windows operating system in computer-equipped classrooms. Monitors were 17–21" in diagonal measurement. All assessments and the PLM were presented on computer, with participants' data being sent to a central server.

3.1.3 *Design*

The experiment was set up to assess effects of our learning technology on speed and accuracy of recognition of algebraic transformations and algebra problem solving. A pre-test was given on one day, followed by 2 days in which students worked on the PLM for 40–45 minutes per day. A post-test was administered the next day. For a subset of subjects, a delayed post-test was administered two weeks later.

3.1.4 *Algebraic transformations PLM*

In the PLM, participants on each trial selected from several choices the equation that could be obtained by a legal algebraic transformation of a target equation. An example is shown in Figure 5. Problems involved shifts of constants, variables or expressions (e.g., $(x-2)$). Accuracy and speed were measured, and feedback was given.

$$6y + 5x - 20 = 43$$

A	$6y - 20 = 43 + 5x$
B	$6y - 20 = 43(-5x)$
C	$6y - 20 = 43 - 5x$
D	$6y - 20 = 43 - x - 5$

Figure 5. Sample problem from the Algebra PLM. A target equation appears at the top and the user selects which of the four choices on the bottom corresponds to a legal algebraic transformation of the target.

Participants were randomly assigned to one of four learning conditions. In Single operation conditions, participants saw problems in the learning module that always involved one operator used to transform the target equation into the correct answer (either subtract or divide). In Double operation conditions, participants saw two different operators during the learning module (on separate trials). Half of the participants in both Single and Double conditions received Unidirectional training, in that they saw problems that required transformation in only one direction, involving the shift of some constant, variable, or expression from left to right. The other half of subjects received Bidirectional training; they saw, on separate trials, either right-to-left or left-to-right transformations. Because these condition manipulations did not figure prominently in the results, we include further details in the Supplementary Materials.

3.1.5 *Assessments*

All assessments were presented on the computer. Three parallel versions were constructed. Corresponding problems on separate versions varied in the specific constants, variables, or expressions appearing in each equation. Each participant saw a different version in pre-test and post-test (and, for a subset, in delayed post-test), with order counterbalanced across participants. Each version of the assessment included two sections: Recognition problems and solve problems. *Recognition* problems were similar to those in the learning module; they required the learner to select a choice that comprised a legal transformation of a target equation. In the assessments, only three choices were used — the correct answer and two distractors. *Solve* problems, requiring the participant to solve algebra equations containing one variable, were used as a transfer test. There were 16 recognition problems, 4 each involving the operators add, subtract, multiply, and divide. The left/right orientation of problems in every category was balanced. There were 17 solve problems, 8 of which were based on the single operators add, subtract, multiply, and divide. The other 9 problems were two-step problems. For example, solving $4=2t/3$ might involve multiplying both sides by 3 and then dividing by 2. Participants first worked on solve-for-variable problems and then transformation problems. These problems were presented individually in random order for each participant.

3.1.6 *Procedures and stimuli*

Depending upon individual progress, participants completed the experiment (pre-test, PLM, post-test) in 2–4 sessions lasting about 45 minutes each and usually taking place on consecutive days. The interval between sessions did not exceed 2 days and the post-test was taken within 2 days of completing the PLM. All problems were presented on the computer. Scratch paper was provided for solve-for-variable problems on the pre-test and the post-test.

On each learning trial, an equation was presented at the top with an equivalent transformed equation given along with three distractor equations (making 4 choices in all). Participants were instructed to select the equivalent equation and to be accurate but respond as promptly as they could. Following either a correct or incorrect selection, portions of the original equation and the equivalent one that were relevant to the transformation were highlighted in red. If the participant chose the correct answer, a green box appeared around that choice and underneath the equations appeared the message "Correct!" and a prompt to press the spacebar to go onto the next problem. If the wrong answer was chosen, a red X crossed out the incorrect choice, a blue box surrounded the correct one, and the message "Incorrect" appeared beneath the equations. A participant timed-out on a problem if there was no response within 30 seconds. In this case, a blue box appeared around the correct answer and the message "Time is up!" appeared beneath the equations.

Following either an incorrect choice or time-out, the participant was required to interact with the feedback. A feedback screen appeared, presenting the original equation and the correct answer choice, marking in red the portions of both equations that related to the transformation. The participant was then given four choices of what operations and terms the transformation involved. If the participant made the correct choice, a green box would appear around it; otherwise, a red cross would mark out the incorrect choice and the correct choice would be highlighted with a blue box around it. The participant was then prompted to press the spacebar to continue.

After each block of 10 trials, a summary feedback screen appeared. It showed graphically the accuracy and mean reaction time for that block and up to nine preceding blocks. Participants performed a minimum of 100 learning trials and ended the learning module according to accuracy and speed criteria. These learning criteria were two blocks with accuracy ≥ 85% and an average reaction time (for correctly answered items) ≤ 8 seconds. Participants either reached learning criteria or performed a maximum of 300 learning trials before proceeding to the post-test.

For the high school participants who finished the learning module on a different day than the day of the post-test, a refresher of 30 learning trials preceded the post-test. This refresher was eliminated for the middle school participants, as it was found to be cumbersome and annoying to participants.

3.2 Results

3.2.1 *Achievement of learning criteria*

Of the 30 participants, 24 reached learning criteria. Six participants retired after 100 trials, 10 between 100 and 200 trials, and an additional eight under 300 trials. Number of operations did not markedly affect learning time but bidirectional conditions took longer than unidirectional ones (see Supplementary Materials for details).

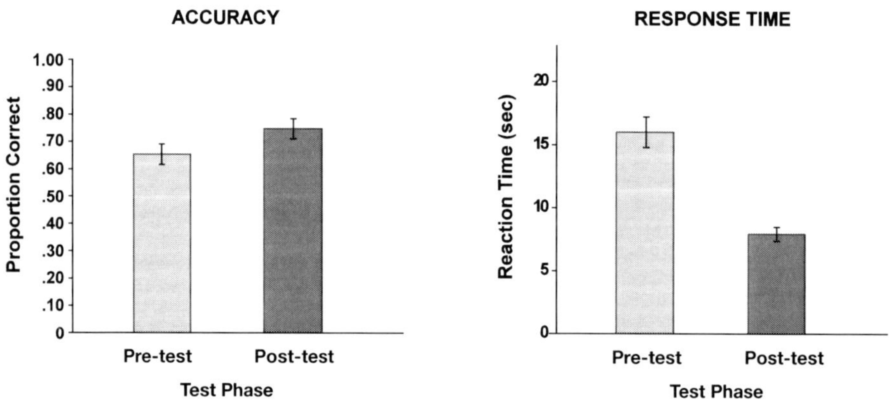

Figure 6. Students' mean accuracy and response times for recognizing algebraic transformations in the pre-test and post-test of Experiment 2. Error bars indicate ±1 standard error of the mean.

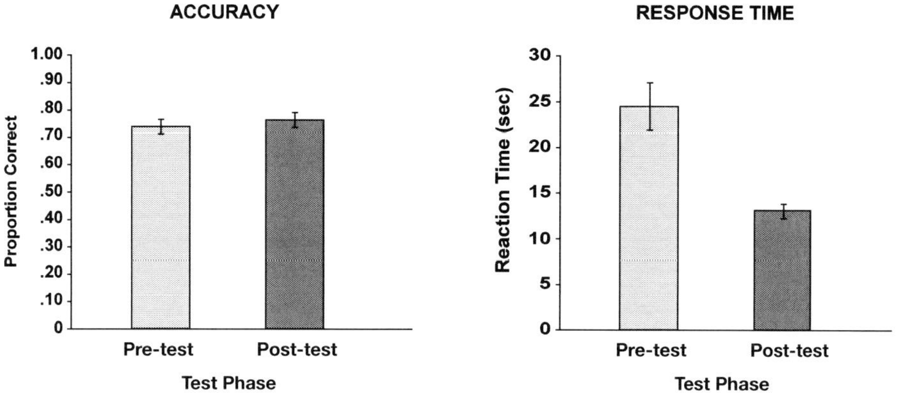

Figure 7. Students' mean accuracy and response times on transfer problems involving solving algebra equations in the pre-test and post-test of Experiment 2. Error bars indicate ±1 standard error of the mean.

3.2.2 *Overview of results*

The main results for performance in recognizing algebraic transformations are shown in Figures 6A and 6B, which present accuracy and response time results respectively. The PLM improved recognition accuracy from pre-test to post-test. There was a robust gain in fluency as well, with response times decreasing about 50%. Figures 7A and 7B show pre-test and post-test results for accuracy and response time on the transfer test, which involved solving open-ended algebra problems. There was little change in accuracy; students in Algebra I performed at a high level (about 80%) in the pre-test and post-test, indicating that as a group, they knew how to solve basic equations. There were, however, large changes in fluency. The data show that for solving simple equations (e.g., $3+y=12$) students in Algebra I take about 25 seconds per problem! Use of the PLM improved the speed of equation solving, producing an average drop in solution time of 46%. Learning effects were for the most part consistent across all conditions; the variations in training conditions produced only modest differences. These findings were confirmed by the analyses, which we consider in separate sections below.

3.2.3 *Recognizing algebraic transformations: Accuracy*

The recognition problems presented in the pre-test and post-tests resembled those presented during the learning module. Accuracy in recognizing algebraic transformations improved in all conditions through the use of the PLM. Recognition accuracy data were analyzed in a 2 (Test Phase) by 2 (Familiar vs. Unfamiliar Problem Type) by 2 (Operators in Learning) by 2 (Transformation Directions in Learning) ANOVA, in which the first two factors were tested within subjects and the latter two between subjects. There was a significant main effect of test phase, indicating overall improvement from pre-test to post-test, $F(1,26) = 9.11$, $p < .01$. There were no other reliable main effects or interactions.

3.2.4 *Recognizing algebraic transformations: Response times*

PLM exposure led to faster performance on recognition problems in all conditions. All but one participant improved. Response times were analyzed in a 2 (Test Phase) by 2 (Familiar vs. Unfamiliar Problem Type) by 2 (Operators in Learning) by 2 (Transformation Directions in Learning) ANOVA, in which the first two factors were tested within subjects and the latter two between subjects. The analysis showed a significant main effect of test phase, $F(1,26) = 56.91$, $p < .001$, reflecting the overall improvement in speed.

3.2.5 *Solving algebra problems: Accuracy*

Accuracy of problem solving was good overall and did not change noticeably, from 74.5% overall on the pre-test to 76.9% on the post-test. Accuracy data were analyzed in a 2 (Test Phase) by 2 (Familiar vs. Unfamiliar Problem Type) by 2 (Operators in Learning) by 2 (Transformation Directions in Learning) ANOVA, in which the first two factors were tested within subjects and the latter two between subjects. The overall effect of accuracy from pre-test to post-test did not reach significance, $F(1,26) = 2.816$, $p = .105$, and there were no other reliable main effects or interactions.

3.2.6 *Solving algebra problems: Response times*

Use of the Algebraic Transformations PLM led to dramatic reductions in response time in algebra problem solving. Whereas Algebra I students after the midpoint of the course do well overall in solving simple equations, remarkably, our response time data indicate that they average 24.7 sec to do so! After the PLM, the average response for the same kinds of problems was 13.2 sec. All but two participants showed faster algebra problem solving after the PLM; most showed robust gains (median = 9.2 sec per problem). These gains appear to be lasting, as shown in a delayed post-test administered to a subset of participants (see below).

Response times were analyzed in a 2 (Test Phase) by 2 (Familiar vs. Unfamiliar Problem Type) by 2 (Operators in Learning) by 2 (Transformation Directions in Learning) ANOVA, in which the first two factors were tested within subjects and the latter two between subjects. There was a substantial main effect of test phase, $F(1,26) = 46.44$, $p < .001$, but no other reliable main effects or interactions.

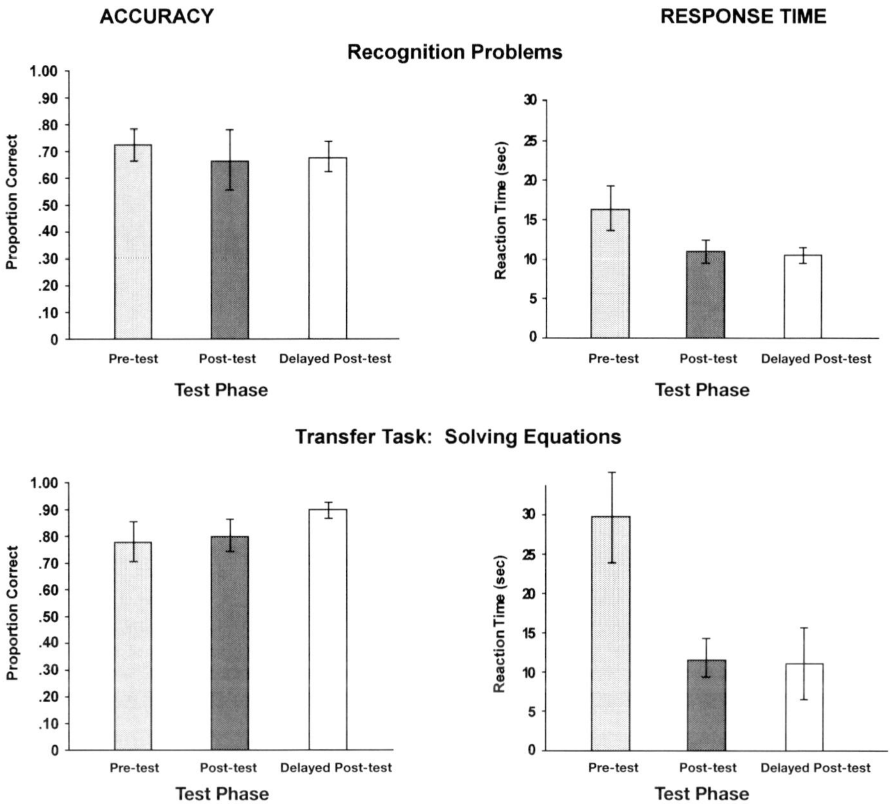

Figure 8. Delayed post-test results for Experiment 2. Pre-test, post-test, and delayed post-test data are shown for the subgroup of students who completed the delayed post-test. Top row: Mean accuracy and response time for recognizing algebraic transformations. Bottom row: Mean accuracy and response time for solving equations. Error bars indicate ±1 standard error of the mean.

3.2.7 *Delayed post-test results*

A small subset of subjects (n = 5) was run on a delayed post-test two weeks after working on the PLM. Figure 8 displays the results from this group. Considering the pre-test and first post-test performance, this subgroup appears reasonably representative of the complete set of participants. They vary somewhat in showing no overall accuracy gain in recognition problems. What the delayed post-tests show is that the learning gains that did occur in this group were completely preserved across a two-week delay. There is a small indication that accuracy for solving equations improved from the first to the delayed post-test. The most conspicuous result, however, is that the data suggest that PLM usage produced relatively enduring gains in fluency.

3.3 Discussion

Use of the Algebra PLM produced substantial learning gains in the recognition of algebraic transformations. Both speed and accuracy improved, and almost all participants showed these gains. Practice in structure extraction and recognition of algebraic transformations also transferred to the task of solving equations. Preliminary data suggested that these effects were lasting, although only a small number of participants were tested after a delay.

These results support the two linked hypotheses that motivate these studies: That changes in information extraction (perceptual learning) are not adequately developed by conventional instruction and that technology embodying PL principles can address these missing dimensions of learning.

Although in presenting the results, we naturally focused on the latter issue — the success of the PLM in improving fluency — our data also speak to the former issue. The declarative and procedural components of learning in algebra do not directly address the perceptual extraction and pattern recognition aspects of learning. Students in this study were past mid-year in Algebra I, and pre-test data showed their high level of competence in solving a range of equations. These results for problem solving, prior to our intervention, gave a strong indication that the students knew the basic declarative and procedural requirements of basic algebra: What to do and how to do it. Yet, the pre-test data also revealed that students at this level require approximately 25 sec per problem. For an experienced adult, it is hard to fathom how someone who knows how to do algebra could take more than several seconds for problems such as $8 = x + 3$. Even for the more complicated problems in our assessment (e.g., $3x + 4 = -8$), it is hard to understand what is going on for 25 sec or more. Our surprise at these response times reflects the fact that we have acquired the experience in extracting structure and seeing transformations in this domain. Early algebra students have not. Nor do the instructional modes they normally encounter do much to facilitate these skills, at least not in the first two-thirds of the course.

Other aspects of the data point to these same crucial and neglected components of learning. Although the different learning groups (differing by number of operations seen and number of directions of transformation) did not differ much in outcomes, there was some interaction of these variables with time to complete the PLM. For example, learners who saw two directions of transformation generally took markedly longer to complete the module. The fact that direction matters (e.g., $x - 4 = 8$ vs. $8 = x - 4$) makes a crucial point about the importance of PL concepts in algebra. Mathematically, there is no important difference between $x - 4 = 8$ and $8 = x - 4$. The equal sign is symmetric, and one hopes that no mathematics teacher has ever presented these cases as different with regard to facts, concepts, or procedures. Yet, in our results, there was both a reliable main effect of mixing directions of transformation and evidence of an interaction: When learning involved more than one possible operator on different trials, it took substantially longer when bidirectional transformations were involved. These outcomes speak to the importance of the "seeing" aspects of algebra proficiency. Bidirectional transformations add to learning time because they place greater demands on the processing of structure and selection of relevant inputs in mapping across transformations.

The greater difficulty posed by bidirectional transformations also suggests connections to the well-documented finding that algebra students often do not recognize the equal sign as signifying the symmetrical relationship of equivalence; instead, they may interpret it as a signal that the preceding operation should be carried out or a marker that the answer follows (e.g., Foster 2007; Knuth et al. 2005, 2006). While interpreting the equal sign operationally rather than relationally has generally been interpreted as a *conceptual* misconception, we suggest that it may arise at least in part from PL principles and from exposure, perhaps prior to algebra, to a biased subset of examples of equations. Unfortunately, perceptual learning is not confined to the instructor's intentions: Given habitual exposure to equations in which x is on the left, students extract this directional structure and attempt to give it meaning.

The present results suggest new opportunities for combining PL technology with declarative and procedural instruction. Issues of how to optimize the technology and combine it with other modes of learning are important priorities for research. One such issue involves learning criteria. In this study, the learning phase ended when a learner achieved 85% correct or better over 20 trials, with average response time below 8.5 sec. One problem with this criterion is that, within the constraints of each condition, different problems were selected randomly. It is possible that learners could sometimes meet the criterion due to a fortuitous selection of problems. Nothing in the design guaranteed that learners had reached competence on particular types of problems. The limitations of the learning criteria may relate to one feature of the data. Although average performance on the final two blocks of the module was well above 85%, post-test performance for recognition was about 75%. Even allowing for the fact that 6 subjects did not reach criterion, these data suggest that performance was slightly lower for the wider range of problems on the post-test than at the end of learning. We explored the issue of learning criteria a bit further in Experiment 3.

4. Perceptual learning in algebra: Experiment 3

Experiment 2 indicated the promise of PLM technology in improving students' abilities to recognize algebraic transformations, and it showed that these improvements transferred to students' fluency in solving algebra problems. Experiment 3 aimed to extend these findings in several respects.

One limitation of Experiment 2 was the small size of the group receiving a delayed post-test. A number of studies have suggested that performance on an immediate post-test may not be indicative of longterm learning (Schmidt and Bjork 1992). If PL interventions are to have value as supplements to conventional mathematics instruction, it is important that they produce lasting effects. Accordingly, we tested our Algebra PLM with a larger sample of students, and we assessed performance after a 3-week delay.

Another goal of this experiment, albeit a preliminary one, was to begin to examine category sequencing in learning technology. Although this initial effort turned out to have little effect on the data, we describe it here because it was included in the design and it gives some introduction to issues of sequencing that we believe are important and which we are pursuing in other research.

Adaptive sequencing for the individual learner, we believe, is one of the greatest potential benefits of learning technology. By assessing and tracking performance through a learning module, items and concept types can be presented at the best times to boost learning for each individual. Items or categories meeting certain learning criteria can be retired from a learning set. Sequencing and retirement allow a number of laws of learning to be implemented in ways that can make learning more efficient, and more durable, for each individual. We have been working with recently patented algorithms[3] that use both the learner's accuracy and speed in short interactive trials to determine when an item or category should recur as learning proceeds. In brief, each item (or category, in category sequencing) is given a priority score that updates each trial, based on accuracy and speed of recent performance, time since last presentation, and other variables. The algorithm, tested previously on fixed learning items (e.g., basic math facts), implements several laws of learning. For example, it prohibits an item from coming up on consecutive learning trials (in order to ensure recall from long-term, rather than short-term memory). It also ensures that missed items recur fairly soon, as their learning strength was likely low. Further, to ensure durability of learning, the retention interval is stretched as learning strength increased (Landauer and Bjork 1978). To do this, response times (for correct responses) are used as a proxy for a hypothetical construct of learning strength. Specifically, the algorithm uses a function of response time to stretch the reappearance interval for that individual on that item, such that faster responses produce longer retention intervals. Earlier work on item sequencing showed it to be particularly powerful in improving learning in conjunction with retirement criteria. When an item has been answered several times accurately and faster than some criterion response time, it is removed from the learning set. The use of dynamically updating priority scores, based on trials since presentation, learner accuracy and speed for each item, allows for optimization of the efficiency of learning the entire set. For memory items (e.g., learning multiplication tables, vocabulary words, or electronic components), sequencing reduces learning time by about 50% and often improves efficiency of learning (learning gains per unit learning trial invested) by 200% or more (Kellman and Massey 2005).

Whereas much is known about laws of learning and retention for individual items, not much is known about perceptual learning of categories, where specific exemplars are novel on each trial. For example, in learning a memory item, it is not useful to have the item appear on consecutive learning trials. Because the answer is still in short-term memory when the second trial occurs, there is little gain in long-term learning strength (Karpicke and Roediger 2007; Landauer and Bjork 1978). In learning a new structural concept, however, such as whether a word in a sentence is an adverb or whether a certain molecule belongs in a certain chemical family, it may be advantageous to have consecutive learning trials relating to the same concept, at least early in learning. Thus, in the present study, we used 4 conditions: Sequenced with retirement (SR), Sequenced with retirement and blocking (SRB), Random with retirement (RR), and random with no retirement (RN). As not much is known about the optimal arrangement of category sequencing, we included blocking of trials as an additional manipulation. Whereas, in item learning, immediate reappearance of a just-tested item is known to be a poor arrangement for learning, the situation could differ in learning category structure. As each instance differs, the learner's extraction of invariance from multiple examples might be facilitated by blocking of trials. Thus, we tested cases in which sequencing operated on single presentations of each category (NB = no blocking) but also a case in which what were sequenced were 3-trial blocks from a given category (B = Blocked).

4.1 Method

The experimental methods were as in Experiment 2, except as noted below.

4.1.1 *Participants*

Participants were 56 high school students (mostly in grade 9) and 38 8th grade middle school students at the same schools as in Experiment 2, all taking Algebra

I. Five students from the middle school and six students from the high school were excluded from the final data set for failing to complete all three phases of the assessments. One of the middle school subjects was removed from the study for disruptive behavior. The final sample contained 34 8th grade students, 42 9th grade students, 6 10th grade students, and 1 11th grade student. There were 40 males and 43 females in the final sample.

4.1.2 *Design*

The experiment was set up to assess effects of our learning technology on speed and accuracy of recognition of algebraic transformations and algebra problem solving. A pre-test was given on one day, followed by 2–3 days in which students worked on the PLM for 40–45 minutes per day. A post-test was administered the next day. A delayed post-test was administered to all participants three weeks later.

4.1.3 *Algebraic transformations PLM*

The PLM was similar to that in Experiment 1, with a few modifications. We reduced the number of choices for each PLM problem to 3, one correct transformed equation and two distractors. Compared to Experiment 2, problems were simplified somewhat, and all participants received all problem types in the learning phase. In addition, whereas transformations relating the target and the correct choice in Experiment 2 had all involved a shift of a term using some operator, Experiment 3 included a wider variety of items. Learning items were defined by type of operation (add, subtract, multiply, and divide) and transformation type (shift or other). Sixty percent of all problems were shift problems, in which the target "moved" from one side of an equation to another, via use of an operation. For example, for a subtract/shift problem with the target $x + 5 = a$, the correct choice would appear as $x = a - 5$. The remaining 40% of learning items involved other kinds of transformations, such as adding a new quantity to both sides of the equation. To ensure little or no repetition of specific problems, 100 exemplars were constructed for each kind of operation.

4.1.4 *Category sequencing*

For purposes of category sequencing, problems were grouped into 8 categories. These were defined by operation (add, subtract, multiply, divide) and by whether the problems involved shifting or not.

Participants were assigned randomly to one of several presentation conditions. Conditions differed in the way categories were arranged for display. They were either selected randomly for use on each learning trial, or they were selected based on the adaptive sequencing algorithm described above, which implemented several laws of learning. Particular learning items did not repeat during the module. Adaptive sequencing involved priority scores and reappearance of *categories* of problems, with problems within categories being chosen randomly within the constraints described earlier. A separate manipulation applied sequencing either to single presentations of each category (NB = no blocking) or to 3-trial blocks from a given category (B = Blocked). A retirement feature was used to remove categories on which the learner had achieved certain learning criteria. The four conditions were then as follows: Sequenced with Retirement with single trials (SRs), Sequenced with Retirement and 3-Trial Blocks (SRb), Random, No Retirement, Blocked (RNb), and Random with Retirement, Blocked (RRb). Although there could be other combinations of these features, these choices were constrained by the limit on available test participants and our own intuitions about what might be most revealing in a first study of category sequencing.

4.1.5 *Learning criteria*

The criteria for retiring a category, when the retirement feature was used, were 5 out of the last 6 problems from that category answered correctly, with an average response time for correct responses averaging 8 sec or less. A participant finished the learning phase when these criteria were met for all 8 categories. Note that in the condition not using retirement, the learning criterion could still be implemented, although problems from "retired" categories could still be presented to the learner. For learners who did not achieve the learning criteria, the learning phase was ended on the third day, and post-test was given the next day.

4.1.6 *Assessments*

The assessments were constructed along the same lines as in the preceding experiment, with some modifications (see Supplementary Materials).

4.1.7 *Procedure*

Testing occurred at the regular class time. The first day included only a pre-test. Days 2–4 (depending on a student's achievement of learning criteria) allowed about 45 minutes per day on the PLM. PLM trials were broken into 10-trial groups, with feedback on accuracy being provided after each 10 trials. Students were encouraged to take short breaks as needed at these intervals. The post-test was given on the day following completion of the PLM. Delayed post-tests were given three weeks later.

4.2 Results

4.2.1 *Achieving learning criteria*

Out of 83 participants, 32 reached criterion. Generally, experimental effects in the group reaching retirement did not differ from those of the full group, although levels of performance were higher and learning effects somewhat clearer in the former group. For brevity, we present statistical results from the full set of subjects only, rather than two full sets of analyses.

4.2.2 *Overview of results*

Figures 9A and 9B show the accuracy and response time results for recognition problems in Experiment 3 by presentation condition. Learners showed clear improvement from pre-test to post-test in accurately mapping algebraic transformations, and these gains were mostly preserved in the delayed post-test (mean =.63). There was a robust gain in fluency as well, with response times decreasing about 29% from pre-test to post-test, and decreasing even more, about 36%, from pre-test to delayed post-test. Figures 10A and 10B show the accuracy and response time results for algebra problem solving before and after completing the learning module. There was no change in accuracy, but large gains in fluency: Problem solving time dropped about 32% from pre-test to post-test, and these gains were preserved in the delayed post-test. Improvements in performance in both immediate and delayed post-tests were seen in all conditions, with little effect of the sequencing, retirement, and blocking manipulations.

These findings were confirmed by the analyses, considered below.

4.2.3 *Recognizing algebraic transformations: Accuracy*

Accuracy was analyzed via a 3 (Phase) by 4 (Condition) ANOVA with repeated measures on Phase (pre-test, post-test, delayed post-test). There was no main effect of Condition, $F(3,78)=.19$, n.s., nor any Condition by Test Phase interaction, $F(6,158)=1.69$, n.s. The overall improvement in accuracy from pre-test to the post-tests was shown by a highly reliable main effect of Test Phase, $F(2,156)=49.5$, $p<.001$. Individual comparisons showed clear improvement from pre-test to immediate post-test, $t(82)=3.82$, $p<.001$, and from pre-test to delayed post-test, $t(82)=3.43$, $p<.001$. There was no reliable difference between performance on immediate post-test and after a three week delay, $t(82)=.35$, n.s.

4.2.4 *Recognizing algebraic transformations: Fluency*

Response times were also analyzed in a 3 (Phase) by 4 (Condition) ANOVA with repeated measures on Phase. Performance did not differ by Condition, $F(3,79)=.84$, n.s., and there was no interaction of Condition and Phase, $F(6,158)=.66$, n.s. Strong

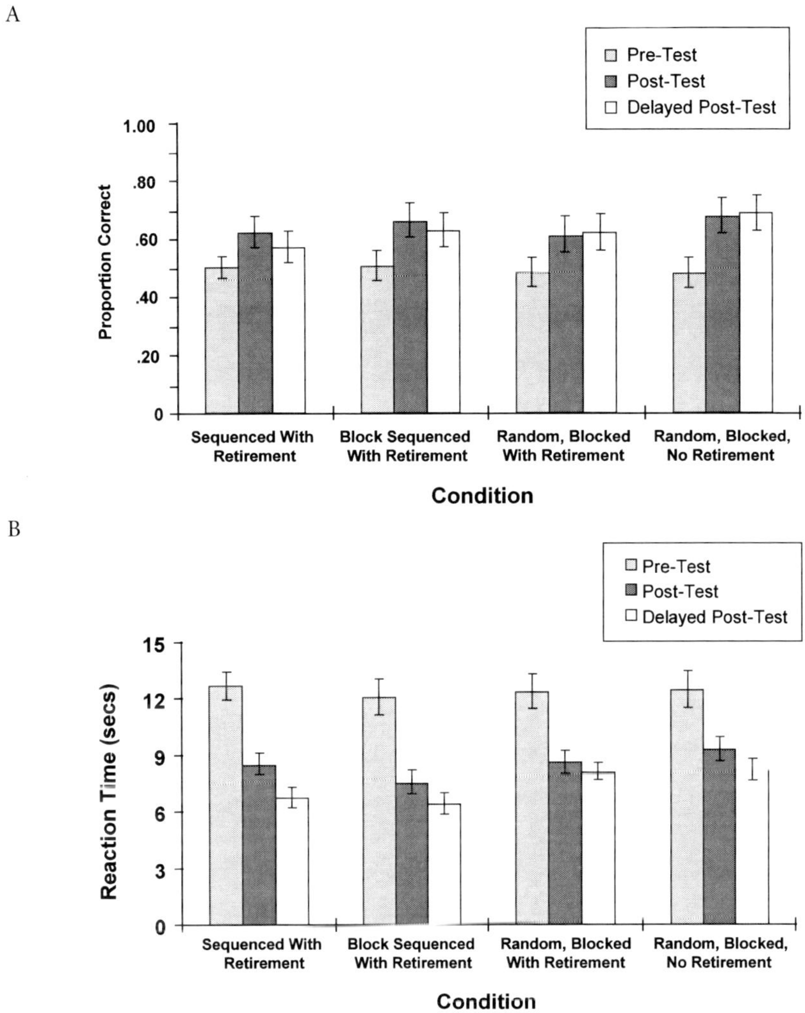

Figure 9. Students' mean accuracy (A) and response times (B) for recognizing algebraic transformations in the pre-test, post-test and delayed post-test of Experiment 3. Data are shown separately for 4 category blocking, sequencing, and retirement conditions (see text). Error bars indicate ±1 standard error of the mean.

learning effects were shown by the main effect of Phase, $F(2,158) = 80.97$, $p < .001$. Individual comparisons showed clear improvement from pre-test to immediate post-test, $t(82) = 6.81$, $p < .001$ and from pre-test to delayed post-test, $t(82) = 9.06$, $p < .001$. Delayed post-test performance was also better than performance in the immediate post-test $t(82) = 2.35$, $p < .02$, suggesting that learners continued to consolidate fluency gains following the study.

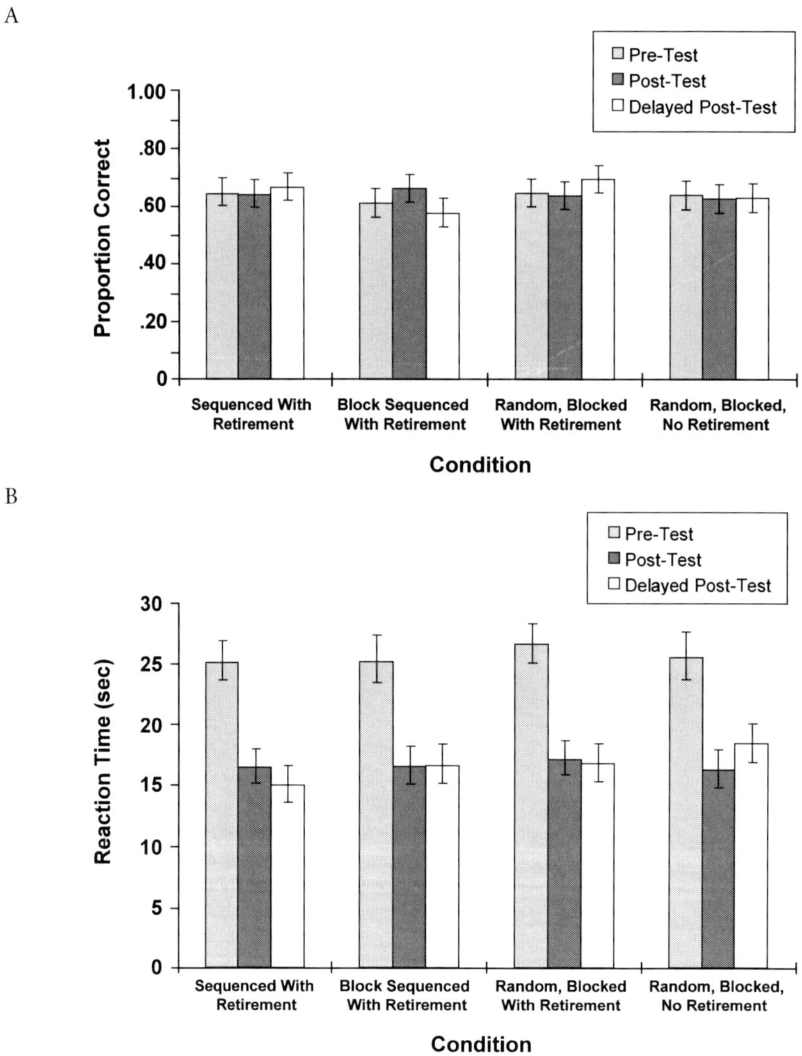

Figure 10. Students' mean accuracy (A) and response times (B) for solving equations in the pre-test, post-test and delayed post-test of Experiment 3. Data are shown separately for 4 category blocking, sequencing, and retirement conditions (see text). Error bars indicate ±1 standard error of the mean.

4.2.5 *Solving algebra problems: Accuracy*

Transfer to problem solving accuracy did not vary as a result of the learning module, remaining level at about .65 in all phases of the study. Accuracy was analyzed via a 3 (Phase) by 4 (Condition) ANOVA with repeated measures on Phase (pre-test, post-test, delayed post-test). There was no main effect of Condition, $F(3,79) = .13$, n.s., nor any Condition by Test Phase interaction, $F(6,158)=1.73$, n.s. There was no overall improvement in accuracy from pre-test to the post-tests (main effect of Phase), $F(2,158)=.10$, n.s.

4.2.6 *Solving algebra problems: Fluency*

Transfer to the speed of algebra problem solving showed strong effects of the PLM. Response times were analyzed in a 3 (Phase) by 4 (Condition) ANOVA with repeated measures on Phase. Learning gains did not differ by Condition, $F(3,79)=.18$, n.s., and there was no interaction of Condition and Phase, $F(6,158)=.65$, n.s. There was a substantial main effect of Test Phase, $F(2,158)=95.75$, $p<.001$. Individual comparisons showed clear improvement from pre-test to immediate post-test, $t(82)=7.24$, $p<.001$ and from pre-test to delayed post-test, $t(82)=6.92$, $p<.001$. Delayed post-test performance did not differ from that in the immediate post-test $t(82)=.08$, n.s., suggesting that learners maintained their improved skills after the experiment.

4.2.7 *Problem type analyses*

Additional analyses were carried out to investigate whether the experimental effects varied for problem types, specifically which operator was used (add, subtract, etc.), and whether the transformation involved a shift or some other change. These analyses also furnished some potentially useful baseline data about the relative difficulty of different kinds of problems for algebra students. The most notable finding was that divide problems were easier for both recognition and solve problems. (See Supplementary Materials section for details.)

4.3 Discussion

The results of Experiment 3 confirm and extend those of Experiment 2. Short interventions using PL technology improved both accuracy and speed in the recognition of algebraic transformations, and they produced conspicuous improvements in the fluency of algebra problem solving. The fluency gains in solving equations, as well as both accuracy and fluency gains for recognition problems, were fully preserved after a three-week delay.

Less informative in this experiment were our initial attempts to study categorization, sequencing, blocking, and retirement. Categorizations of problem types figured in two efforts — to begin to look at category sequencing and to be able to track particular components of learning, provide practice where it is most needed, and lead learners to meet objective criteria for each category.

Although we strongly believe in the importance and ultimate potential of these concepts, the present results make clear that their study is just beginning. There were few indications of effects of sequencing, blocking, or retirement in this study. Unfortunately, these negative findings are difficult to interpret. One reason was that fewer than half of participants met the learning criteria. Obviously, tests of manipulations involving learning criteria must be long enough to allow students to meet the criteria. Moreover, in retrospect it is not clear that the experimenters' categories (e.g., categorization of problem by operator type and by shift vs. "other" transformation) tapped different learning components for the learners. Benefits of category sequencing, blocking, and retirement hinge heavily on using categories that have validity for the learner. Finding ways to determine such categories and optimizing sequencing, blocking, and retirement schemes is a challenging but exciting priority for future research.

5. General discussion

Perceptual learning contributes enormously to expertise. It allows selective extraction of information for specific tasks, reduces required effort and attention, leads to chunking of important patterns in the input, and enables the discovery of higher-order invariance. Although these changes in information pickup can develop unsystematically through experience, attempts to address them directly in instruction have been lacking.

We hypothesized that interventions in middle school mathematics designed to foster and accelerate PL, in the form of PLM technology, might produce learning gains in pattern recognition and fluency, and that such gains might transfer to problem solving. We chose the domains of fraction learning and algebra due to their difficulty for many students and their importance in the curriculum.

The results of three experiments in two different learning domains confirm our hypotheses. In fraction learning, PLM interventions markedly improved performance on fundamental learning tasks such as solving problems involving fractions and comparing fractional quantities. Although response times were measured in the learning phase as an indicator of student progress, only accuracy in these tasks was measured in the assessments. We interpret the large learning gains across all item types in the assessments to reflect advancement of students' abilities to extract relevant relations from fractional notation and other representations, including word problems, and map them accurately across representations. The observed gains from this intervention are encouraging, especially when one considers that these students had previously had considerable exposure to fractions in their normal coursework. We found that classroom instruction combined with PLM interventions produced learning gains that exceeded and persisted beyond those gotten from classroom instruction alone. Notably, our classroom component, focusing on extracting structure and mapping structures across representations, also produced noticeable learning improvements relative to students' initial levels. This suggests that there may be value in specifically discussing relevant stuctures and structure mapping, even in conventional instructional modes. The enhanced learning produced by PLMs, however, indicates that PL technology can most directly and effectively address these aspects of learning. The results showed lasting, not transitory, changes brought about by PLMs: Learning gains survived intact over a 9-week delay.

The fraction research is special among the studies reported here in that it combined instructional techniques. This synergy underscores an important element of our approach. Although we believe that PL techniques are a sorely needed addition to most instructional contexts, they do not replace declarative and procedural components of learning. Finding the right blend of introducing facts, concepts, and procedures, along with accelerating pattern recognition and fluency through PL technology, is likely to be of maximal benefit to learning in mathematics and many other domains. The role of the teacher in introducing concepts and procedures and the role of PL technology in developing pattern recognition and fluency are complementary. Improving students' latter abilities during individual computer-based learning will allow teachers to make better use of class time. When students become fluent with basic structures and representations, their cognitive load is reduced, allowing them greater capacity to focus on new concepts or applying their knowledge. The question of how to optimize learning by combining instructional modes remains a prime question for further research.

Our experiments testing PL technology in algebra showed improvements in recognition of algebraic transformations and major gains in speed on the transfer task: Solving equations. In contrast to the fraction study, students started out with high levels of problem solving accuracy. Having recently passed the halfway point of Algebra I, they demonstrated a command of basic concepts and procedures of algebra. Students' performance illustrated vividly, however, the split between the knowing and seeing aspects of doing mathematics: In both studies, students started out requiring, on average, about 25 sec to solve simple equations. The data suggest that Algebra PLMs helped students by directly addressing pattern recognition and transformation abilities in this domain. Students practiced, not the solving of problems, but the mapping of equations onto other equations. Two to three 40-minute sessions of the Algebra PLMs improved students' accuracy and speed in recognizing algebraic transformations and produced a nearly 50% drop in the time required to solve equations. These gains proved to be lasting.

5.1 Discovery and fluency effects in PL

Earlier we distinguished discovery and fluency effects in perceptual learning. When might we see one or the other in particular PLM interventions? When learners have not yet identified what the important structures are, which parts or relations in a representation are relevant to a given task, or which features in one representation map onto those in another, one might expect that effective PLMs will produce gains in discovery, most evident in students' accuracy on assessments. Where the relevant information is known, but pattern extraction is effortful, slow and piecemeal, effective PLMs will tend to produce fluency gains.

5.2 Accuracy and speed in mathematics learning

We must also note, however, that in practical applications, such as those considered in this paper, accuracy and speed are to some degree interchangeable. As in typical psychophysical experiments, we could no doubt have changed the measured fluency differences into accuracy differences by limiting problem exposure or problem solving time. The important point for mathematics and other learning domains is not that PL discovery and fluency effects are indistinguishable. We believe these effects are different, and the present results furnish some evidence of this. The point is that both fluency and accuracy should be considered equally important in mathematics (and many other learning domains). Although this contention is hardly novel, it is unusual in educational contexts to measure response times item by item. (A test period may be time-limited, but individual problems are usually not.) The reason fluency and accuracy should be considered together is that, as students progress in mathematics, earlier learning is assumed as a foundation for new material. The student who must stop to consider the structure of fraction notation will necessarily be left behind when fractions appear in the context of a chemistry problem. And it is not just the speed at which new material appears, but its cognitive load. For many purposes, not knowing and knowing too slowly will have indistinguishable effects in impeding students' progress.

5.3 A paradox: Natural PL vs. PL technology

We claimed earlier that PL is not systematically addressed in typical instruction, but we also noted that PL is a natural, implicit learning process. The process we are trying to add into instruction and enhance through technology is the same process that allows three-year-olds to learn to classify new instances of dogs, toys, and trucks, or squares and triangles, or natural concepts of any sort. If such a process occurs naturally for three-year-olds (without lectures on the distinguishing features of dogs and cats), perhaps perceptual learning also happens in ordinary instructional settings as teachers present examples and students work problems. If so, what is the special role of systematically constructed PL technology?

There are two, related answers to this question. First, some advance in the learning and pickup of structure surely does come from seeing examples and working problems. However, this happens haphazardly, and such activities probably comprise "low doses" of PL, ultimately (perhaps years later) effective for some students but less so for others. Second, systematic targeting of PL through PLM technology can accelerate learning, through a variety of features. These include providing many more classification instances in short periods of time, systematically arranging instances to allow learning of invariance as well as learning what variation is irrelevant to a given classification, and tracking, adaptively sequencing, and retiring particular categories and classifications.

That PL technology can provide such advantages is shown in our data. In the Fractions PLM, for example, several examples and a great deal of discussion of relevant structure were presented in the control group; yet, participants in PLM groups showed greater learning gains. In the Algebra PLMs, students had seen numerous in-class and homework examples over the first 2/3 of the school year (not to mention in Pre-Algebra), but this seemed to produce little fluency, as documented in pre-test performance. Large and lasting improvements in the fluency of problem solving were produced by the PLM in only two to three class periods.

5.4 Other features of learning technology

Our discussion has emphasized novel PL techniques for mathematics instruction, but some other features of learning technology play complementary, facilitative, or in some cases, unknown roles. We required students to interact with feedback after errors, because we have learned in other work that without this feature some students may not attend much to, nor benefit much from, feedback. Although its role was not explicitly tested here (because it was always present), we highly recommend this feature for learning technology, especially when the learning activity has many short trials. Our style of reversing the question in interactive feedback may also be considered a PL manipulation, in that it again draws attention to the structure, and often, to the mapping across representations, developing flexibility in the direction of mapping. Other features, such as category sequencing, blocking, and optimal use of retirement features, were tentatively explored, but not much illuminated, by Experiment 3. These features of learning technology in a PLM format will likely prove important, but their optimal deployment will require further investigation.

We began by noting some persistent problems in mathematics learning. The present results suggest that PL technology can help address many of these issues. Theoretically, we believe PL is a neglected dimension of learning, one that requires special techniques to address systematically. The present work suggests that PLMs of relatively short duration can produce large gains in the fluency and accuracy of structure extraction, and that these gains can transfer to the fluency and accuracy of mathematics problem solving. This approach to learning technology also offers significant promise in tracking separate components of learning, continuing learning until mastery criteria are met, and incorporating response time measures to assess fluency and to include it in learning milestones. If we are correct in the assessment that most instruction does not much address PL, that pattern recognition and fluency issues arise for many students, and that these problems compound as one advances through the curriculum, then interventions made possible by principles of PL and digital technology are vitally needed. Nor do we think these issues are limited to mathematics. It is hard to think of any learning domain in which advanced performance does not rely heavily on fluent extraction of features and patterns, and on detection of invariance in changing contexts. Whether in other academic subjects, such as science or language learning, or in professional fields, such as electronics, radiology or air traffic control, the need for and promise of PL technology seem unlikely to be overestimated.

Notes

* This work was supported by the National Science Foundation under Grant REC-0231826 to PK and CM. Any opinions, findings, and conclusions or recommendations expressed in this material are those of the authors and do not necessarily reflect the views of the National Science Foundation. We gratefully acknowledge Whitney Huston, Patricia McCarrin, Eric Irwin, and Donna Perretta for their assistance and cooperation in implementing the Fractions study, and Christina Schofield and Lindsey Engle Richland for assistance in the first Algebra experiment.

1. Without further discussion, the label "perceptual" may seem overly restrictive to some. If so, the terms "structural learning" or "pattern recognition" may be used instead. In any case, what we intend should be become clear regardless of terminology, and we consider issues regarding the scope of perceptual learning below.

2. Obviously, systems that learn, either through feedback or in an unsupervised manner via the statistics of the input, would be exempt from this characterization. Such systems have been used to model human perceptual learning.

3. System and Method for Adaptive Learning, US Patent 7052277, issued May, 2006. Insight Learning Technology, Inc. holds the rights to the use of this patent. For further information, contact Insight at info@insightlearningtech.com.

References

Ahissar, M. and Hochstein, S. 1997. "Task difficulty and learning specificity". *Nature* 387: 401–406.

Anderson, J.R., Corbett, A.T., Fincham, J.M., Hoffman, D., and Pelletier, R. 1992. "General principles for an intelligent tutoring architecture". In J. Regian and V. Shute (eds), *Cognitive Approaches to Automated Instruction*. Hillsdale, NJ: Lawrence Erlbaum, 81–106.

Anderson, J.R., Corbett, A.T., Koedinger, K.R., and Pelletier, R. 1995. "Cognitive tutors: Lessons learned". *The Journal of the Learning Sciences* 4(2): 167–207.

Barsalou, L. W. 1999. "Perceptual symbol systems". *Behavioral and Brain Sciences* 22: 577–660.

Behr, M.J., Harel, G., Post, T., and Lesh, R. 1992. "Rational number, ratio, and proportion". In D. Grouws (ed), *Handbook of Research on Mathematics Teaching and Learning*. New York: Macmillan, 296–333.

Bryan, W.L. and Harter, N. 1899. "Studies on the telegraphic language. The acquisition of a hierarchy of habits". *Psychological Review* 6(4): 345–375.

Chandler, P. and Sweller, J. 1991. "Cognitive load theory and the format of instruction. *Cognition and Instruction* 8: 293–332.

Chase, W.G. and Simon, H.A. 1973. "Perception in chess". *Cognitive Psychology* 4 (1): 55–81.

Fahle, M. and Poggio, T. (eds). 2002. *Perceptual Learning*. Cambridge, MA: The MIT Press.

Foster, D. 2007. "Making meaning in algebra: Examining students' understandings and misconceptions". *Assessing Mathematical Proficiency* 53:163–176.

Garrigan, P. and Kellman, P.J. 2008. "Perceptual learning depends on perceptual constancy". *Proceedings of the National Academy of Sciences, USA*. 105(6): 2248–2253.

Gibson, E.J. 1969. *Principles of Perceptual Learning and Development*. New York: Appleton-Century-Crofts.

Gibson, J.J. 1966. *The Senses Considered as Perceptual Systems*. Boston: Houghton Mifflin.

Gibson, J.J. 1979. *The Ecological Approach to Vision Perception*. Boston: Houghton Mifflin.

Gibson, J.J. and Gibson, E.J. 1955. "Perceptual learning: Differentiation or enrichment?" *Psychological Review* 62: 32–41.

Goldstone, R.L. 1998. "Perceptual learning". *Annual Review of Psychology* 49: 585–612.

Goldstone, R.L. 2000. "Unitization during category learning". *Journal of Experimental Psychology: Human Perception & Performance* 26 (1): 86–112.

Hackenberg, A.J. 2007. "Units coordination and the construction of improper fractions: A revision of the splitting hypothesis". *Journal of Mathematical Behavior* 26: 27–47.

James, W. 1890. *The Principles of Psychology* (1983 ed.). Cambridge, MA: Harvard University Press.

Karpicke, J. and Roediger III, H.L. 2007. "Expanding retrieval practice promotes short-term retention, but equally spaced retrieval enhances long-term retention". *Journal of Experimental Psychology: Learning, Memory, and Cognition* 33(4): 704–719.

Kellman, P.J. 2002. "Perceptual learning". In R. Gallistel (ed), *Stevens' Handbook of Experimental Psychology, Vol. 3. Learning, Motivation, and Emotion, Third Edition*. New York: Wiley, 259–299.

Kellman, P.J. and Arterberry, M.E. 1998. *The Cradle of Knowledge: Development of Perception in Infancy*. Cambridge, MA: The MIT Press.

Kellman, P.J. and Kaiser, M.K. 1994. "Perceptual learning modules in flight training". *Proceedings of the 38th Annual Meeting of the Human Factors and Ergonomics Society*, 1183–1187.

Kellman, P.J. and Massey, C. 2005. "Background and validation research on perceptual learning and adaptive sequencing technologies". Unpublished Technical Report, Insight Learning Technology, Inc.
Knuth, E.J., Alibali, M.W., McNeil, N.M., Weinberg, A., and Stephens, A.C. 2005. "Middle school students' understanding of core algebraic concepts: Equivalence & variable". *Zentralblatt für Didaktik der Mathematik* 37(1): 68–76.
Knuth, E.J., Stephens, A.C., McNeil, N.M., and Alibali, M.W. 2006. "Does understanding the equal sign matter? Evidence from solving equations". *Journal for Research in Mathematics Education* 37(4): 297–312.
Lamon, S. 2001. "Presenting and representing: From fractions to rational numbers". In A. Cuoco and F. Curcio (eds), *The Roles of Representation in School Mathematics. 2001 Yearbook*. Reston, VA: National Council of Teachers of Mathematics, 146–165.
Landauer, T.K. and Bjork, R.A. 1978. "Optimum rehearsal patterns and name learning". In M.M. Gruneberg, P.E. Morris, and R.N. Sykes (eds), *Practical Aspects of Memory*. London: Academic Press, 625–632.
Landy, D. and Goldstone, R.L. 2007. "How abstract is symbolic thought?" *Journal of Experimental Psychology: Learning, Memory, and Cognition* 33(4), 720–733.
Mayer, R.E. and Moreno, R. 1998. "A split attention effect in multimedia learning: Evidence for dual processing systems in working memory". *Journal of Educational Psychology* 90: 312–320.
Merzenich, M.M., Jenkins, W.M., Johnston, P., Schreiner, C., Miller, S., and Tallal, P. 1996. "Temporal processing deficits of language-learning impaired children ameliorated by training". *Science* 271(5245): 77–81.
Mettler, E. and Kellman, P.J. 2006. "Unconscious discovery in concrete and abstract perceptual learning". *Paper presented at the Annual Meeting of the Psychonomics Society*, Houston, Texas.
Michotte, A. 1962. *The Perception of Causality*. Andover, MA: Methuen.
Michotte, A., Thines, G., and Crabbe, G. 1964. *Les Compléments Amodaux des Structures Perceptives* [The Amodal Complements of Perceptual Structures]. Louvain: Publications de l'Université de Louvain.
Olive, J. 1999. "From fractions to rational numbers of arithmetic: A reorganization hypothesis". *Mathematical Thinking and Learning* 1(4): 279–314.
Olive, J. 2001. "Connecting partitioning and iterating: A path to improper fractions". In M. van den Heuvel-Panhuizen (ed), *Proceedings of the 25th Conference of the International Group for the Psychology of Mathematics Education* (PME-25, Vol. 4). Utrecht: Freudenthal Institute, 1–8.
Olive, J. and Steffe, L.P. 2002. "The construction of an iterative fractional scheme: The case of Joe". *Journal of Mathematical Behavior* 20: 413–437.
Olive, J. and Vomvoridi, E. 2006. "Making sense of instruction on fractions when a student lacks necessary fractional schemes: The case of Tim". *Journal of Mathematical Behavior* 25: 18–45.
Paas, G. W. C. and van Merrienboer, J. J. G. 1994. "Variability of worked examples and transfer of geometrical problem solving skills: A cognitive load approach". *Journal of Educational Psychology* 1: 122–133.
Petrov, A.A., Dosher, B.A., and Lu, Z. 2005. "The dynamics of perceptual learning: An incremental reweighting model". *Psychological Review* 112(4): 715–743.

Post, T.R., Behr, M.J., and Lesh, R. 1986. "Research-based observations about children's learning of rational number concepts". *Focus on Learning Problems in Mathematics* 8(1): 39–48.

Recanzone, G.H., Schreiner, C.E., and Merzenich, M.M. 1993. "Plasticity in the frequency representation of primary auditory cortex following discrimination training in adult owl monkeys". *Journal of Neuroscience* 13(1): 87–103.

Schmidt, R.A. and Bjork R.A 1992. "New conceptualizations of practice: Common principles in three paradigms suggest new concepts for training". *Psychological Science* 3(4): 207–217.

Schneider, W. and Shiffrin, R.M. 1977. "Controlled and automatic human information processing: I. Detection, search, and attention". *Psychological Review* 84 (1): 1–66.

Shiffrin, R.M. and Schneider, W. 1977. "Controlled and automatic information processing: II. Perceptual learning, automatic attending and a general theory". *Psychological Review* 84(2): 127–190.

Shipley, T.F. and Zacks, J.M. (eds). 2008. *Understanding Events: From Perception to Action.* NY: Oxford University Press.

Silva, A. and Kellman, P.J. 1999. "Perceptual learning in mathematics: The algebra-geometry connection". In M. Hahn and S.C. Stoness (eds), *Proceedings of the Twenty-first Annual Conference of the Cognitive Science Society.* Mahwah, NJ: Lawrence Erlbaum, 683–689.

Steffe, L.P. 2002. "A new hypothesis concerning children's fractional knowledge". *Journal of Mathematical Behavior* 20: 267–307.

Sweller, J., Chandler, C., Tierney, P., and Cooper, M. 1990. "Cognitive load as a factor in the structuring of technical material". *Journal of Experimental Psychology: General,* 119(2): 176–192.

Tallal, P., Merzenich, M., Miller, S., and Jenkins, W. 1998. "Language learning impairment: Integrating research and remediation". *Scandinavian Journal of Psychology* 39(3): 197–199.

Thompson, P. 1995. "Notations, convention, and quantity in elementary mathematics". In J. Sowder and B. Schapelle (eds), *Providing a Foundation for Teaching Middle School Mathematics.* Albany, NY: SUNY Press, 199–221.

Thompson, P. and Saldanha, L. 2003. "Fractions and multiplicative reasoning". In J. Kilpatrick, G. Marti, and D. Schifter (eds), *Research Companion to the Principles and Standards for School Mathematics.* Reston, VA: National Council of Teachers of Mathematics, 95–114.

Tzur, R. 1999. "An integrated study of children's construction of improper fractions and the teacher's role in promoting the learning". *Journal for Research in Mathematics Education* 30 (4): 390–416.

Wise, J.A., Kubose, T., Chang, N., Russell, A., and Kellman, P.J. 2000. "Perceptual learning modules in mathematics and science instruction". In D. Lemke (ed), *Proceedings of the TechEd 2000 Conference.* Amsterdam: IOS Press, 169–176.

On foundations of technological support for addressing challenges facing design-based science learning*

Swaroop S. Vattam and Janet L. Kolodner
Georgia Institute of Technology

Design experiences can provide valuable opportunities for learners to improve their understanding of both science content and scientific practices. However, the implementation of design-based science learning (DBSL) in classrooms presents a number of significant challenges. In this article we present two significant challenges, *bridging the design-science gap* and *overcoming time and material constraints*, and a strategy for addressing them through software design in which explanation-construction scaffolding integrates with modeling and simulation. We present two software systems (SIMCARS and SHADE) developed based on our strategy and guidelines for integrating them into DBSL practices. We present a pilot study (involving SIMCARS), the findings of which support the potential of our technology for responding to the identified challenges. A follow up study (involving SHADE) is presented which shows the affordances of our technology for improving the quality of classroom discourse, suggesting the potential of our strategy to enhance collaborative understanding and social construction of knowledge in DBSL environments.

Keywords: design-based learning, external representations, knowledge construction, science education, simulation and modeling, technology-based scaffolding

1. Introduction

Learning science through design activity has been shown to be a productive way to promote deep science learning (Hmelo et al. 2000; Kolodner et al. 2003; Penner et al. 1998; Resnick 1996; Fortus et al. 2004). In design-based science learning (DBSL), the goal of designing a working artifact contextualizes all inquiry learning. Design is used as a vehicle through which scientific knowledge is constructed and real-world problem-solving skills are cultivated. The design challenge provides impetus for identifying what needs to be learned and for sustaining engagement in inquiry over time, as well as providing need for cultivating and using a variety of skills.

But while learning science through design activity can lead to deep science learning, not all teachers are expert at facilitating its enactment, and even in classes where the teacher is proficient, not all students are able to connect their design experiences to generalized science concepts (Kolodner et al. 2003; Ryan and Kolodner 2004). There are a variety of reasons for this. Some students need more time and opportunities experiencing a concept, attempting its application, and using it for explanation than there is time for in a classroom; some students need more variation across those opportunities; and some need more guidance than might be available. In these situations students can still be successful at completing a design challenge without gaining targeted scientific understanding.

A variety of approaches have been tried to alleviate these problems, some in the context of design-based learning and some in other inquiry contexts: (i) introduction of software that scaffolds and allows simulation of phenomena under a variety of conditions, usually with animated graphical visualizations (e.g., Thinkertools (White 1993), SimQuest (Van Joolingen and De Jong 2003), RIDES (Munro et al. 1997)); (ii) use of modeling software that scaffolds and allows learners to model situations on the computer rather than in the real world (e.g., Model-It (Soloway et al. 1996), StarLogo (Resnick 1994), Articulate Virtual Laboratory (Forbus et al. 1999)); and (iii) introduction of software that encourages articulation and provides scaffolding as students are attempting explanation construction (e.g., ExplanationConstructor (Sandoval 2003; Sandoval et al. 2003)) or argument articulation (e.g., Belvedere (Suthers et al. 1995)).

But none of these approaches are entirely consistent with the intentions of design-based learning. Simulation systems usually focus on targeted scientific phenomena but not on their *application* in the context of the design challenge students are working on. Contrary to design-based learning, where learners are building tangible artifacts, model-building systems usually focus on modeling systems that are impossible for a learner to experience closely or manipulate firsthand (e.g., an ecosystem or a chemical production plant). The major deficiency of software for scaffolding explanation is similar. No software for scaffolding explanation has been designed with design-based learning in mind. In the best of those systems (e.g., ExplanationConstructor (Sandoval 2003; Sandoval et al. 2003)), learners are asked to give causal accounts of observations after they have been introduced to the science content. In a DBSL situation, however, learners are motivated to predict and explain the behavior of artifacts they are designing based on incomplete scientific understanding, as well as incomplete understanding of what a good explanation is.

Our broad research goals are twofold. With respect to technology, we want to (i) understand the functions simulation and modeling software should have when integrated with design-based learning and (ii) provide guidelines for designing the interactions between learners and the software for ease of use and to promote personal and epistemological connections among learners. With respect to learning, we wish to understand which practices for interleaving physical design and testing with computer simulation, modeling, and explanation scaffolding will result in deep science learning among learners. Our efforts have been focused on middle-school (grades 6 to 8) learners.

Within this broader context, and in this article, we address some narrower goals: To articulate two of the significant challenges to implementing DBSL in classrooms, *bridging the design-science gap* and *overcoming time and material constraints*; to identify guidelines for designing software to address those two challenges; to begin to identify strategies for integrating such software into DBSL curricula; and to identify specifics about the affordances of such software for promoting science learning in DBSL environments and the challenges that remain. We present two studies. A pilot study conducted in spring 2005 supports the potential of such software for responding to the two identified challenges. A more formal study showed the same potential using a different curriculum and different version of the software and further showed affordances of such software for improving the quality of classroom discourse, suggesting its potential to enhance collaborative understanding and social construction of knowledge in design-based science classrooms.

2. Design-based science learning: Promises and challenges

In design-based pedagogy, the goal of designing a working artifact contextualizes all curricular and inquiry activities (e.g., Kolodner et al. 2003; Fortus et al. 2004). Design-based science pedagogy, at its best, presents students with a design challenge that requires, for its success, using some targeted science content and scientific reasoning to design and build a working device. While attempting to understand the design challenge, and perhaps during first attempts to achieve the challenge, students identify the science content they need to apply for success, and they move between learning that content and applying it to achieve the design challenge. In the best of enactments, learning is active, expertly facilitated by the teacher, and includes opportunities for publicly articulating science understanding, debating understandings, explaining phenomena, and debugging those explanations. In such an environment, as students iteratively move toward better design solutions, they iteratively move toward better understandings of science concepts and laws, generalizing from the particular experiences they are having as they design.

But research shows that generalization from experiences of particular phenomena or devices to broader science concepts and laws does not always happen naturally (Crismond 2001; Kolodner et al. 2003; Ryan and Kolodner 2004). Design challenges can often be achieved to a degree that students (and teachers) find them satisfactory without students making this progression from particular to general. Because of this we have had to devise strategies to bridge the gap between (i) design — the concrete world of direct experiences and creation of products and (ii) science — the abstract world of physical laws and causal explanation, i.e., between (i) the phenomena they are experiencing and trends they see and (ii) the science that explains those phenomena and trends.

2.1 Learning by Design™: Fulfilling the promises of DBSL

Our own research group has developed an approach to DBSL called Learning by Design™ (LBD) (Kolodner et al. 2003) that orchestrates classroom activities in ways that afford the kinds of facilitation and scaffolding needed so that the affordances of DBSL will be fully realized.

Figure 1. The Learning by Design cycle

Each LBD unit begins by introducing students to a design challenge. The students work in small groups, *messing about* with materials or devices that will help them understand what they need to learn to successfully achieve the challenge. They get together as a class around a *whiteboard* to share their experiences and ideas for achieving the challenge and to articulate what they need to learn for success. From there, the class decides which are the most important of the questions and divides into small groups, each of which designs and runs an investigation aimed at answering their question. Students report to each other in a *poster session* about their methods and results, and peers ask questions and make suggestions. *Design rules of thumb* are generalized from their investigation results to help learners connect the science they are learning to its application. Then groups move on to making a first pass at achieving the challenge. The groups present their design ideas to the class in a *pin-up session*, reporting to the class about their design decisions, why they think each is a good one, and predicting how their design will behave when constructed. Then they move on to constructing and testing their designs. Finally, students present their experiences to each other in a *gallery walk*, soliciting feedback from others which could lead to more questions and additional investigations. This cycle, shown in Figure 1, is repeated until an appropriate degree of success is reached.

Within this sequencing are embedded a number of strategies for promoting science learning. One such strategy is our Rules of thumb (RT) practice (Crismond et al., 2001; Ryan and Kolodner 2004), designed to serve the *cognitive purpose* of generalizing a theory from observations and broadening its context, and the *design purpose* of making those abstract laws more usable in the context of designing. The RT practice involves, first, identifying trends in experiments in terms of rules of thumb (e.g., the larger the surface area of the canopy, the longer time it will take for the parachute to fall). Before moving on to use those rules, the teacher asks why a rule of thumb might be true. This provides an opportunity for learners to associate scientific explanations with the observed trends in their experiments, and it provides a *need* for them to visit relevant science content. Students then plan their designs based on the identified rules of thumb and use the explanations associated with those rules to describe the reasons behind their design choices. As such, the RT practice has students generate trends that need to be explained, work towards explanations, use those rules and explanations to predict outcomes, and then, as the rules and their explanations are applied, iteratively revise their explanations. This practice is consistent with what is recommended by other studies in science education. Studies show that making explanation demands of inquiry explicit can improve students' efforts in inquiry (Dunbar 1993; Schauble et al. 1995).

2.2 The challenges

Our studies show that even rudimentary implementation of the RT practice in the LBD-style classrooms results in science learning that is more advanced than that of students in comparable non-LBD classrooms (Kolodner et al. 2003). Further, our studies show that differences in the way the RT practice is implemented can produce differing outcomes in student learning (Ryan and Kolodner 2004). Students who participated in better implementations of this practice showed a better understanding of the targeted science concepts and demonstrated better applicability of those concepts to their designs than those who engaged in a version of the practice that focused less rigorously on connecting their experiences to the targeted science. The more the teacher had students revisit and refine their explanations of the rules of thumb, the deeper was their science learning.

Additionally, the success of the RT strategy depends significantly on the quality of the rules of thumb generated by the students with the help of their teacher. The best rules of thumb and best science learning we identified were in the classrooms of a teacher who orchestrated the elements of the practice well and guided the classroom participation based on her deep understanding of the science (Ryan and Kolodner 2004). This teacher was fluent enough with the science to help the learners diagnose their "troubled" designs from a science perspective, and she created an environment where students found it meaningful to generate rules of thumb and understood the purpose of generating those rules. But not all teachers can do this well.

Another set of pragmatic challenges for design-based learning also shows itself in our evaluations of LBD. Because there is only limited time in a classroom to cover any specific science topic, the speed with which learners can construct and then refine their designs greatly effects the number of experiences they will have revisiting and refining the science. Furthermore, noise in the real world combined with students' novice construction capabilities lead to difficulties collecting fully consistent and precise enough data needed to identify the trends. In addition, the real world does not easily provide the variety some students need for understanding. For example, in one of our units dealing with the design of model cars, students can experience the effects of 2-inch wheels and 5-inch wheels, but they cannot easily experience the effects of other sizes. They can put 3 balloon engines on a vehicle, but they cannot build one with 6 engines because it is too hard to blow up 6 balloons at the same time.

Our investigations show that the better these two challenges, *bridging the design-science gap* and *overcoming time and material constraints*, are addressed, the better students will learn science content and scientific reasoning from their DBSL experiences.

3. Addressing DBSL challenges through software assistance

Our software challenge, then, is this: Can we devise a technological innovation (or a set of them) that addresses these challenges — (i) sharing with the teacher some of the burden of helping learners bridge the gap between design experiences and scientific explanations and (ii) allowing for more varied and more exact experiences? If so, what should the nature of this technology be? What features should it have? When, where, and how should it be used? Two classes of technology seem well suited for addressing these challenges if they can be integrated with each other and with other classroom activities in effective ways — *explanation-construction tools* and *simulation and modeling tools.*

3.1 An explanation-construction tool to bridge the design-science gap

One can think about enhancing students' experiences connecting physical phenomena to scientific explanations by providing software tools that will scaffold their ability to explain phenomena they experience. They might use such a tool after they have derived rules of thumb and wish to attach scientific causes underlying their rules. This would expose students to the relevant science and to connecting science to experienced phenomena (i.e., bridging design-science gap). It might also promote discussions of science concepts among classmates during group presentations and whole-class discussions, which are otherwise more design focused.

Studies have shown such beneficial effects of using software-based explanation-construction tools (e.g., Sandoval et al. 2003; Bell and Linn 2000; Suthers et al. 1995). From that research, we can derive some guidelines for including explanation activities in our design-based curriculum and for developing technology for aiding students to become better explainers and better learners in the process. (i) It is important for the students to understand the goals for the products that their inquiry processes are intended to produce. With respect to the explanations, this means that students must understand that scientific explanations are efforts to construct causal accounts for how or why things happen. (ii) A technology designed to scaffold explanation generation should provide both domain-general and domain-specific supports. At a domain-general level, the tool should help students to satisfy criteria of good explanations: They should capture causality, they should be parsimonious, and they should account for observations. At a domain-specific level, the tool must provide explanation templates that visually represent a framework of domain concepts, presented as a chain of causally connected components. (iii) It must encourage students to support explanations with specific data, by providing facilities to link data generated in their investigations to specific explanation components. (iv) It must encourage students to explicitly consider alternative explanations and question which is best. (v) It must help students recognize the limitations of specific explanations. (vi) It must provide avenues for explanation evaluation via critiquing, to encourage students to reflectively evaluate their work using the criteria mentioned above.

3.2 Simulation and modeling software to overcome time, materials, and other environmental constraints

One can think about enhancing students' experiences with designing and testing physical artifacts with the opportunity to do further exploration of like artifacts on the computer in a simulation and modeling environment. But simulation and modeling environments provide rich and engaging learning experiences only under certain conditions. Papert (1993) and Resnick et al. (1996) suggest that it is crucial to design such environments taking into account the need for learners to be engaged in activities that are personally meaningful and that promote epistemological connections. In our context, *personally meaningful* has two parts to it. First, models and simulations should connect to learners' interests and passions, generating learner interest in engaging with them. Second, learners have to be able to easily sense the connections between models they are manipulating within the software and real world experiences. *Epistemologically meaningful* means that when they run their model or test their design, its failures raise questions for them that they can handle by using the domain concepts. Failure has to be just beyond their capabilities, within their zone of proximal development (Vygotsky 1978). Experience with simulation manipulatives, however, shows that it is quite difficult to design toolkits that themselves provide a complete set of learning affordances for all learners. Rather, as we have found in our LBD classrooms, additional help is usually needed from outside the software for many learners.

Examination of the larger literature on simulation and modeling for promoting learning suggests to us three guidelines for designing the simulation and modeling portion of our software. (i) Software to be integrated into a design-based learning environment should focus on both model building and simulation. (ii) Modeling and simulation systems for integration into design-based classrooms should be built so that at least some of their primitive elements match the parts of the physical artifacts learners are already manipulating. (iii) Modeling software to be integrated into design-based learning environments should include in it facilities for helping learners learn from their modeling experiences. This means helping them decide what explorations to make next, remember why they were making those explorations, make predictions about the behavior of their model before running it, explain the model's behavior after running it if the behavior is different than what was expected, and recording and saving their experiences in a way that they can easily understand and easily access later.

3.3 Integrating the two software functionalities

These guidelines for designing software environments effective for promoting science learning in DBSL environments suggest ways of integrating explanation-construction scaffolding with simulation and modeling functionality. The guidelines suggest that *explanation construction should be directed by the investigation and design revision goals of learners.* That is, explanation construction should be situated in the context of design questions and design consequences learners are investigating. Such integration affords asking learners to provide explanations at times when it feels like explanations are *authentically* needed. They can be asked for predictions when they set up a design investigation and be prompted to explain their predictions. They can be asked to identify what they learned through that investigation and be prompted to generate accurate explanations by comparing their predictions with what actually transpired. This brings goal-orientedness to learners' use of science because scientific explanation is situated in the context of issues they are investigating.

Our approach recommends integrating software into the design-based curriculum with the purpose of enhancing real world investigation and design activities. We do not intend to imply that software should substitute for those activities. Designing and conducting experiments on real artifacts has significant value for learning. Producing tangible artifacts is sometimes more motivating and promotes a deeper sense of having actually "made" something. Also, interaction with real world artifacts affords feeling and sensing effects of variations in more tangible ways. Further, real world provides more manipulability, thus allowing more subtle and creative variations in solutions. *Through our investigations we want to learn how exactly to integrate software modeling and simulations with physical modeling and testing in ways that promote the affordances of both.*

4. The plausibility of proposed software solution: A pilot investigation

The objective of our pilot study was to put our design principles into a software design and to integrate it into a DBSL environment to learn more about its feasible use. Some of the research questions for this study were: (i) how does integrating a simulation and modeling-based virtual design environment implemented according to our guidelines contribute to the learning experiences of learners; (ii) how well does the design and use of an explanation-construction tool implemented according to our guidelines help learners generate good explanations, and (iii) how well does the practice of explanation generation through such a tool contribute to the bridging of the design-science gulf among learners and contribute towards enhancing scientific understanding? We designed and built our first software environment, SIMCARS (Vattam and Kolodner 2006), to be integrated into LBD's *Vehicles in Motion (VIM)* unit (Kolodner et al. 2003), which focuses on learning about forces and motion in the context of designing miniature vehicles with propulsion systems.

4.1 Context of the investigation: The *Vehicles in Motion* unit

The design challenge of *Vehicles in Motion (VIM)* involves designing and constructing a model car and its propulsion system that will travel as straight as possible and cover the longest distance possible within a single run. Throughout the unit, students test several engines to propel the car across a test track that has varying surfaces and small hills. The unit is designed such that in each of its modules, students are addressing engineering challenges associated with making the vehicle function as it should and in that context are investigating science issues that will help them address those engineering challenges. Initially in the unit, a *grand challenge* is presented to the students — to design a vehicle and its propulsion system that can go over several hills and then travel straight and long under its own propulsion. Learners *mess about* with toy cars to identify the criteria and constraints of their challenge, what they already know about propulsion and forces, and questions they will need to answer to achieve the challenge. Then, students attempt to make a car powered by a ramp travel as far and straight as possible. This mini-challenge (Coaster Car Challenge) provides a context for answering questions about how to make a vehicle go long and straight, with a need to understand gravity and friction as forces and how forces interact with each other. Next, the students attempt to make a car powered by a balloon engine travel as far and straight as possible. They attempt to run this car over a test track made of carpet and containing small hills. This mini-challenge (Balloon Car Challenge) provides a context for answering questions about how to get a vehicle started and how to keep it going, providing the need to better understand the ways forces interact with each other and for grasping issues of equal and opposite forces. Upon attempting to run their designs over a hill, learners realize they still have more to learn about combining forces in such a way that they can generate enough forward force for their vehicle to counter the force of gravity as it goes up a hill. Next, students investigate the behavior of cars powered by rubber-band and falling-weight engines and test them under similar conditions. Finally, they bring together what they have learned to design a car with a hybrid propulsion system. Table 1 summarizes the science concepts targeted by each learning module. In each module, students follow the LBD cycle (Figure 1) and adopt the various LBD practices discussed in Section 2.1.

Table 1. Concepts addressed in various modules of the *Vehicles* unit

Module	Science concepts
Coaster car	Gravity, Forces, Friction, Newton's First Law of Motion, Velocity
Balloon car	Acceleration, Force, Net Force, Newton's Second and Third law
Rubber-band car	Newton's Laws of Motion, Torque, Friction

4.2 The design of *SIMCARS* software

In accordance with our technological strategy for addressing the challenges involved in implementing the VIM unit (see Sections 3.1 and 3.2), SIMCARS includes two main functions: (i) a simulation and modeling-based virtual design environment where the students can quickly design and test virtual model cars, and (ii) an explanation-construction tool that scaffolds construction of scientific explanations in the context of designing.

SIMCARS' virtual design environment: A learner can interact with SIMCARS' design environment in two operational modes: Explore and Experiment.

Explore mode supports *messing about*, helping learners become familiar with the design space. Through guided play, learners come up with potential design possibilities and questions they need to investigate. Exploring possible designs generates design-related issues and science-related questions to be investigated in greater detail. In a typical classroom session, students explore at most three or four design variations. Exploring designs in SIMCARS' environment affords quicker and more expansive *messing about* than when done with physical models, leading to more opportunities for inquiry. As shown in Figure 2a, learners can quickly configure a car in SIMCARS by clicking on the various parts of the car and adjusting their parametric values. As shown in Figure 2b, learners can also easily test the performance of their model under a variety of different conditions, some of which are not available in the real world (e.g., zero gravity, zero friction). Learners can also compare two or more designs with the help of relevant visualizations (Figure 2c).

(a) (b) (c)

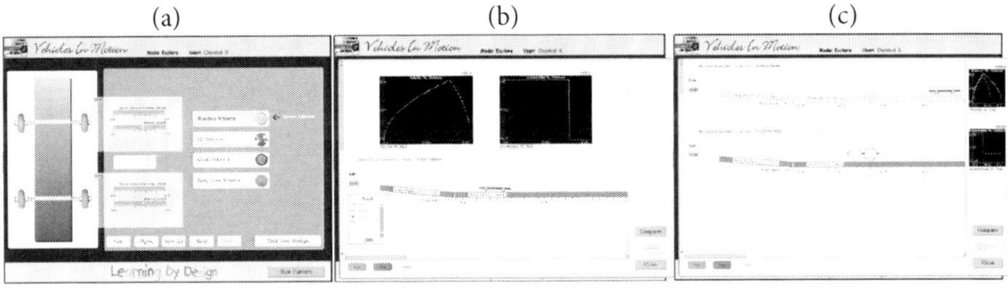

Figure 2. The Explore mode in SIMCARS: (a) Design area, (b) Test area, (c) Design comparison area

Compared to exploration, experimentation is more structured and hypothesis-driven. Here, once a question to be investigated is identified, being able to design and run an experiment and get reliable results is desirable. But neither is completely achieved in classrooms because real world construction takes time and the real world is inherently complex and noisy. Interaction with SIMCARS in the *Experiment* mode takes the user sequentially through steps involved in designing and running an experiment: (i) capturing the question being investigated (Figure 3a), (ii) setting up an experiment by configuring a control design and a test design (Figure 3b), (iii) predicting the outcome of the experiment and explaining the scientific reasons behind the prediction (Figure 3c), and (iv) running the experiment and getting feedback on the outcome of the experiment (Figure 3d).

SIMCARS' Explanation-construction tool: The explanation-construction tool consists of an explanation template that serves as an external discursive representation (Sandoval et al. 2003). A discursive representation is one that represents elements of an explanation. Scaffolding for explanation construction in this tool takes the form of partially filled templates (Figure 3e). Each template captures a portion of the mechanism behind what will be observed in the form of cause-linking statements. For example, *"friction in the control car is less than friction in the variable car; therefore, net force experienced by the variable car is less than the net force experienced by the control car; therefore, the acceleration of the control car is greater than the acceleration of the variable car;..."* Providing the right explanation is reduced to completing an explanation template. Further scaffolding is provided through menus of terms for filling the unfilled blanks in the template, allowing multiple-choice selection. The explanation templates and menus of terms match the science content of the *Vehicles* unit.

Integration of SIMCARS into the *Vehicles* unit: We determined that experiments would provide a good context for learners to engage in explanation activity because this is a key activity where they systematically investigate the effects of structural changes in their designs. The explanation-construction tool would be best launched in the Experiment mode, between step 2 (after setting up the control and test designs (Figure 3b)) and step 4 (before seeing the outcome of the experiment (Figure 3d)), in accordance with the integration strategy outlined in Section 3.3. Upon launching, the explanation-construction tool helps students make predictions about the outcome of their experiment. For instance, they would predict that "the control car will go farther than the test car." Then there is an option for them to explain their prediction. If they choose to explain, the explanation tool scaffolds them in generating an explanation. They then run their experiment and see results as well as visualizations of important phenomena (size of forces, speed, etc.) They run the explanation tool again to help them identify trends in their data and to explain expected and unexpected results.

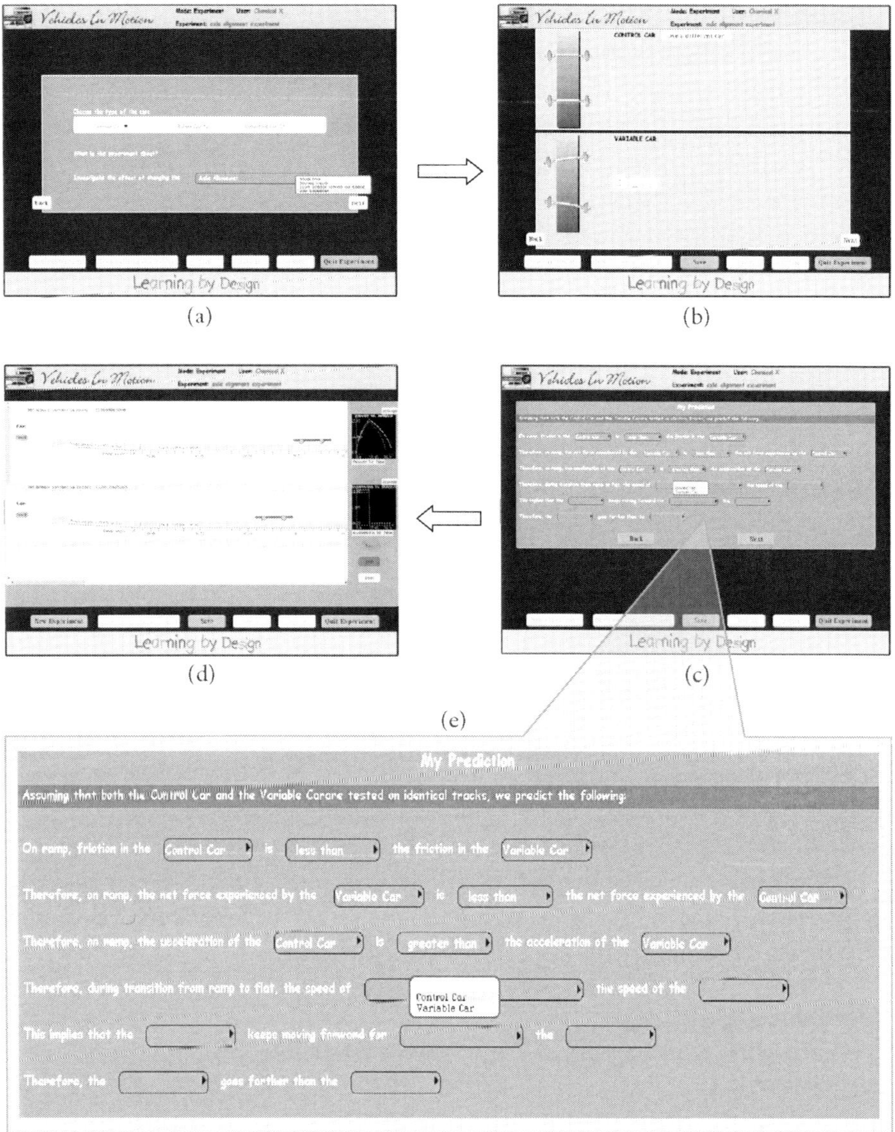

Figure 3. The Experiment mode in SIMCARS: (a) capturing experiment objective, (b) control and test designs specification, (c) prediction and explanation capture, (d) experimental run and results, (e) explanation template

4.3 The pilot study details

We conducted a pilot study using SIMCARS in the context of the *Vehicles* unit in spring 2005. The study was conducted as part of an after-school program in a suburban independent school. Participants were 16 6th graders (ages 11–12), all of whom volunteered to participate with permission from their guardians. We implemented a short version of the *VIM* curriculum, making sure the adapted version retained the "flavor" of the original unit. Students focused on the Coaster Car Challenge to learn about forces, friction and gravity and then on the Balloon Car Challenge to learn about combining forces.

Learners built a physical car as a first pass of the messing about activity. They then explored design variations in SIMCARS' design environment in *Explore* mode. Learners then discussed the different factors that seemed to affect the performance of their cars and identified which factors they wanted to investigate in detail. They conducted experiments to investigate these factors using SIMCARS in *Experiment* mode. Using SIMCARS, they gathered evidence, created and justified design rules of thumb, and provided explanations using the explanation-construction tool. Students then engaged in design in the physical world after collecting and interpreting data as they would have in the original Vehicles unit, and they built, tested, and revised their vehicles to address each of the challenges.

As suggested by LBD, students moved back and forth from small-group exploration, investigation, interpretation, building, and testing activities to full-class presentations and discussions. The teachers for this implementation were two researchers, the first author of this article being one of them. Though not experienced teachers, they did their best to facilitate small-group work and class discussions as an experienced teacher would. Data was collected in the form of video recordings of the sessions and retrospective field notes written by the instructors/researchers immediately after each session. Video recordings consisted of all whole-class discussions, all discussions of small groups while testing and attempting to explain their vehicles' behavior on the test track, and other small-group discussions on an ad-hoc basis. Data analysis focused on student discourse. Those utterances dealing with design concepts, science concepts or both were identified as "science talk" and noted. Patterns of science talk during each session were identified (e.g., design talk only, design talk grounded in scientific explanations). Then changes in the patterns of science talk were tracked over time.

4.4 Preliminary findings

Use of SIMCARS enhanced science talk: During initial stages of the unit, consistent with the "design-science gap" problem mentioned above, we noted from data that some students were indeed "lost" in the world of design and did not relate their design activities to the science concepts underlying their designs. Their designs were more informed by trial and error than by their conceptual understanding. We inferred this based on student discourse about their design decisions and rules of thumb during whole-class and small-group discussions. For instance, in response to an instructor's question about why one choice of axle-wheel arrangement (axle is fixed and the wheels spin around the axle) was better than the other (wheels and the axle spin as a single unit within a straw acting as a bearing), the student replied:

> Student: ... because with the wheels spinning instead of the axle, [it] will create more friction, because spinning of the wheel will [create] friction with the axle. Then the car slows down.

As the sessions progressed, however, science talk became more sophisticated. In sessions following investigation using SIMCARS, we found that the explanations were not only maturing, but also that students' "science talk" mirrored the explanations elicited from them using SIMCARS' explanation-construction tool. That is, when students were trying to explain some of their design decisions or rules of thumb, they naturally incorporated the structure of discourse that was present in the templates of the explanation-construction tool. For instance, after SIMCARS was deployed, in response to an instructor's question regarding why a group made a bearing's length shorter, the following conversation with the *same* student ensued:

> Student: ... they rub against the nut, against the wheel, which is bad, [be]cause the rubbing causes the friction.
> Instructor: We'll know what happens then, right?
> Student: the car won't go very far
> Instructor: why?
> Student: well, if the friction is more, the car has less force pushing it on the ramp compared to a less friction car, causing less speed up. So, when the car comes off the ramp, it carries less speed with it.
> Instructor: So less speed means
> Student: less speed means less travel, car doesn't go that far.

Portions of the above explanation maintained the cause-linking structure present in the explanation-construction tool (see discussion on explanation-construction tool in Section 4.2). This case of a student's explanation discourse mirroring the format of templates in the explanation-construction tool was impressive on two accounts. First, it happened in the context of whole-class discussion, i.e., outside of the context of the tool (indicating transfer). Second, it happened naturally — during whole-class discussions students were free to structure their discourse in any way they wanted.

To summarize, our analysis showed that the reasons and explanations offered by at least some students incorporated appropriate scientific vocabulary after they used the explanation-construction tool. This was in accordance with our prediction about the effects that "bridging" design and science would bring about.

SIMCARS promoted more design-space exploration and more question asking: It is not possible for us to accurately know how many designs every group explored using SIMCARS. But we closely followed one group's messing about activity, with and without SIMCARS. Using SIMCARS, that group explored twelve different variations of designs during one session, compared to three or four when working with physical models. More extensive exploration of the design space also helped at least some students in their discovery of variables affecting the performance of their vehicles. For example, early in the Balloon Car Challenge, students constructed and tested their first physical versions of their cars. In the classroom discussion that followed, we asked them to identify the variables that affected their vehicle designs. They were able to identify only two variables — the number of balloons on the engine, and the number of straws forming the nozzle of the balloon engine — both easily perceivable. The actual number was at least four. They had left out the length of the straws (nozzle) and the number of layers of balloons. The SIMCARS exploration activity followed. In the discussion that followed that, students identified all four variables. Using SIMCARS, learners explored more of the design space and were able to identify more factors that cause variation and are worth investigating.

4.5 Discussion

Our pilot investigation results suggest that integration of a software tool designed according to our guidelines into a DBSL learning environment will have a positive impact. The benefits of using the virtual design environment helped our participants meet some of the difficult challenges of learning from design activity in a shorter period of time, addressing one of the challenges that we identified earlier — overcoming time, material, and other environmental constraints.

Our results also suggest that the design and integration of SIMCARS' explanation-construction tool has the potential to provide the necessary connections between science content and design activity, addressing the design-science gap. Some students who used this tool demonstrated deeper understanding even though the facilitation was handled by inexperienced instructors. Further, their "science talk" mirrored the explanations that they gave using the explanation-construction tool. This was an important side effect of using the explanation-construction tool that we investigated further in our next study.

5. A Formal investigation: How might use of an explanation-construction tool influence classroom discourse?

Our pilot study showed the feasibility of continuing our line of research. It showed that at least one way of implementing the design principles articulated in Section 3 of this article had the potential to positively affect learning from design-based activities in science class. But that investigation was carried out over a period of time too short for us to see or collect evidence of deep and lasting learning. In that short time, however, we were able to see the beginning of explanation capabilities developing among students. Students' mirroring of the science talk patterns from the software seemed significant to us. It suggested that providing patterns for explanatory discourse to students would begin to scaffold their explanation capabilities, which in turn provided the necessary connections between science content and design activity. We sought to investigate that more closely. Would an explanation-construction tool influence classroom discourse in predictable ways? If we introduced explanatory discourse more systematically, what specific effects would that have? Would the classroom discourse be more systematic? Would it contain more or better causal explanations?

These questions hold two-fold interest. First, if indeed we find that an explanation-construction tool positively influences the classroom discourse by bringing in more systematicity in terms of including more causal explanations, we can hypothesize that it will lead to better collaborative learning in DBSL settings. Second, discursive representations have been a subject of much study in the context of scientific knowledge construction (Bell and Linn 2000; Sandoval et al. 2003; Scardamalia and Bereiter 1994; Toth et al. 2002; Vattam and Kolodner 2006). A majority of those studies, including our earlier SIMCARS research, have focused on its role in constructing understanding among learners, either in solitary or small group setting. Only some of them have examined the role of such representations as *mediational resources* (Roschelle and Teaslay 1995) facilitating classroom-wide collaborative interactions. Suthers and Hundhausen (2002) reported the effect of representations of argument structures on learner discourse in the context of within-group collaboration. Perhaps we would be able to show the same for our representations, but on a classroom-wide basis.

We carried out this investigation in the context of an intensive week-long design-based unit on hovercraft science. We created a short LBD-type unit for a science summer-camp and the software (called SHADE) to go with it. We chose hovercraft science for two reasons. First, it is appealing to middle-school students, both boys and girls. Second, we had available to us kits from a company called Goldstein Hovercraft that make it relatively quick and easy to design, test and refine hovercraft models. We first provide an overview of the *Hovercraft* unit. Then we present the design of SHADE. We then present the study.

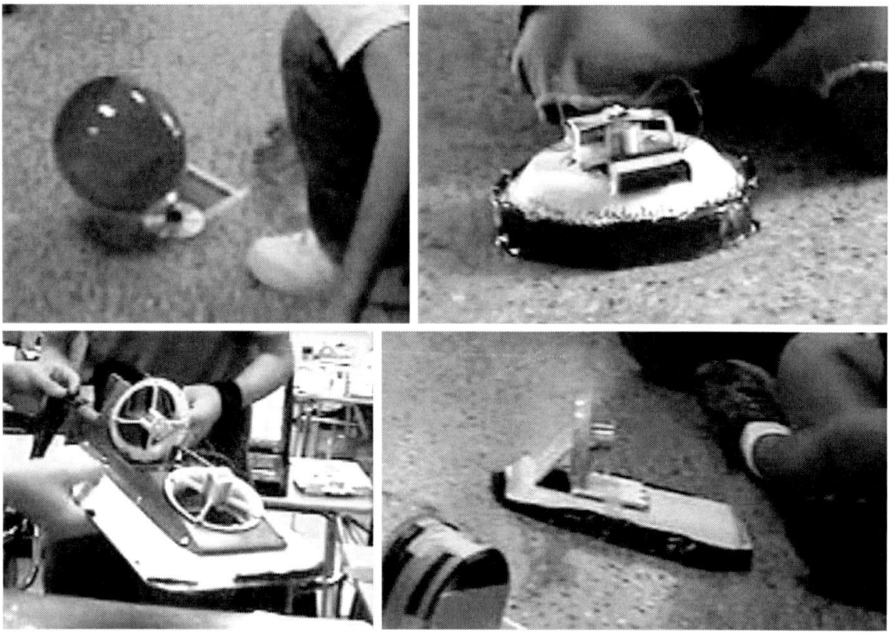

Figure 4. Model hovercrafts developed by learners in the Hovercraft unit

5.1 Context of investigation: The Hovercraft unit

Hovering around GeorgiaTech was developed to teach physics concepts related to hovercrafts and to teach explanatory practices of designers and scientists. This one-week LBD unit was broken down into four hovercraft design challenges that increased in complexity. Participants designed a balloon hovercraft, a flying saucer hovercraft, a 2-fan hovercraft, and a 1-fan hovercraft. Figure 4 shows typical models of each kind. This was followed by a final presentation to an external audience at the end. The sequence of activities for each mini-challenge was similar to the sequencing in each of the modules of the *Vehicles* unit.

5.2 The design of SHADE software and its integration into the *Hovercraft* unit

The design of SHADE is similar to its predecessor, SIMCARS. To bridge the design-science gap, SHADE was developed to promote specific "explanation-construction" interactions in the classroom culture and in the context of learners' design and investigation needs. To overcome time and material constraints, its virtual design environment imitates the real world in a way that both expands the design space for the learners and allows for more efficient exploration of the space. SHADE incorporates a simulation-based virtual design environment, in which learners can explore variations of the four hovercraft designs mentioned above.

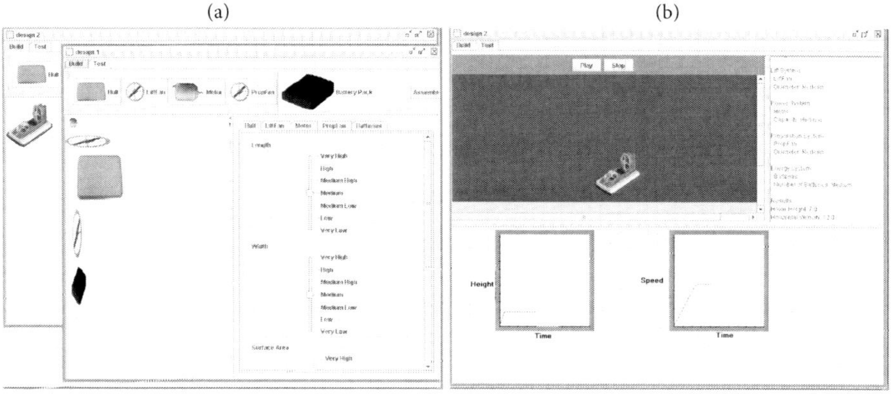

Figure 5. SHADE's exploration facilities: (a) Design area, (b) Test area

The virtual design environment of SHADE has a design area and a test area. Figure 5a shows the design area in SHADE where one can see the correspondence between virtual crafts and the real models depicted in Figure 4. In the design area, users can quickly configure a hovercraft to match their conceptual design by clicking on the various parts and adjusting their parametric values. Figure 5b shows the test area. Learners can test their design in the test area, which animates the behavior of their design and shows a graph that plots the hover height versus the hover time. They can also pause and step through the simulation.

The explanation-construction tool in SHADE is embedded in the design comparison feature of SHADE. The Design comparison feature of SHADE (Figure 6a) is analogous to the Experiment mode in SIMCARS with one difference — in SHADE, one can compare multiple designs side-by-side as opposed to only two

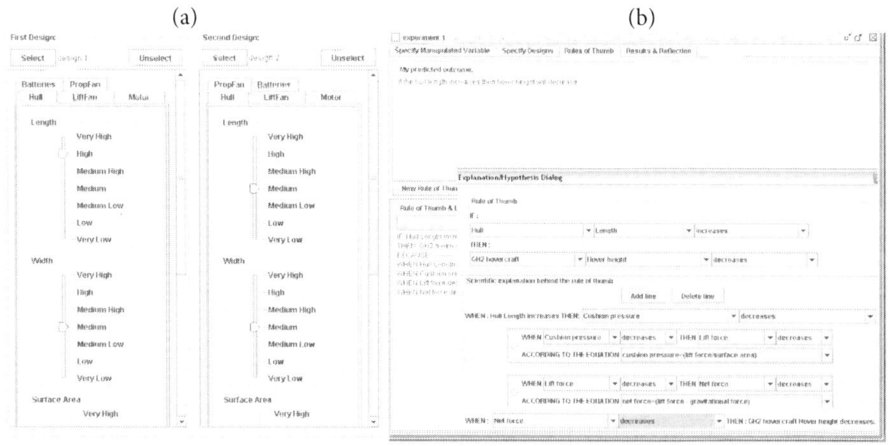

Figure 6. (a) Design comparison, (b) Explanation-construction tool

in SIMCARS. After choosing the designs for comparison, learners have the option of (i) predicting the outcome of running those designs side-by-side, and (ii) generalizing the prediction as a rule of thumb, and explaining the science behind the predicted outcome.

For instance, let us assume that learners were comparing 3 designs (D1, D2 and D3) similar in every respect except that the weight of D3 was greater than the weight of D2, which in turn was greater than the weight of D1. Based on discussions already had in class, learners might predict that "D3 will have the lowest hover height." After running the investigation to see if indeed that was true, they could extract a general rule of thumb, "to maximize the hover height, keep the hovercraft weight as low as possible." But the prediction and the rule of thumb alone will not account for the underlying science that would explain them. At this stage, there is an option for learners to launch the explanation-construction tool to back up their prediction or justify their rule of thumb. Figure 6b shows the prediction and the rule of thumb that a learner entered and the corresponding explanation entered by the same learner in the explanation-construction tool. The design of SHADE's explanation-construction tool is similar to that of SIMCARS and includes partially-filled templates with menus of terms to choose from in order to formulate an explanation.

5.3 Locale, setup, and participants of the study

This study was conducted as part of a science summer camp organized by the Center for Education Integrating Science, Mathematics, and Computing (CEISMC) at Georgia Tech. It attracted a socio-economically diverse set of rising 7th and 8th graders (ages 13 and 14) from the Atlanta metropolitan area. One teacher collaborated with the researchers to implement the same *Hovercraft* unit three times in three successive weeks. The teacher was neither an expert in the science content nor an expert at facilitating design-based learning. However, she was enthusiastic about learning to use design as a context for science learning. In each week, we had a different set of learners. There were 16, 13 and 18 participants in Weeks 1, 2, and 3 respectively, all of whom volunteered to participate with permission from their guardians.

5.4 Procedure

Our intention was to carry out iterations of a design study (Barab and Squire 2004; Collins 1992; Collins et al. 2004) over the three weeks of the summer camp. We intended to integrate SHADE into Week 1 with one set of participants, and based on findings, refine its ways of promoting explanatory discourse and enact the curriculum again in Week 2 with a different set of participants. Based on the findings of second week, we would refine SHADE again and enact the curriculum a third time with yet another set of participants in Week 3. However, due to technical difficulties in the software, we were unable to deploy SHADE during Weeks 1 and 2 of the camp. In Weeks 1 and 2, we implemented the *Hovercraft* unit without the SHADE software. By Week 3, SHADE was ready for deployment. In Week 3, the *Hovercraft* unit was implemented with SHADE integrated into it. We therefore had three sets of participants, two of which (Weeks 1 and 2) participated in the *Hovercraft* curriculum unit without the software and one (Week 3) which had the benefit of both the curriculum and the software. Instead of a design study, our investigation became a quasi-experiment, comparing explanatory discourse and explanatory capabilities across learners who had used the software (Week 3) and those who had not (Weeks 1 and 2). We chose to compare participants in Week 1 and Week 3 and did not include the data from Week 2. This was because, based on the analysis of Day 1 dialog of all three groups, we found that the Week 3 participants were more similar to Week 1 participants than Week 2 with respect to background knowledge and maturity levels.

Comparing the results of Weeks 1 and 3 allowed us to compare development of explanation capability among participants with similar backgrounds and developmental capabilities, with and without the scaffolding provided by the explanation tool. Participants in Week 1 received support from the teacher to articulate their explanations, and they ran their experiments in the real world and used paper-and-pencil based tools to capture their explanations. Participants in Week 3 followed the same unit with the same teacher but used the software to run experiments and to articulate their explanations. All the sessions were videotaped using two cameras. The two cameras were positioned such that we were able to capture the whole-class interactions during discussions, presentations, and lectures.

5.5 Findings and analysis

To understand SHADE's impact on explanatory discourse, we analyzed discourse during whole-group discussions in both Weeks 1 and 3, at the beginning of the week, several times during the week, and at the end of the week as shown in Figure 7.

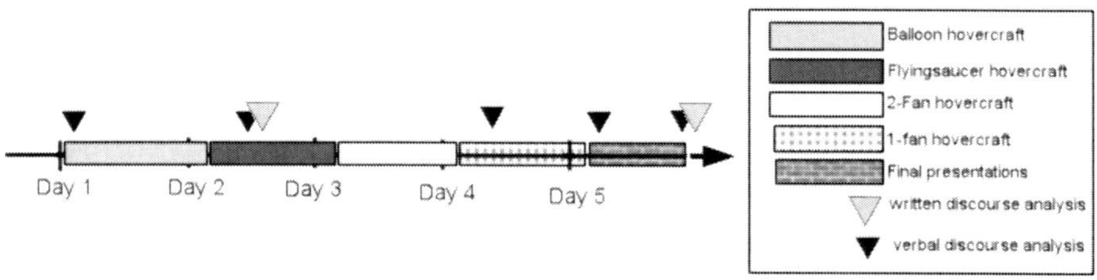

Figure 7. Stages in the unit when discourse analysis was carried out

5.5.1 *Discourse analysis at the beginning of the week*

Day 1 in both conditions started in a similar fashion with an informal class-wide discussion about what participants already knew about hovercrafts and science. Discussions in both weeks were anchored in the question "What does hovering mean?" This discussion was useful in assessing the initial knowledge and explanatory capabilities of participants across the weeks. Discussions during the first morning session for both Weeks 1 and 3 were qualitatively similar, consisting of fragmented knowledge of Newton's laws and ideas about hovering.

5.5.2 *Explanatory discourse early in the week*

We show samples below of written and verbal discourse from the afternoon of Day 1 of each session, when participants were working on the balloon hovercraft challenge. Groups were asked to investigate ways of making a hovercraft using balloons, bottle caps, and CDs. In both weeks, within thirty minutes, most groups had grasped the techniques needed to assemble a device and had put together a basic working hovercraft. After demonstrating their craft to each other, the teacher reviewed experimental method and presented the nomenclature of a hovercraft, including hull, air cushion, cushion pressure, power system, and lift system. It was at this point that activity during the two weeks diverged. During Week 1, participants conducted investigations in the real world, and during Week 3, participants used SHADE to conduct investigations and to (optionally) provide explanations during those investigations. In the poster session that followed in both weeks, groups were encouraged to include results in their posters along with appropriate written explanations. The teacher helped participants as needed in both weeks. We analyzed the written and verbal discourse of participants after their experiments with balloon hovercraft. This early written discourse comes from what small groups of learners had written on posters in preparation for "poster sessions" where they presented results of balloon hovercraft investigations. We analyzed the written discourse with respect to its form, content, and correctness.

Looking at the representative explanations below, we see that Week 3 groups structured their explanations as "*if X then Y, because when X then A, when A then B ... and when D then Y*". The structure of explanations of Week 1 groups, on the other hand, varied from "*since X therefore Y*" to "*X because Y, and Z*". We think the structure of Week 3 explanations was better and more similar across groups because participants modeled it on the cause-linking framework modeled for them in the software. When we look at the content of written discourse, the Week 3 groups used more intermediate causal concepts such as *net force* and *lift force* in their explanations than did Week 1 groups. We also see that in Week 1, participants typically provided only one-level explanations. As far as correctness is concerned, groups in Week 3 show more correctness. But we do not believe that that can be

Representative written discourse, early in each week:	
Week 1 (no software condition)	Week 3 (with software condition)
(i) *"the larger the air [volume], the longer the hovering time* *Why? Because the air is the power."* (ii) *"The larger the balloon, the longer it hovers and the higher it goes.* *Why — because there is more air that comes out of the balloon and it goes longer."* (iii) *"The smaller the nozzle, the higher the H[over]T[ime]. The larger the nozzle, the higher the H[over]H[eight].* *Why: when the air passes through a smaller nozzle, the air is more concentrated & blows at a steadier weight, and air passes through a larger nozzle a bust of air lifts the H[over]C[raft] height."*	(i) *"If hovercraft has a smaller diameter, it will less surface area and a greater hover height.* *IF: CD diameter decreases* *THEN: Balloon hovercraft [hover height] increases* *BECAUSE: WHEN CD diameter decreases THEN lift force increase* *WHEN lift increases THEN Balloon hove[r height increases]"* (ii) *"IF: Nozzle Diameter decreases,* *THEN: Balloon Hovercraft Hovertime increases* *Because…* *WHEN: Nozzle diameter decreases THEN [Lift] Force decreases* *WHEN: Lift force decreases THEN Balloon hovercraft hover time increases"*

attributed to SHADE alone because the teacher had improved her understanding of the concepts by Week 3. Therefore, we do not take correctness into account in this analysis.

Our analysis of verbal discourse from that same poster session shows similar differences. We video taped and analyzed each of the presentations made during that poster session and the discussions that ensued. As can be seen in the typical samples of verbal discourse below, participants in Week 1 offered more impoverished explanations with respect to science content and focused primarily on the designed artifact. The verbal discourse of participants in Week 3, on the other hand, was more sophisticated in form and content and mimicked the explanations that they had articulated using SHADE.

Typical Week 1 explanation (no software condition)	Typical Week 3 explanation (with software condition)
Student: *If I change the size of the balloon it will hover longer.* Teacher: *… change the" if" statement to make it better* Student: *If I increase the balloon…* Teacher: *Good, if I increase the balloon size then it will hover longer.*	Student: *when the lift force is greater than the gravitational force then the net force will be directed upward, but if the gravitational force is greater than the lift force then the net force will be directed downward and the hovercraft would not move.*

A fuller analysis of the same data shows that the best Week 1 discourse was equivalent to the typical Week 3 discourse and that the best Week 3 discourse was significantly better than the best Week 1 discourse as depicted below.

Best Week 1 explanations (no software condition)	Best Week 3 explanation (with software condition)
(i) Student1: *Because adding weight to the hull is going to push more gravity down and it is going to push the air cushion down and have less air cushion"* (ii) Student2: *With every action there is an equal and opposite reaction...[so] air under the hull must overcome gravity*	Student: *If fan diameter increases then flying saucer hovercraft hover height increases because, when fan diameter increases then the cushion pressure increases. [When] cushion pressure increases lift force increases. [When lift force increases] then net force increases. When net force increases then flying saucer hovercraft hover height increases.*

5.5.3 *Discourse at the end of the week*

On the last day of the week, small groups presented their experiences in the camp to an external audience including their family members. The latter part of the morning session of the final day was dedicated to preparing posters for their presentations. Student groups were given a list of topics to choose from for their posters. They were also free to choose their own topics. Participants in Week 3 had the software available to refer to as they were working on their posters. They did not, however, choose to use it. The content of posters and verbal presentations of all groups in Weeks 1 and 3 were compared to analyze the differences in learners' discourse towards the end of the unit. While the analysis early in the week told us about the effects with use of the software, this analysis allows us to begin to identify effects of using the software.[1]

To analyze the final posters and presentation, we first counted the total number of statements made by the students that warranted an explanation, including recommendations and rules of thumb. We rated each statement as a *simple statement of cause and effect* (Type 1), a *statement with rudimentary explanation* (Type 2), or a *statement with a good explanation* (Type 3). For example:

i. **Type 1 (simple statements)** — "*...small [balloon] — has the least power, medium [balloon] — has medium power, large [balloon] — has the most power...*"
ii. **Type 2 (rudimentary explanations)** — "*...if the surface area increases then the hovercraft hover height decreases... [because]... the cushion pressure beneath the hovercraft will decrease....*"
iii. **Type 3 (good explanations)** — "*... [Skirt] contributes to the hovercraft ... increases the cushion pressure underneath the hovercraft causing the lift force, net force, and hover height to increase.*"

Good explanations (Type 3) contained coherent causal explanations. Rudimentary explanations (Type 2) contained either simple causal explanations without intermediate causal concepts or mere reproduction of formulas without showing any understanding of the formulas. Simple statements (Type 1) are statements without justification of any sort. Type 3 statements are the most sophisticated, and Type 1 the least sophisticated.

Table 2 captures the findings about explanatory statements from participants in Week 1. As one can see, most statements are Type2 — rudimentary explanations (8 out of 13, 61.53 %). Most of the rest are simple statements (Type1) with no explanations associated with them.

Table 2. Results of analysis of Week 1 posters and presentations

Poster and presentation theme	Simple statements	Rudimentary explanations	Good explanations
Hull weight	0	0	1
Surface area	1	0	0
Motor power	1	2	0
1 fan vs. 2 fans	0	2	0
Best flying saucer	2	2	0
Balloon hovercraft	0	2	0
Total (13)	4	8	1

Table 3 shows the data from Week 3. In Week 3, posters and presentations had significantly fewer simple statements (Type 1) and contained an equal number of rudimentary and good explanations (Type 2 and 3). Most statements contain either rudimentary (5 out of 11, 45.45 %) or good (5 out of 11, 45.45 %) explanations.

Table 3. Results of analysis of Week 3 posters and presentations

Poster and presentation theme	Simple statements	Rudimentary explanations	Good explanations
Difference in 1 & 2 fan	0	0	2
The effect of weight	0	1	0
Surface area	0	0	1
Best flying saucer	0	2	0
Best balloon	1	1	0
What's a skirt?	0	1	1
Hovercraft 101	0	0	1
Total (11)	1	5	5

The consolidated results in Figure 8 show the overall differences between Weeks 1 and 3 with respect to the statement types. While 30% of the statements in Week 1 were simple statements (Type 1), only 9% were simple statements (Type 1) in Week 3. While only 7% of explanations in Week 1 were good explanations (Type 3), almost half (45%) in Week 3 were good explanations (Type 3).

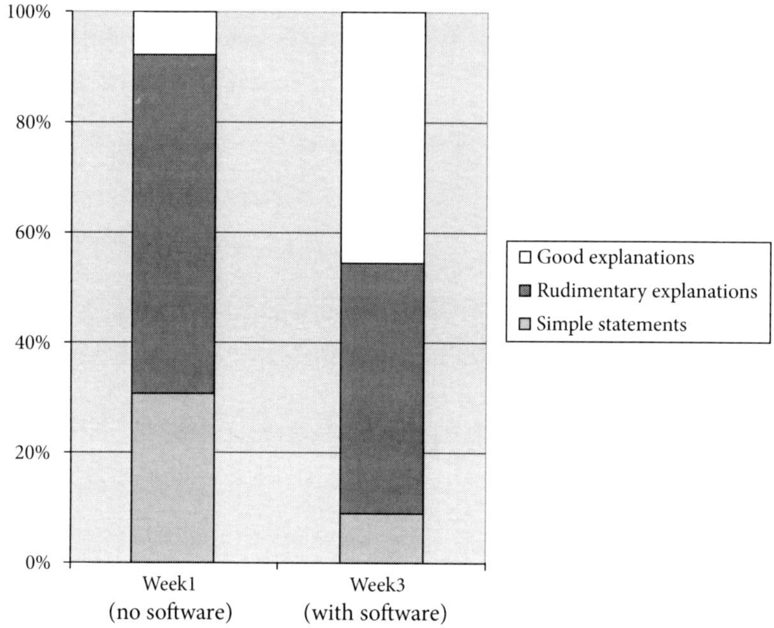

Figure 8. Results comparing findings across Weeks 1 and 3

5.6 Discussion

This study sought to explore the affordances of a mixed modeling/simulation and explanation-construction tool for enhancing learners' explanatory discourse and explanation construction. We hypothesized that learners who used the explanation-construction tool would engage in better explanatory discourse by the end of the *Hovercraft* unit in comparison to learners who did not use the tool, even if all received similar teacher support throughout the unit. Our results support this claim. Both written and verbal discourse of participants who used the explanation-construction tool in Week 3 were more sophisticated than discourse of participants in Week 1 who did not have access to the tool. Specifically, changes were noticed in three areas. First, participants in Week 3 felt the need to explain more. More of their claims and findings were communicated with causal explanations when compared to participants who did not use the tool. Second, participants from Week 3 maintained a more coherent structure in their explanations, consistently across groups and throughout the unit, as a direct effect of just having used the software and more indirectly after having used it several times. Third, the content of explanations from Week 3 was more elaborate and contained more intermediary causal concepts (like lift and net force) compared to explanations from Week 1.

The participants in Weeks 1 and 3 had similar knowledge and capabilities at the start of their hovercraft experiences, but the teacher knew a bit more about hovercraft science and design-based learning by Week 3. So there are two possible reasons why the learners in Week 3 might have performed better: The teacher's increased understanding might have influenced the learners' understanding and capabilities and/or use of the software might have been responsible. We believe we can rule out the teacher's influence as the major contributing factor. This is because, while the teacher's understanding of science concepts had improved by Week 3, her explanatory discourse and her methods of teaching were essentially the same in both weeks. This suggests that use of SHADE's explanation-construction tool was primarily responsible for the better quality of explanatory discourse among Week 3 participants. Our explanation of the increased number of good explanations in Week 3 is that situating SHADE's explanation-construction tool in the context of design investigations gave participants practice both in explaining observations and also in identifying opportunities to explain. A possible explanation of the differences in the form and content of the explanations between Weeks 1 and 3 is that learners who received structured explanation support in SHADE developed better conceptual frameworks in which to organize the various concepts they learned, and the external discursive representation gave participants a better understanding of the form of a good explanation. This account is in line with the foundational literature we drew on in SHADE's design, which suggested that explanation support would provide specific guidance about the nature of scientific explanations.

Although the software had an equal potential to impact the teacher's discourse, SHADE influenced learners more than the teacher during this study. That can be explained by the fact that the teacher did not use SHADE at all. The constant presence of researchers during all the 3 weeks did not necessitate the teacher's use of the tool to integrate it into her teaching. Under normal circumstances, though, we can expect that the teacher would use SHADE before and during the implementation of a unit. We believe such software use has the potential to influence teachers' discourse as well, in the same way that the software usage influences the learners. We also expect that resulting change in teacher's discourse can be an additional influence in enculturating classroom learners into becoming better scientific explainers. A useful extension of this study would combine the kind of analysis presented here with discourse analysis of teachers in the classroom after they actively use and integrate the SHADE software into their teaching.

6. Conclusion

Perhaps the most important lesson of the experiences presented here pertains to the role of technology in design-based science learning (DBSL). In trying to understand the challenges in implementing LBD units, we noticed some issues that one might encounter in implementing a design-based learning approach. Although DBSL has strong affordances for promoting learning of science content through design activity, realizing its benefits requires learners to make explicit connections between design activity and science concepts. Technologies such as the explanation-construction tools in SIMCARS and SHADE can be very useful in addressing this issue. Some of the features that make such technology useful in design-based contexts include (i) articulation of causal mechanisms using domain concepts and quantities, (ii) embodying simple templates to scaffold articulation, and (iii) allowing growing of explanations in an incremental fashion. Our conclusions regarding the integration and usage of explanation-construction tool are (i) by contextualizing explanation in design needs of learners, we can encourage them to want to explain, (ii) by contextualizing explanation in design exploration and investigation, learners will get direct experience at explaining their observations, and (iii) by employing a representational framework that models explanatory discourse, learners will be scaffolded into generating more conceptually and structurally elaborate explanations during whole-class discussions and presentations.

Our approach to enculturating learners into the practice of explanation construction has other advantages. We demonstrated that a software tool like SHADE makes a difference in how learners engage in collaborative learning to become better scientific explainers. Our in-depth discourse analysis suggests that the explanation-construction tool has the potential to affect collaborative knowledge construction. Often, teachers' lack of expertise in facilitating knowledge construction in design-based inquiry environments hampers development of scientific understanding among learners. But if students can use the language of a domain in well-formed explanations, there is a better chance that they can articulate their science understanding in a way others can comprehend. Such expression is essential to productive collaborative knowledge construction. Our results suggest that technologies like SIMCARS and SHADE, which model appropriate discourse, have an important role to play as mediational resources in facilitating collaborative interactions in the classroom.

Regarding promoting learning through simulation and modeling, encouraging sufficient and efficient exploration of a design space, especially those regions of the space that normally go untouched, has affordances for promoting the identification of issues that lead to deeper investigation. But promoting such exploration can pose a significant challenge during implementation because the extent of exploration is limited not only by time and material constraints in the real world, but also by the inherent properties of the real world itself. Simulations should be a good way of addressing this issue, as simulations can adapt their time scales, facilitate quick designing, allow exploration of features of the world that cannot be changed in the real world (e.g., the value of g), include a lot of different types of materials, and provide visualizations of invisible and hard-to-see phenomena alongside the behavior of a designed artifact. Further, use of a simulation environment that parallels but extends the real world provides an infrastructure to hang an explanation-construction tool onto, and makes that tool available at times when learners might be seeking explanations. Such integration provides a natural and an authentic context for making explanations.

One of the significant insights gained from our studies is the indirect influence of simulation and modeling tools and associated explanation-construction tools and their potential for impact on learning in DBSL settings. It may be, though, that this indirect role is exactly the right one for such tools. But we recognize the need for further research on better understanding how those influences unfold in the classrooms, and how different tools interact with each other, with teachers' practices and with students' work. Mapping out such relationships will lead to better educational tools and more effective use of those by teachers and students.

Notes

* This research was supported in part by a grant from the National Science Foundation We wish to thank Goldstein Hovercraft, LLC (http://www.gohover.com), Tony Docal and Megan McCollum for their support in this research effort. We wish to also thank Christopher Kramer, Hyungsin Kim, and other members of the LBD group who have contributed immensely to this project. Finally, we acknowledge students, teachers and other staff members of the Galloway school who gave us an opportunity to conduct our pilot study.

1. Salomon et al. (1991) discuss "effects with" and "effects of" educational software. Effects "with" are what we see participants capable of when they are using the software. Effects "of" the software are what participants are capable of as a result of having used the software earlier. Early in the week, participants created their posters based on what they had just finished doing with the software. These end-of-week data are farther removed from explicit software use and thus count as "effects of".

References

Barab, S. and Squire, K. 2004. "Design-based research: Putting a stake in the ground". *The Journal of the Learning Sciences* 13(1): 1–14.

Bell, P. and Linn, M.C. 2000. "Scientific arguments as learning artifacts: Designing for learning from the web with KIE". *International Journal of Science Education* 22(8): 797–817.

Collins, A. 1992. "Towards a design science of education". In E. Scanlon and T. O'Shea (eds), *New Directions in Educational Technology*. Berlin: Springer, 15–22.

Collins, A., Josephs, D., and Beilaczyk, K. 2004. "Design research: Theoretical and methodological issues". *The Journal of the Learning Sciences* 13(1): 15–42.

Crismond, D. 2001. "Learning and using science ideas when doing investigate-and-redesign tasks: A study of naïve, novice, and expert designers doing constrained and scaffolded design work". *Journal of Research in Science Teaching* 38(7): 791–820.

Crismond, D., Camp, P.J., Ryan, M., and Kolodner, J.L. 2001. "Design rules of thumb: Connecting science and design". Paper presented at the *Annual Meeting of the American Educational Research Association*, Seattle, WA.

Dunbar, K. 1993. "Concept discovery in a scientific domain". *Cognitive Science* 17: 397–434.

Forbus, K.D., Kuehne, S.E., Whalley, P.B., Everett, J.O., Ureel, L., Brokowski, M., and Baher, J. 1999. "CyclePad: An articulate virtual laboratory for engineering thermodynamics". *Artificial Intelligence* 114(1–2): 297–347.

Fortus, D., Dershimer. C.R., Krajcik, J.S., and Marx, R.W. 2004. "Design-based science and student learning". *Journal of Research in Science Teaching* 41(10): 1081–1110.

Hmelo, C.E., Holton, D.L., and Kolodner, J.L. 2000. "Designing to learn about complex systems". *Journal of Learning Sciences* 9(3): 247–298.

van Joolingen, W.R. and De Jong, T. 2003. "SimQuest: Authoring educational simulations". In T. Murray, Blessing, S., and Ainsworth, S. (eds), *Authoring Tools for Advanced Technology Educational Software: Toward Cost-Effective Production of Adaptive, Interactive, and Intelligent Educational Software*. Dordrecht: Kluwer Academic Publishers, 1–31.

Kolodner, J.L., Camp, P.J., Crismond, D., Fasse, B., Gray, J., Holbrook, J., Puntambekar, S., and Ryan, M. 2003. "Problem-based learning meets case-based reasoning in the middle-school science classroom: Putting Learning by Design™ into practice". *Journal of the Learning Sciences* 12(4): 495–547.

Munro, A., Johnson, M.C., Pizzini, Q.A., Surmon, D.S., Towne, D.M., and Wogulis, J.L. 1997. "Authoring simulation-centered tutors with RIDES". *International Journal of Artificial Intelligence in Education* 8, 284–316.

Papert, S. 1993. *The Children's Machine*. New York: Basic Books.

Penner, D.E., Lehrer, R., and Schauble, L. 1998. "From physical models to biomechanics: A design-based modeling approach". *Journal of the Learning Sciences*. 7(3–4): 429–449.

Resnick, M. 1994. *Turtles, Termites, and Traffic Jams: Explorations in Massively Parallel Microworlds*. Cambridge, MA: The MIT Press.

Resnick, M. 1996. "Towards a practice of constructional design". In L. Schauble and R. Glaser (eds), *Innovations in Learning: New Environments for Education*. Mahwah, NJ: Lawrence Erlbaum, 161–174.

Resnick, M., Bruckman, A., and Martin, F. 1996. "Pianos not stereos: Creating computational construction kits". *Interactions*, 3(6): 40–50.

Roschelle, J. and Teaslay, S.D. 1995. "The construction of shared knowledge in collaborative problem solving". In C.E. O'Malley (ed), *Computer Supported Collaborative Learning*. Berlin: Springer, 69–97.
Ryan, M.T. and Kolodner, J.L. 2004. "Using 'rules of thumb' practices to enhance conceptual understanding and scientific reasoning in project-based inquiry classrooms". In *Proceedings of the International Conference of the Learning Sciences (ICLS 2004)*. Los Angeles, CA: Lawrence Erlbaum Associates, 449–456.
Sandoval, W.A. 2003. "Conceptual and epistemic aspects of students' scientific explanations". *Journal of the Learning Sciences* 12(1): 5–51.
Sandoval, W.A., Crawford, V.M., Bienkowski, M., Hurst, K., and Millwood, K. 2003. "Effects of explanation support on learning genetics". Paper presented at the *Annual Meeting of NARST 2003*, Philadelphia, PA.
Scardamalia, M. and Bereiter, C. 1994. "Computer support for knowledge-building communities". *Journal of the Learning Sciences* 3(3): 265–283.
Schauble, L., Glaser, R., Duschl, R.A., Schulze, S., and John, J. 1995. "Students' understanding of the objectives and procedures of experimentation in the science classroom". *Journal of the Learning Sciences* 4: 131–166.
Salomon, G., Perkins, D.N., and Globerson, T. 1991. "Partners in cognition: Extending human intelligence with intelligent technologies". *Educational Researcher* 20(3): 2–9.
Soloway, E., Jackson, S.L., Klein, J., Quintana, C., Reed, J., Spitulnik, J., Stratford, S.J., Studer, S., Jul, S., Eng, J., and Scala, N. 1996. "Learning theory in practice: Case studies of learner-centered design". In *Proceedings of the Conference on Human Factors in Computing Systems: Common Ground (CHI '96)*. New York: ACM Press, 189–196.
Suthers, D. and Hundhausen, C.D. 2002. "The effects of representation on students' elaborations in collaborative inquiry", In G. Stahl (ed), *Proceedings of Computer Support for Collaborative Learning: Foundations for a CSCL Community 2002*. Mahwah, NJ: Erlbaum, 472–480.
Suthers, D., Weiner, A., Connelly, J., and Paolucci, M. 1995. "Belvedere: Engaging students in critical discussion of science and public policy issues". In Greer, J. (ed), *Proceedings of Artificial Intelligence in Education (AI-ED 95)*, AACE, Charlottesville, VA, 266–273.
Toth, E., Suthers, D., and Lesgold, A. 2002. "Mapping to know: The effects of representational guidance and reflective assessment on scientific inquiry skills". *Science Education* 86:264–286.
Vattam, S. and Kolodner, J.L. 2006. "Design-based science learning: Important challenges and how technology can make a difference". In *Proceedings of the International Conference of the Learning Sciences (ICLS 2006)*. Bloomington, IN: Lawrence Erlbaum Associates, 799–805.
Vygotsky, L.S. 1978. *Mind in Society: The Development of Higher Psychological Processes*. Cambridge, MA: Harvard University Press.
White, B. 1993. "ThinkerTools: Causal models, conceptual change, and science education". *Cognition and Instruction* 10(1): 1–100.

Index

In the series *Benjamins Current Topics (BCT)* the following titles have been published thus far or are scheduled for publication:

28 **GULLBERG, Marianne and Kees de BOT (eds.):** Gestures in Language Development. 2010. viii, 139 pp.
27 **DROR, Itiel E. (ed.):** Technology Enhanced Learning and Cognition. 2011. ix, 265 pp.
26 **SHLESINGER, Miriam and Franz PÖCHHACKER (eds.):** Doing Justice to Court Interpreting. 2010. viii, 246 pp.
25 **ANSALDO, Umberto, Jan DON and Roland PFAU (eds.):** Parts of Speech. Empirical and theoretical advances. 2010. vi, 291 pp.
24 **ARBIB, Michael A. and Derek BICKERTON (eds.):** The Emergence of Protolanguage. Holophrasis vs compositionality. 2010. xi, 181 pp.
23 **AUGER, Alain and Caroline BARRIÈRE (eds.):** Probing Semantic Relations. Exploration and identification in specialized texts. 2010. ix, 156 pp.
22 **RÖMER, Ute and Rainer SCHULZE (eds.):** Patterns, Meaningful Units and Specialized Discourses. 2010. v, 124 pp.
21 **BELPAEME, Tony, Stephen J. COWLEY and Karl F. MACDORMAN (eds.):** Symbol Grounding. 2009. v, 167 pp.
20 **GAMBIER, Yves and Luc van DOORSLAER (eds.):** The Metalanguage of Translation. 2009. vi, 192 pp.
19 **SEKINE, Satoshi and Elisabete RANCHHOD (eds.):** Named Entities. Recognition, classification and use. 2009. v, 168 pp.
18 **MOON, Rosamund (ed.):** Words, Grammar, Text. Revisiting the work of John Sinclair. 2009. viii, 124 pp.
17 **FLOWERDEW, John and Michaela MAHLBERG (eds.):** Lexical Cohesion and Corpus Linguistics. 2009. vi, 124 pp.
16 **DROR, Itiel E. and Stevan HARNAD (eds.):** Cognition Distributed. How cognitive technology extends our minds. 2008. xiii, 258 pp.
15 **STEKELER-WEITHOFER, Pirmin (ed.):** The Pragmatics of *Making it Explicit.* 2008. viii, 237 pp.
14 **BAKER, Anne and Bencie WOLL (eds.):** Sign Language Acquisition. 2009. xi, 167 pp.
13 **ABRY, Christian, Anne VILAIN and Jean-Luc SCHWARTZ (eds.):** Vocalize to Localize. 2009. x, 311 pp.
12 **DROR, Itiel E. (ed.):** Cognitive Technologies and the Pragmatics of Cognition. 2007. xii, 186 pp.
11 **PAYNE, Thomas E. and David J. WEBER (eds.):** Perspectives on Grammar Writing. 2007. viii, 218 pp.
10 **LIEBAL, Katja, Cornelia MÜLLER and Simone PIKA (eds.):** Gestural Communication in Nonhuman and Human Primates. 2007. xiv, 284 pp.
9 **PÖCHHACKER, Franz and Miriam SHLESINGER (eds.):** Healthcare Interpreting. Discourse and Interaction. 2007. viii, 155 pp.
8 **TEUBERT, Wolfgang (ed.):** Text Corpora and Multilingual Lexicography. 2007. x, 162 pp.
7 **PENKE, Martina and Anette ROSENBACH (eds.):** What Counts as Evidence in Linguistics. The case of innateness. 2007. x, 297 pp.
6 **BAMBERG, Michael (ed.):** Narrative – State of the Art. 2007. vi, 271 pp.
5 **ANTHONISSEN, Christine and Jan BLOMMAERT (eds.):** Discourse and Human Rights Violations. 2007. x, 142 pp.
4 **HAUF, Petra and Friedrich FÖRSTERLING (eds.):** Making Minds. The shaping of human minds through social context. 2007. ix, 275 pp.
3 **CHOULIARAKI, Lilie (ed.):** The Soft Power of War. 2007. x, 148 pp.
2 **IBEKWE-SANJUAN, Fidelia, Anne CONDAMINES and M. Teresa CABRÉ CASTELLVÍ (eds.):** Application-Driven Terminology Engineering. 2007. vii, 203 pp.
1 **NEVALAINEN, Terttu and Sanna-Kaisa TANSKANEN (eds.):** Letter Writing. 2007. viii, 160 pp.